FIRST STEPS IN
PROGRAMMING
THE PSION SERIES 3

by
Mike Shaw

FIRST STEPS IN PROGRAMMING

THE PSION SERIES 3

An Introductory Guide

by
Mike Shaw

To Dad, and in loving memory of Kay

Published by
KUMA COMPUTERS LTD.

First Published 1991

Kuma Computers Ltd.
Unit 12, Horseshoe Park
Horseshoe Road, Pangbourne
Berkshire RG8 7JW
Printed in Great Britain by Bookcraft (Bath) Ltd.

ISBN 07457-01450

FOREWORD

Way back in 1987, Psion created a revolution with the introduction of their Organiser II, a device which looked rather like a calculator, yet which provided numerous facilities and utilities over and above the usual calculator functions. It was the electronic answer to 'pocket sized' loose leaf diary systems, and sold in the hundreds of thousands.

Organiser II went from strength to strength - four models, each with increased capability, being introduced over the ensuing years. It was copied by many other companies, but never equalled in overall performance, the significant difference between the Psion Organiser II and the rest being its powerful, built-in programming language, 'OPL'.

The ability to program an Organiser II gave it a distinct advantage: it could be tailored, by the user, to perform additional facilities to suit the user's own needs. The language is a clever mix of BASIC (a language specifically developed to help beginners learn to write programs) and 'C' (a highly structured language used by professional programmers), and as such is both structured and comparitively easy to learn. The original OPL had about 120 'key' words, enabling users to develop their own comprehensive databases for business use, navigational aids, and so on.

With the new Psion Series 3, the whole concept has been taken a giant leap forward. The language, an extension of the original, now comprises more than 200 words. Yet, for the most part, it is as straightforward and as easy to learn. Indeed, those who learned to program their Organisers will have little difficulty in adapting to the new, more powerful OPL built into the Series 3, with its considerable extension in capability and its ability to produce graphics.

Psion Series 3 differs from the Organiser - and any other hand held of its ilk on the market - in that its operating system has been especially designed from the outset to provide a *graphic* interface, and 'multitasking'. (Multitasking is the ability to handle more than one job simultaneously, such as printing out a document whilst allowing the user to examine his database or make calculations).

The programming language allows the user to access the new graphics capabilities - thus enabling very sophisticated programs to be produced.

Yes, the language is now more comprehensive than the original and it embodies a number of new features: but the user need not be concerned by this, it is still a fairly easy language to learn, if taken a step at a time.

And that is the purpose of this book.

It will take the complete novice through to the stage where he or she can develop useful programs to solve a variety of requirements. It will explain, where necessary, the programming concepts entailed - but only to the depth required for an understanding of the process. It will also give those with some programming experience, perhaps in another language or the original OPL, an insight into the power of the new graphics OPL.

For those with OPL experience, please note that although the new OPL is an extension of the original, programs written on an Organiser II cannot be transferred directly to the Series 3: they must be re-written.

Learning to program a computer such as the Series 3 is extremely satisfying and gratifying, and by no means as difficult as it may sound. Compare it, if you like, to learning a foreign language: it has a 'vocabulary' of words which the computer will understand, and it has a syntax - a way of using those words. The difference between a computer language and a foreign language is that the computer will not tolerate any mistakes. It expects that the rules will be obeyed precisely. Understand these rules, and you will join the growing ranks of those for whom programming is not just an enjoyable pastime, but a valuable asset.

Now, let's get to it!

Mike Shaw
October 1991

Acknowledgements

This book was written using a Series 3 Version 1.58F kindly
supplied by Psion, to whom I am deeply indebted not just
for making the machine available, but also for the generous
help and support provided.

In particular, I would like to thank H.P. in the OPL
development team for patiently and diligently answering
questions about the many facets of the new OPL language:
without such help, this book may never have seen the light
of day.

CONTENTS

PART 2. The Graphics

xi

PART 3. Files & Data Handling

EPILOG

PART 1

The Basics

In this Part of the book, you will be introduced to the principles of programming, and how to use the basic elements of the OPL language to create programs.

STEP ONE

How Does It All Work?

This Step introduces you to the concept of computers and how they work. It will give you a broad understanding of
* *A computer's structure*
* *How information is stored*
* *The binary system*
* *How Series 3 operates*

Why do you need to know?

When programming a computer, it is helpful to have a broad understanding of how the machine works. Insight into what goes on when programs are run helps to explain in part why some things have to be done in a certain way. Such knowledge provides a useful background and shows that, in reality, computers can do only what they are told to do. Consequently, a brief description is given here as the first step in programming your Series 3: this description is presented in an analogous form rather than the actual technicalities, to make it easier to follow. If you have an understanding of the way computers work and handle information, you may skip this Step completely. Otherwise, a few minutes reading the rest of this Step will be time well spent...

The Warehouse Concept

Any computer, the Series 3 included, can be considered as a large warehouse with thousands upon thousands of storage boxes neatly laid out in an orderly fashion. Each box is individually numbered, rather like the houses in a street. And like the houses in a street, this number is called the 'address'. It enables the box to be located very quickly when the need arises.

The boxes are used to store simple instructions and information for the running of the warehouse. They are known as the memory. The size of the memory is simply the number of boxes available for information storage.

The Basics

Two slots on the Series 3 cater for additional storage space - consider them as doors to the warehouse to which can be driven pantechnicons containing even more boxes (up to two million at a time). These storage areas can be changed at will, whereas those inside the warehouse - or Series 3 - are always there.

There are two distinct types of storage box within the Series 3, and we will examine these briefly later.

A busy office

Tucked away in the heart of the warehouse is a very busy Office, the nerve centre of the entire operation. Virtually everything that happens in the warehouse is under the control of this Office. Even when the warehouse is closed (Series 3 is switched off), activity inside it abounds, and it continues to abound as long as power is available. It works very fast indeed - performing thousands of actions every second. Its 'staff' are capable managing a variety of operations at the same time. The only time it stops work is when there is no power supply (i.e when both the two main AA batteries and the back-up lithium cell are removed from the Series 3).

The technical name for this Office in a computer is Central Processor Unit, or CPU for short. For the time being at least, we'll continue to refer to it as the Office: it sounds less daunting.

Keeping in touch

The Office would be absolutely useless if we had no way to communicate with it, or if it had no way to communicate with us. We are, after all, the 'customers' who decide what we want the warehouse to do for us.

Our instructions are communicated to the Office through the keyboard. The Office keeps a close eye on what happens there, and does its level best to interpret our requirements. Tap the icon key for a specific application - such as the Word Processor - and the Office sees to it that that application is made available immediately. It then waits for the 'word processing' instructions.

In the main, the Office communicates with us through the screen. If we ever get stuck over what to do next, pressing the HELP key will have the Office jumping into action to provide useful hints and guidance on the screen.

If the warehouse is 'closed for business' - so that the screen is not active, the Office can keep in touch with us by bleeping on the loudspeaker. For example, we may have requested an alarm call to remind us about an impending appointment: the ever alert Office, aware of our need, will attract our attention through the loudspeaker. Switching on, the appropriate message is then displayed on the screen.

To achieve these and similar activities, the Office has to keep in constant touch with other departments in the warehouse - a master 'clock', for example. However, these other departments need not concern us. It is sufficient to know that when we communicate with the Office, it must understand our requirement. It doesn't have human intelligence, and so can only understand the precise instructions it has been taught. Fortunately, those instructions have been made very easy for us to understand too.

How the boxes store information

Let's now take a closer look at the storage boxes, because it is quite important when programming that you appreciate just how they store information.

Essentially, there are two types of box: with the first type you can look in to see what's there, you can 'read' or take a copy of the information it contains, but you cannot change that information. This type of box is called *Read Only Memory*, or ROM for short. The instructions and information for running your Series 3 are contained inside boxes of this type. They don't need any power supply to retain their information, and since you cannot change anything, your Series 3 will always be able to run the programs or 'software' that has been built into it by 'looking at' the information in these boxes.

The second type of box is far more interesting to us, because the information it contains can be changed. Our programs and data are held in boxes of this type: we can 'write' information into a box, we can look at it or 'read' it, and we can change it or clear it out altogether. Collectively, boxes of this type go by the name *Random Access Memory*, or RAM for short.

The snag with this type of box is that it needs a power supply to keep it active. No power supply, no information. It's as simple as that. This is the reason Series 3 has a back-up lithium cell: if ever the main batteries fail, or you're changing them, the lithium cell keeps all the RAM boxes 'alive' until the batteries are re-installed. Providing you don't take longer than a few months...

The way these boxes operate is in many respects similar to the cassette tape in your recorder. Each time you record ('write') new information to the tape, you first erase what was there before. The same is true in the boxes - when new information goes in, the old information is lost. But this is no more of a problem than re-using a cassette tape: in fact in a computer there's less likelihood of making a mistake and recording over wanted information.

The Basics

What's in the box

It is fairly important to understand the way information is stored inside the boxes, particularly those that we can change. It would be rather nice to think that a box contains a specific 'chunk' of information, such as a complete address, or a shopping list.

Unfortunately, it doesn't. It doesn't even contain one word. In fact all that the box can contain is a number from 0 to 255 inclusive. That's 256 'numbers' in all, if you count zero. What's more, the number in the box can represent an instruction or part of an instruction, it can represent a character, such as the letter 'A' or the figure '2', or it can represent an actual value in real terms, that is, a number that can be used for mathematical operations such as adding or multiplying.

Here's the first important thing to note: as far as the computer is concerned a character '2' is quite different from a value '2'. To the computer, characters are just shapes that we humans use to communicate with each other. So a character '2' is just a shape. Values on the other hand are bits of information the computer can use for any mathematical operation we care to throw at it.

On the face of it, things are starting to look very complicated indeed - here we have a box that can contain a number from 0 to 255, and that number can represent an instruction, a character or a value: how on earth are we supposed to know which it is? The answer is, we don't have to know, most of the time, because the computer sorts it out for us. The only time we need to be concerned about what's going into the boxes is when we use 'variables' when writing programs, and at this point in time, we don't even have to worry about what a variable is.

The other question that has probably crossed your mind is 'if a box can only store a value up to 255, how are larger values stored?'. The simple answer is that boxes are used in combination.

The more complicated answer is that numbers are stored in computers using the *binary* system. Many people are unnecessarily frightened by the thought of a system that doesn't have any numbers in it other than a '0' and a '1'. You don't have to know anything at all about the binary system unless or until you want to get really deep into programming, so you can skip this next bit if you wish: on the other hand, why not dip in and see how easy it is?

Counting the binary way

In our normal, every day life, we use the decimal system of counting. We have ten numbers - '0' through to '9'. Yes, in this context, '0' is a number. If we're counting, when we get to '9', we have run out of numbers. So we add '1' to the column to the left - increasing it from '0' to '1', and start again. We can now count from 10 to 19. And so the process goes on until we get to 99 - then we move to the next column to the left, and so on.

Each column in the decimal counting system has ten values - from 0 to 9. We're so used to it, we don't even think of how it works. But given a number such as '352', for example, you'll know that this means '3 hundreds, plus 5 tens, plus 2 units'. That's because the right column represents units, the middle column represents tens, and left column represents hundreds.

Now, what happens if we have only '0' and a '1' to play around with? The highest we can count up to is '1', *unless* we do what we do in the decimal system - add 'one' to the column to the left. So, counting this way we get

	0	(0 in the decimal system)
	1	(1 in the decimal system)
(add one to left)	10	(2 in the decimal system)
	11	(3 in the decimal system)
(add one to left)	100	(4 in the decimal system)
	101	(5 in the decimal system)
	110	(6 in the decimal system)
	111	(7 in the decimal system)
(add one to left)	1000	(8 in the decimal system)

and so on. You can see that it works just the same as the decimal system - add one to the next left column when you've run out of numbers, then start counting up again from 0. Trouble is, these binary numbers look like gibberish to us mortals more used to the decimal system. But there is an easy way to work out what the binary number is in decimal terms.

Take a look at the binary equivalents of the decimal numbers 1, 2, 4 and 8. They are 1, 10, 100, and 1000 respectively. And I can tell you that 16 is 10000 in binary and 32 is 100000. In other words, whereas in the decimal system each column to the left is another multiple of ten (10, 100, 1000, 10000), in the binary system each column to the left represents another multiple of 2 (2, 4, 8, 16, 32). So binary '100001' is 33 in decimal, and binary '100010' is 34 in decimal.

Basically, that's all there is to the binary system. The reason it is used in computers is that it is very easy to have devices with two states (on or off, magnetised or not magnetised, up or down), but not so easy to have devices with more states. Inside each of our storage boxes, there are, in effect, eight 'switches' which can be either 'on' or 'off'. If 'on' they represent a '1', and if 'off' they represent a '0'. With eight switches, to represent eight 'columns' of binary numbers, we can count all the way up to 11111111 - which in decimal, is the number 255. Voila!

By taking two boxes together, we can count up to 1111111111111111 in binary, which is 65535 in decimal.

Just to finish of this little discussion, each of the 'switches' inside a memory box is known as a bit (short for Binary digIT), and eight *bits* together- one 'box-full' are known as a *byte*. And just so that you are aware of it, whereas 'k' in the decimal system stands for '1000', in the world of computers and binary, 'k' stands for 1024. So a memory of 1kbyte actually means 1024 memory boxes.

How characters are stored

If a box can store only a number from 0 to 255, how on earth does it hold a *character* like the letter 'A'? That's where our Office comes in - and another department inside the computer which is rather like a library. Most of the time, the Office is clever enough to know (or to be able to work out) when the contents of box are meant to be a character.

Each number in the box is associated with a 'pattern' in the 'library'. When displayed on the screen, we'll recognise this pattern as a character, such as 'A'. If it knows, or is told that a box contains a character, the Office checks with the library for the corresponding pattern and if required, displays it on the screen. Later on, we'll write a little program that will let you see the character patterns associated with most of the 255 numbers a box can hold: some numbers are actually used as 'instructions', like 'start a new line on the screen or printer', or 'bleep the loudspeaker'.

How real values are stored

If you read the paragraphs on the binary system, you'll know that two boxes together can save values up to 65 thousand odd. In practice, the range of values goes from -32768 to +32767 (one of the switches is used to indicate minus or plus). These are all whole numbers, called *integers*: they have no decimal point. By using two more boxes (four in all), larger integer values in the range -2147483648 to +2147483647 can be stored: later on, we'll see how we tell the computer when we want the boxes to be used for these larger values (called *long integers*) instead of ordinary integers.

Of course, these values are fine as far as they go, but what about values with a decimal point in them, such as 4.5. Well, these are stored quite differently, using more boxes and a system that you don't have to worry about (sighs of relief): all you *do* have to remember when programming is to tell the computer when you want the boxes to store a number with a decimal point in it, and as you'll see, that is very easy indeed. So don't panic.

As a matter of interest, values with a decimal point in them are called *floating point* numbers, the 'floating' bit meaning that the decimal point can be anywhere we like. The range of floating point values that can be stored is truly astronomical - far larger than you'll ever need.

How instructions are obeyed

At the 'Office' level, computer instructions are really just a series of numbers: each number, or little group of numbers, is an instruction to the Office to perform some task or other. To program a computer using just these numbers is a very difficult task - so much so that, even for professional programmers, ways are devised to convert what's wanted into the numbers that the computer Office can understand. Fortunately for us, OPL, the language built into Series 3 to allow us to create programs, is very 'English', and, once you get the hang of it, very easy to understand and to use.

But, given that the Office only accepts 'numbers' as instructions, how does it work? First of all, it must be stated that each number (or group of numbers) represents the simplest of instructions. One instruction, for example, would be 'Go to a box, and copy whatever number you find there into another box', with the addresses of the boxes concerned forming part of the instruction group.

All the instructions for running the Series 3 are contained in memory boxes of the 'read-only' type (ROM). There's over 300,000 of them - so as you can see, there's a lot that Series 3 is capable of doing even without us adding instructions!

Inside the Office, there is a 'meter' which is called 'The Program Counter'. It is set to the address of the box containing the next instruction to be dealt with. When Series 3 is powered up for the very first time, the Office jumps into action, looks at the Program Counter meter, sees a '0' (it resets to zero when there is no power at all), and immediately has a look in Box 0. The Office examines the instruction, obeys it, and re-adjusts the Program Counter. It then rushes off for the next instruction, and so on. It is capable of obeying thousands of instructions every second.

Once the power is on, the Office is active, even though nothing may be appearing on the screen. Much of what the Office does goes on in the background, or behind the scenes. For example, tucked away in the warehouse is a counting device, like a clock, which counts hundreds of thousands of times a second at a very precise rate. The Office keeps a close watch on this device, and every time it reaches a certain number, the Office jumps into action to perform its 'background' duties. These could include things like checking to see whether it's time to ring an 'alarm' to let you know about an appointment, or more simply to add another second to the clock display, or to check whether anything has happened at the keyboard recently and, if not, to save power by closing down the display - 'switching off'. The Office is, in fact, capable sharing its time between a number of specific duties - including the tasks we give it as well as those that go on in the background.

As we shall see when we come to program Series 3, instructions can run around in loops. For example, when Series 3 is switched off, the instructions will be saying to the Office something like *Go and see whether the ON key has been pressed*. The next instruction will be saying *If it has, go do what's necessary to switch-on (jump to instruction so-and-so). But if it hasn't, then go back to the last instruction, which says Go and see if the ON key ... '*. Loops, and the ability to branch off according to the results of a test are very common in programming.

And that's all you really need to know about the way a computer works. Easy, isn't it!

STEP TWO

Let's Get Started!

At the end of this Step, you will know how to
*   *Start and name a new program*
*   *Enter a program*
*   *Handle syntax errors*
*   *Run a program*
*   *Load a program Module for editing*
*   *Copy and rename Modules and programs*
*   *Delete a Module or program*

The mechanics of programming
Let's get those itchy fingers working to show that learning to program is really quite an easy process. We'll start by looking at how programs are put together, then we'll enter a very simple program, run it, and see how it works. We will then discuss how to run it from the main System screen, how to edit it, and how to delete it.

The main objective of this Step is the actual *mechanics* of using Series 3 to write and edit programs. Follow the discussion and instructions given carefully, so that you become familiar with the processes involved.

How a program is constructed
The first thing to understand is the way that a program is put together on Series 3. (*Those familiar with programming the Psion Organiser II, please note that Series 3 allows you to enter more than one procedure at a time ... read on!*).

A complete program is made up of one or more *procedures*. A procedure is a programming unit that performs a distinct action. It may be the entire program, or just a part of a program, that is to say, one of a series of procedures that together perform the overall requirement. Every procedure *always* starts with the word PROC, and *always* ends with the word ENDP.

11

The Basics

A number of procedures can be written, one after the other, and saved as one *Module*. All the procedures in one Module could, together, form one complete program. However, a program need not be completely contained in one Module: there are occasions when it is more convenient to use several Modules.

Each *procedure* must have a name, and each *Module* must have a name. Generally speaking, you'll use the same name for the Module and for the *first* procedure in that Module, though this is not necessary.

The *Module* name is the one that will appear under the RunOpl icon, so you will usually give it a name that reflects the overall function of the program. *Procedure* names, on the other hand, should reflect the operation of that particular piece of the program. Consequently you will name *procedures* and *Modules* according to what they do, so that you will be able to remember them.

To summarise:

1)   A *Module* can consist of one or more *procedures*.
2)   A *program* can consist of one or more *Modules*.

We will start with *single* procedure (and hence, *single* Module) programs, so that you become familiar with the concept. Later on in the book, we will deal with programs that consist of two or more procedures contained one Module.

Starting a new program

First, here are the steps you'll take every time you want to start a new program.

1)   Switch ON your Series 3 (good start!)
2)   Select the Program icon on the screen using the arrow (cursor) keys *or*
        Press the Program icon button under the screen display.
        You can, if you wish, now press ENTER: this takes you straight into the Program Editor. However, the next steps will do the same...
3)   Press the MENU button
4)   Select the 'File' option from the list at the top of the screen, and then select the 'New file' option from the list that 'drops down' (use the arrow keys to 'highlight' an option, and press ENTER to 'select' it).
        A 'dialog' box will appear. You now have to name the *Module* that the program is going to be saved as.

12

Module names can include *up to* eight letters or numbers, in any order. *Procedure* names, on the other hand, must *never* start with a number.

We'll call this first program 'MYFIRST', so type in MYFIRST as the File Name. (It doesn't matter whether you use capital or small letters). You'll see two other options in this Dialog Box - 'Disk', and 'Use Template'. Unless you have a RAM SSD fitted, make sure that 'Disk' is set to 'Internal': programs should be developed using RAM (re-writable) memory. Also, it is best to set the 'Use Template' to 'Yes' (if it isn't already set that way), since this gives automatic indents and sets up the start of the program for you. Use the left and right arrow keys to change these options if necessary.

Then press the ENTER button.

5) The screen will clear, and you will see the 'PROC :' on the top line, and spaced below it, the word ENDP. Our program (a single procedure) will be written between these two lines.

> **Note**: You are now in the Program Editor, which is similar to the Word Processor in Series 3. For ease of reading your programs, you should press MENU, select 'Special', then 'Set Preferences', and ensure that 'Monospaced' character widths have been selected: this makes all characters, including spaces, the same width and easier to check. You can, of course use the proportional face if you choose. You may also wish, in the 'Show as symbols' option, to set Tabs, Spaces and Carriage returns to 'Yes' so that they can be seen. You may also wish to see that the 'Auto-indentation' is switched 'on' and that the indent spacing is set to match the listings in this book (the 'Prog - Indentation' menu options). The 'Outline' option under 'Special' lists all of the procedures (when they exist) in the current Module.

We must now name the procedure (the rules are almost the same as for Module names: no more than eight characters in total, but *always* starting with a letter), and this is done by entering the name after the word PROC and before the colon (the cursor - that flashing line - should be in position ready for you). We will give this procedure the same name as the Module, so type in 'MYFIRST' but *don't* press enter. Your screen should now look like this

```
PROC MYFIRST:

ENDP
```

Remember that every procedure must have the word PROC (which stands for PROCedure) followed by the procedure's name and a colon as the first line, and must end with the word ENDP, which stands for END Procedure. This is so that both we and the Series 3 knows what the procedure is called, and where it begins and ends.

6) We are now ready to start entering our procedure-cum-program. Press the *down arrow* key (*not* ENTER) to position the *cursor* on the next line. If you press ENTER, the colon, which is an integral part of the procedure's name, will also jump to the next line down. That's not what we want.

> **Note:** Refer to the Word processing part of your User's Manual for details on how to use the various keys on the keyboard to enter and edit text.

You will notice that the cursor is indented under the word PROC, as though the TAB key had been pressed. Indenting is a useful way to keep your programs easy to read and decipher at a later time. The OPL style automatically indents for you, until you want a further indent.

7) Type in

```
PRINT "Hey look! I can program!"
```

followed by the ENTER key. Make sure you type in the quotation marks - they are important! The line you have just entered is a program *statement*, or an instruction to Series 3 to do something. Before we go any further, let us have a look at the conventions used in this book to help you when entering programs.

a) OPL language words are written in CAPITAL letters, to help you to identify them. In practice, these can be entered as small letters if you wish, but it won't be so easy to distinguish the OPL words when examining your programs.

b) In this book, the type face used for program lines is *monospaced*: in other words, every character and space has the same width. This should match up with your Series 3 display, and will help you to identify where the spaces are.

8) The cursor should be on the next line down and indented, so now enter each of the following lines the same way, remembering to press the ENTER key after each line. Pressing ENTER tells Series 3 that one statement has been completed - and it will also position the cursor on the next line for you, already indented. (*From now on, it will be assumed that you press the* ENTER *key at the end of each program line*).

```
PAUSE 40
BEEP 16,400
PRINT "Heck, It ain't so hard!"
PRINT "Press any key to finish"
GET
```

9) Your complete program should now look like this on the screen:

```
PROC MYFIRST:
    PRINT "Hey look! I can program!"
    PAUSE 40
    BEEP 16,400
    PRINT "Heck, It ain't so hard!"
    PRINT "Press any key to finish"
    GET
ENDP
```

That's it. Not the most exciting program in the world, but we have to start somewhere. At the moment, our program is written in a way that *we* understand (you will! you will!), but it is not quite in the form that the Series 3 can use. So, the next step is to get Series 3 to *translate* it for us - and at the same time, a check will be made for the things we may have done wrong when entering the program - such as spelling mistakes.

10) Press the MENU key, select the 'Prog' option at the top of the screen, and then select 'Translate' from the drop-down list. Note the alternative '*short-cut*' keypress combination - PSION KEY and 'T' key pressed at the same time. You'll soon get into the habit of using this combination, as it is quicker and easier than using the MENU key and selecting the options you require.

The Basics

If you made any mistakes when entering the program, now is the time they'll show up, because a message such as '**Syntax Error**' will be displayed on the screen. If this has happened to you, the flashing cursor will *usually* (but not always) jump to the point where Series 3 had a problem. The ball's now in your court, but check that you have spelt the words correctly, that you have spaces in the correct places (between the key word that start each line and the 'instruction' that follows it), and check that you have used numbers for the '40' - and not the letter 'O'. Computers know the difference between the letter 'O' and the number '0'. Be careful. If you did have an error, correct it, and 'Translate' it again as before. You can re-check the type of error that has occurred by selecting the 'Show error' option from the 'Prog' menu item, or by pressing the short-cut keys PSION and 'E'.

If you get a '**Memory full**' message, refer to your User's Guide on how to free up some memory before you try to Translate the program again. Series 3 needs room to translate and run your programs.

When there are no mistakes in your program after it has been translated, Series 3 will display a message asking you if you want to run it. Usually you will want to test it out straight away, so

11)   Press the 'Y' key ... and there it is! The screen will display

        Hey look! I can program!

followed soon after by a 'bleep', and the two lines:

        Heck, It ain't so hard!
        Press any key to finish

Press any key on the keyboard, and you will be returned to the Program Editor screen, with everything just as you left it.

There shouldn't be any problems running this program, but you ought to be aware that sometimes, even when a program *translates* satisfactorily, it doesn't always *run* properly because of other types of error. These are called 'run-time' errors, and usually relate to things that Series 3 hasn't been properly informed about. We'll discuss this type of problem later on.

Re-running your program

Before we see how this little program works, you'll no doubt like to run it all again: otherwise it would have been a lot of effort for such short lived glory.

To run a program whilst you're in the Program Editor of the Series 3:

1) Select 'Prog' from the menu at the top (MENU key first, remember), and select 'Run' from the list of options, *or*
Press the PSION and 'Z' keys at the same time. This is the *short-cut* method.

2) A dialog box will appear, asking you for the name of the program *Module* you wish to run: when you have a lot of translated programs, you can choose the name of any of them by using the left or right arrow keys. You'll also be able to choose where the Module was saved (if you have SSDs fitted). When the Module you want is on display (which it should be now), press ENTER.

Note that only *translated* programs can run, so if you make changes to a procedure or program but don't translate it, it is the unchanged *translated* version that will run. Always translate a program after you have made changes to it!

One of the things that happens when a Module is successfully translated is its name appears under a special 'RunOpl' icon (identified by the word OPL in a speech bubble, without a 'document' box round it) on the main 'System' screen display .

To run MYFIRST from the System screen, either:

a) Press the 'SYSTEM' button to bring up the System screen display. Use the arrow keys on the keyboard to move the 'highlight' until it's at the RunOpl icon and over 'MYFIRST', then press ENTER. (When you have more Modules translated, they'll all be listed. You select with the up and down arrow keys).

or

b) Press both the CONTROL key and the PROGRAM button at the same time (that's another 'short-cut' key combination: it takes you to the RunOpl icon, whatever you are doing in Series 3). Then select 'MYFIRST' as in a) above, and press ENTER.

What does it all mean?

OK, we've entered our first program. But what does it all mean? First of all, each line is a separate instruction or *statement* to the Series 3 to do something. The first word on each line in our program is either a *command*, or a *function*.

The Basics

Series 3 understands over 200 different *commands* and *functions*: we've just met a few of them. A *command* is generally an order to do something, while a *function* is generally an instruction to get or evaluate and 'return' some information. Most of the time, a *function* is not the first thing that will appear on a line, but we'll worry about that later on. Let's have a brief look at what the words in this particular program mean (we'll cover most of them again in greater detail).

The word PRINT in the first line is a command. It tells Series 3 that we want it to print something on the screen. What we want printed forms the second part of the statement: "Hey look! I can program!". So that Series 3 can differentiate between words and other things like *variables*, we put those words between quotation marks. The format is

> PRINT "*what we want printed on the screen*"

Whenever you want to spell out what will appear on the screen, that's the format to use. What happens if you just have PRINT, without anything following it? You get a blank line on the screen. We'll deal with PRINT in more detail in a later Step. The next program line

> PAUSE 40

is another command.

PAUSE   tells Series 3 to spin its wheels for a while - the time it spends spinning its wheels being given by the number after the word PAUSE. This number tells Series 3 how many *twentieths* of a second to wait. So the '40' in our program will cause Series 3 to wait for 2 seconds. (40 twentieths). This number can also be negative - we could have written, for example PAUSE -40: this tells Series 3 to wait for 2 seconds *or* until a key is pressed, whichever comes first. We could also have written a '0' as the number. This is a special instruction: it doesn't mean don't wait, it means wait until a key is pressed.

The next line is another command. BEEP tells Series 3 to make a noise at the loudspeaker. The length of the beep is given by the first number, which is a measure of *thirty-seconds* of a second. So 16

ιere means half a second. The second number gives the frequency
ιy a rather wondrous formula - which we'll discuss in another Step.

There follows two more PRINT command lines, and then the line
ιhich simply says

```
GET
```

ιhis is a function, and is usually preceded by something else. It is
ιn instruction to Series 3 to wait until a key is pressed, and to then
ιeturn the character code for that key: by 'return', we mean save it
ιomewhere so that we can act on it if we want. The character code is
ιhe value that Series 3 uses to determine what character pattern to
ιut on the screen. We didn't need to know what key had been
ιressed in our program, so we haven't bothered to save the
ιnformation.

Why use GET instead of PAUSE 0? To show you that, when
ιrogramming, there is invariably more than one way to do
ιomething! Why use GET at all? Because without it, the program
ιould end and vanish from the screen before you'd had a chance to
ιead anything! You have to tell Series 3 to 'hang on', before it obeys
ιhe next instruction - which is to end running the program - and
ιeturn to the previous screen display.

Starting a new Module from the Program Editor

ιf you are already using the Program Editor, you can start a new
ιlodule by simply
)   Pressing the MENU key
)   Selecting 'File' from the options at the top (press ENTER), then
         'New File' (press ENTER), and enter the new Module's name.

ιf you aren't already in the Program Editor, then you start a new
ιrogram Module in the same way we started MYFIRST.

Note that, on the System display, the Module that is currently
ιeady' for editing is in bold letters.

Editing an existing Module

ιrom the System display (press the 'System' button), cursor along to
ιhe OPL program menu, then cursor down to the name of the Module
ιou wish to edit, and press enter.

From the Program Editor, either
         Press the MENU key, select the 'File' option, then select the
         'Open file' option, *or*
         Press the short-cut combination PSION and 'O' keys.

The Basics

Either way, a Dialog Box will open, and you can use the left an
right arrow keys to select the Module you wish to edit (if there's mor
than one). Make your selection and press ENTER.

Deleting a Module

The procedure for deleting an OPL Module from your Series 3 is th
same as that for deleting any file:

1) Press the 'SYSTEM' button to bring up the System scree
display. Use the arrow keys on the keyboard to move th
highlight until it's at the RunOpl icon, then use the arrow keys
necessary to select the program Module you wish to delete.
or Press both the CONTROL key and the PROGRAM button at th
same time to get to the RunOpl icon, then select the Module yo
wish to delete using the arrow keys.

2) If the Module you have selected is in bold lettering, it means th
Module is 'active'. You must make it *inactive* before you can dele
it. So
Press the DELETE key. A Dialog Box will appear, askin
you if you want to 'quit' the selected Module (i.e. make
inactive). Press 'the 'Y' key.

3) Press the MENU key, to display the option list at the top of th
screen, select 'File', and press ENTER, then select 'Delete File
(short-cut is PSION and 'D' keys). Now when you press ENTER th
selected Module will be displayed: as before, you can sele
another Module to delete, if any are present, using the left an
right arrow keys.

4) Press ENTER to continue, (or ESC to abort the deletion). Anoth
Dialog Box will appear asking you to confirm the deletion (or no
by pressing the 'Y' or 'N' key. If you press 'Y', the Module will b
deleted. If you press 'N', you will be returned to the previou
Dialog Box: press ESC to abandon the deletion.

When you delete a Module, you delete it for ever. Consequently you shoul
be absolutely sure you have no further use for the Module before deletin
it! Having said that, many of the procedures in this book are of a trivi
nature, written purely to help you understand a particular process. They d
take up valuable space, so when you feel happy about it, delete them to fre
up memory.

Deleting a translated program

The procedure for deleting a translated program is exactly the same as that for deleting a Module. The only difference is, you will select the program from the list under the RunOpl icon.

Duplicating a Module

There may be times when you want to make changes to a Module, but don't want to lose the 'original'. You can do this two ways: by first saving the Module again under a different name, and secondly by copying the Module.

To save the Module again under a different name:
1)   From the System display, or from the Program Editor, first select the Module concerned and press ENTER to make that Module 'active'. Then, from the Program Editor, either press MENU and select 'File' and 'Save as', *or* use the short-cut combination PSION and 'A' keys. (Don't use PSION and 'A' from the System display - that does something else!)
2)   A Dialog Box will appear, prompting you for the new name for the file or Module: make your entry (remembering the rules for Module names) and press ENTER. Don't worry about the 'Use new file' option: that's for the styles in Word. The Program Editor has its own style.

To copy a Module:
1)   Press the System button. Examine the name of the file you wish to copy: if it is in bold letters, it is active, so press the DELETE key to make it inactive. Make sure the highlight is at the Program icon, then *either* press MENU, select 'File' and then 'Copy file', *or* press the PSION and 'C' keys at the same time.
2)   Press ENTER, and a Dialog Box will appear. At 'From file: Name' select the file you wish to copy using the left or right arrow keys. Then cursor down to the 'To file: Name', and type in the name for your new file, and press ENTER.

Having saved your Module under a new name, remember that it will need to be translated again before it can be run under the new name.
    You can now select the original or the newly named file for further editing.

The Basics

Renaming Modules or Translated Programs

On the System display, set the highlight over the name of the Module or Program name you wish to rename. Make sure it is 'inactive', pressing the DELETE key if necessary, and *either* press MENU, select 'File' and 'Rename file' and press ENTER, *or* press PSION and 'R' together.

A Dialog Box will appear. If the file you wish to rename isn't the one selected in the 'From: Name' option, select it using the left or right arrow keys. Then cursor down to the 'To: Name' and enter the new name, finishing by pressing the ENTER key.

The selected Module or translated program will be renamed.

Your first taste

You have now written your first program, translated it, and run it. You should know how to handle your Modules for editing, and so on. And you should have a general, though perhaps sketchy idea of what it's all about. Let's summarise it all.

A program is made up of one or more *procedures*. The program we have written has just one procedure. A procedure starts with the word PROC followed by its name and a colon, and ends with the word ENDP. The procedure name must never be more than eight characters (and that includes an *identifier*, which we'll come to later), and must start with a letter.

Each line of a procedure is an instruction or *statement* telling the Series 3 to do something. These statements use a key word which is either a *command* (an instruction to do something), or a *function* (an instruction to get some information and, usually, save it somewhere). You are advised to type in the key words in capital letters, so that they're easy to spot.

A few final points that haven't been mentioned yet, and you're ready to start on Step Three.

1)   You *can* have more than one statement on a line, provided that each of the statements is separated by a space and a colon. Thus

```
PAUSE 40 :BEEP 16,400
```

However, this can sometimes make programs harder to read and 'debug'.

2)   A procedure in one Module can 'call' or use procedures in *other* Modules, by *loading* those Modules first. More about this at the right time...

3) When a Module contains more than one procedure, it is the *first* procedure that is executed when the Module is run. The other procedures in the Module are, in effect, 'sub-procedures', which must be 'called' in order to be executed. This, too, we'll deal with later on.

4) The name of a program that is *running* is shown in bold under the RunOpl icon on the System screen display. The name of a Module being *edited* in the Program Editor is also shown in bold, under the Program icon on the System display.

5) When you are 'in' a program that is *running*, you can stop it by pressing the PSION and the ESC key at the same time. To pause a program that is running, press the CONTROL key and the 'S' key at the same time. You can resume running the program by pressing CONTROL and 'S' again.

Finally, from now on only when appropriate will a *Module name* be suggested to you (that's the name the procedure or procedures will be saved as, remember, and the name that will appear under the RunOpl icon). While working through this book, each *single* procedure should be saved as a separate Module: if you try to tack other procedures to an existing Module, those procedures won't run unless specifically called by the first procedure in the Module. You can give the Module any name you choose, but is recommended that you give it the same name as the procedure.

The Basics

STEP THREE

Planning The Program

After this Step, you'll have an insight on how to plan your program properly ... a process often ignored by would-be programmers at their peril.

The way it was...

Not too many years ago, newcomers to the world of programming used a language called 'BASIC'. It was (and still is) an easy language to learn, but in the early days, it had no 'structure': programs written in BASIC tended to be one long, ghastly string of statements.

Invariably a program needs to 'branch off' under certain conditions, and these 'branches' were just tacked in among the rest of the program lines. The result was that at the end of the day, such programs were very difficult to add to, or change, because they were so convoluted and involved.

To give an example of why a program may need to branch, consider a routine for making a hot drink (if only our Series 3 could be so programmed!). The program may start off by asking "Tea or coffee?", and according to our choice, it will branch off to perform the necessary operations. All branches could well come back to one 'end' point - where the computer proudly announces "*Your* (whatever the choice was) *is made, sir!*"

Now such a program *could* be written in one long listing, but what a mess it could look, especially after you decided to add a few more drinks, and options (*with or without milk? do you want sugar?*).

The solution is what has become known as *structured programming*: breaking the program up into little blocks, as separate routines or procedures, and then having just one, short(ish) main or master procedure that calls the others as and when they're needed.

The Basics

The way it is

You'll be delighted to know, Series 3 is designed to let you structure your programs. It makes life much easier, and means that you can design 'blocks' which can be used in a number of different programs, so you don't have to keep re-inventing the wheel. Once you have designed a neat procedure to perform a particular task, you can use it over and over again in other programs by *loading* it into those programs.

Structuring a program means you have to think about it a bit before you actually start writing the code. You have to ask yourself what exactly do you want the program to achieve, how will the user interact with it, and so on. A very large program can in many respects be like building a house. To simply start digging foundations and then plod away tacking on a bit here and a bit there without any planning is a recipe for a pretty grim looking house which may or may not, at the end of the day, serve its purpose. And when it comes to adding another room, or a service such as central heating ... the mind boggles.

The problem is nowhere near as pronounced for short, simple programs: these can be, and in most instances are, written in one 'chunk'. But as soon as there is a routine or a set of instructions that needs to be repeated, then the program should be broken up into sections or *procedures*.

Let us take an example. Let us suppose you wish to write a game program that requires a dice throw. If you had to write the dice-throw routine every time it is needed, you'd have the routine repeated a number of times unnecessarily. If, on the other hand, the dice-throw routine is written as one discrete procedure, that procedure can be 'called' whenever it is needed. The dice-throw routine becomes one of the 'blocks' in your program. Later on should you wish to make changes to the dice-throw routine - to simulate the throw of *two* dice, perhaps, it is a simple matter to make the change. Once.

Right way or wrong way?

One of the interesting facts about programming is that, if you were to give each of 100 programmers the task of writing a program to perform a particular task on a particular type of computer, you'd end up with 100 different programs. They may look the same when running, but if you were to examine the actual instructions, they'd almost certainly be different.

Some of the programs will require a lot of memory while others will use very little memory. Some will operate very fast, and some will be comparitively slow. Some will be easy to understand, and others look extremely complex. Some will be 'user-friendly' - that is, have lots of prompts to guide the user through what is required, while others will leave the user wondering what he is supposed to do next.

The reason why each solution will be different is because everyone has their own ideas on how to tackle the requirement. The truth of the matter is there is no *right* or *wrong* way to write a program: only good ways and bad ways. If it works and does the job expected of it, it is 'right'. If it doesn't - then it's wrong.

Later on, when more experienced, you'll be able to look back over a program and think "I could have written that better - to run faster or take up less room, or to be more user-friendly". And if you used the modular approach, you'll be able to make your improvements fairly easily.

So, when you first start to write your own programs, don't worry about whether they're right or wrong: worry about whether or not they're going to work!

Define your requirement

As previously mentioned, the first thing to do when writing a program is to define what you want it to do as clearly as possible. Not in your head. On paper. Make sure that you cover everything, including how you will want to use the program.

Once you have a little knowledge of the programming language, you can start the task off by writing 'pseudo' code: this isn't the exact instructions, but an outline of the instructions that you want performed. For example, let us suppose that you're in the carpet business, and you want to write a program that will quickly tell you how many square yards of carpet are needed for a particular sized room, and what the cost is going to be given the price of the carpet per square yard.

In broad terms, the program needs to do the following:

1) Get the size of the room.
2) Work out the area in square yards.
3) Round *up* the answer to the next nearest square yard, and display the answer.
4) Get the cost of the carpet per square yard.
5) Work out the cost of carpeting the specified room, and display the answer.

The Basics

We have defined the basic requirement. But the program can go further: we can provide a 'loop', allowing the user to enter another room size, or another carpet cost, or both, without having to re-run the program each time.

Getting the room size and working out the square yards of carpet needed is one entire action. Provided that the area is known, getting the cost of the carpet per square yard and calculating the carpeting cost is another complete action. We could therefore create two 'blocks' or procedures to do the donkey work:

a) Get room size and work out square yardage of carpet needed.
b) Get cost of carpet and work out cost of carpeting room.

Block or procedure (a) we shall call *area*, and (b) we shall call *cost*. Now we can have another *main* procedure, which we will call *carpet*, to do the following:

1) Get *area*
2) Get *cost*
3) Another cost? *Yes*　Repeat from (2) again
　　　　　　　　 No　 Go on to (4)
4) Another area? *Yes*　Repeat from (1) again
　　　　　　　　 No　 End the program

If you follow this last routine through step by step, you will see that it starts off the same way as before, but having worked out the cost of a carpet for a particular room, it will allow us to change the cost of the carpet and come up with the new answer, or go right back and get a whole new room size entirely.

The illustration setting out our requirements diagrammatically and shown on the next page is known as a *flow chart*. This one is fairly straightforward, but nevertheless, as you can see, a flow chart helps in understanding the problem. It also makes programming easier, because we can take each box as a separate unit, and code it accordingly. (At a later Step, we'll write the code for this program).

The "CALL" in the top two boxes is a way of saying 'go and do the separate procedure, and then come back here'. You will see that there are various ways of making 'calls' to other procedures - and as it happens, the actual OPL word 'CALL' is *not* one that we will be using in this book: it is one of the words that is used for writing

28

ode at the 'machine's own level' and as such is beyond our scope.
Be assured, you won't need to use it yet!

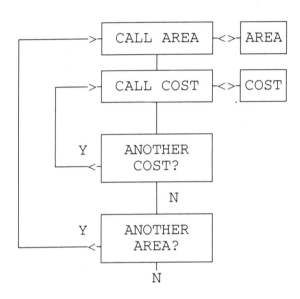

Fig. 3.1 Flow Chart for the Carpet Program

Note the calculations

Having worked out what we want our program to do, and defined a
structure for it in the form of a flow chart, the next stage before
settling down to write and test the code is to make a note of any
calculations the program may need to make, and write them down.
This step may not always be necessary: for the program under
discussion, the calculations are fairly trivial, and could easily wait
until we're actually preparing the code. However, as we shall be
concentrating on other matters in later Steps, we'll deal with the
mathematics of our program now.

Floor area is given by the very simple formula, *length x breadth*.
We want the answer in square yards, but will most likely want to
input the measurements in feet. Thus we can say

$$\text{area in sq yds} = \frac{\text{length x breadth in feet}}{9}$$

The Basics

Whatever the area is, we need to round it up to the next whole number. So if the answer works out to be 11.2 square yards, we need to round that up to be 12 square yards. There are a number of ways we can do this. One is to check whether there is any 'decimal value' to the answer, and if so, add one to the 'whole number' or integer part. Any decimal values will be dropped, of course.

Having obtained an area in square yards, the next thing we need is simply the cost of the carpet required. This is given by

Carpet cost = area in sq yards x cost per sq yard

It can sometimes happen, when evaluating the mathematics required for a program, that another routine may be called for. A particular calculation may appear in several different places throughout the program: if this is the case, then a procedure - or *function* - can be prepared to handle that calculation. And it is at the planning stage you need to know whether such a procedure will be necessary, so that you can write the program accordingly.

Planning a program properly before it is started is a stage that many would-be programmers tend to ignore. Professional programmers excluded, a small proportion of programmers can afford to ignore in depth planning for their programs - they can call upon previous experience and skills. Unfortunately, the rest believe they belong to that small proportion, then find they waste a considerable amount of time trying to 'debug' their programs. Or writing to authors of books like this to help them out!

'Debugging' is an expression that comes from the early days when computers used valves and relays. Insects, attracted to the bright lights emitted by the valves, would sizzle themselves on the hot glass and fall, very dead and very inconsiderately, into the delicate circuitry below. It is reputed that on one notable occasion a moth, sizzled and singed, dropped carelessly between the contacts of a relay, causing mysterious operational problems. The fact that those problems were caused by a mere bug have remained part of the colourless folk law of computing ever since. As punishment for the thoughtless behaviour of one moth, the whole bug race is now blamed for anything, absolutely anything that goes wrong with software written by super human beings. Almost without exception, 'bugs are the result of human error: so planning to avoid them is a good human practice!

STEP FOUR

The Variables

After this Step, you will know

* *What variables are, and the different types used by OPL.*
* *How to name variables, and to tell Series 3 about them.*
* *The difference between LOCAL and GLOBAL variables.*
* *The scope of GLOBAL variables.*
* *How to pass values to other procedures.*
* *How to return a value from a function procedure to the calling routine using the OPL word RETURN.*
* *About variables that don't need declaring*
* *How to use constants wisely.*

The unknown quantities

It's now time to get started on the language itself in earnest, and our first step in this direction is to look at the various ways there are of saving information that is likely to change ... the *variables*.

Whenever you write a program or procedure, you will almost always need to work with different sets of figures or characters each time the program is run. Taking the 'Carpet' program outlined in Step 3 as a typical example, each time we run the program we will want to enter the room's measurements at the keyboard, and we will want to enter the cost of the carpet. This information has to be stored somewhere for subsequent action: the alternative is to actually re-write the program with the relevant figures each time it is used, and that, obviously, is an utter waste of time and programming effort.

What we do is to tell Series 3 that we have unknown quantities to be stored - quantities that could be different each time the program is run. We do this by telling Series 3 to set aside memory boxes specially for these quantities, and, to make it easy for ourselves and the Series 3, we give those memory boxes names.

The unknown quantities are called *variables*.

Before we discuss how to tell Series 3 to set aside the appropriate numbers of boxes for each variable, let us look at the nature of the variables themselves.

31

The Basics

TYPES OF VARIABLE

There are two fundamental *categories* of variable. First there are those that hold numbers of one kind or another - that is, values that are going to be used for mathematical operations of some sort: these are called *numeric* variables. Then there are the variables that hold *characters*, which can be letters or numbers or any other symbol that can be entered from the keyboard. These are called *string* variables and cannot be used *directly* in mathematical operations, although as we shall see later, it is possible to convert them into numeric values if they contain numbers.

Let us examine these two types separately.

Numeric variables

You may recall, from Step One, that numbers for mathematical operations can be stored in memory boxes in various ways. For example, we can use two boxes to store whole numbers in the range -32768 to +32767, and four boxes to store whole numbers in the range -2147483648 to +2147483647. These two types are called *integers* and *long integers* respectively.

Numbers that have a decimal point in them are called *floating point* numbers, and have to be stored in a different way, using more boxes. *Integers* and *long integers* can never have a decimal point in them, and it is important that you understand this when you use integer variables (and constants) in program calculations.

String variables

String variables require as many boxes as there are characters to be saved or stored, plus a few more that you needn't worry about. If you want to use a *string* variable, you have to know when you start programming how many boxes you want Series 3 to set aside (ignoring those extra ones just mentioned - Series 3 sees to those on your behalf).

Array variables

The numeric and string variables described above are just *single* variables: that is to say, they hold just one value. But there are many occasions when you'll want a group of variables of the same type - which you will want to give the same basic name to. For example you may wish to store the first three letters of each month of the year - JAN, FEB, MAR and so on. You could put these into their own individual memory boxes, but it is better to create an *array* of boxes called, say, MON$(). (Don't worry about that dollar sign or the brackets yet). With such an array, it is easy to get at any of the individual elements very quickly. For example, once the program had been initiated and set up, 'JAN' would be defined as MON$(1), and 'FEB' as MON$(2), and so on.

Similarly, numeric values of like types and of the same grouping can be placed into arrays for easy access during the running of the program. 'Like types' means integers, or long integers, or floating point numbers. And 'like groupings' means being able to share the same basic variable name, such as 'Items'.

NAMING VARIABLES

We now come to the rules that *must* be obeyed when you name a variable. First, you must know the variable's *type*, so that you can *identify* it for the Series 3: Series 3 must know how many boxes to allocate for that variable, remember.

Variable names are effectively in two parts: the name part which enables us - and Series 3 - to know which group of memory boxes we're talking about (the name in effect replaces the numeric address, just like a house name can replace its numeric address). This is followed by an *identifier* part that tells Series 3 how many memory boxes to allocate for the job.

The name part

* Can be up to eight characters long, and no more, *including* the identifier.
* Must *always* start with a letter, but after that, can be any combination of letters and numbers.
* Must *not* be one of the OPL function or command words - that is, words that are part of the OPL language itself.
* *Must* end with the identifier symbol which describes the type of variable, with the sole exception of *floating point* variables - which have no identifying character.

The identifying symbols are as follows:

%	Integers
&	Long Integers
$	Strings
	Floating point

Finally, it doesn't matter whether you use capital or lower case letters: Series 3 takes them both to be the same. Thus CARpet% is the same as carPET% is the same as CARPET% is the same as carpet%. But quite different from carpet$ (the last one is a *string* variable, the rest are *integer* variables).

When naming variables, it is useful for your later understanding of the program to give meaningful names. Where memory space is at an absolute premium, it is equally wise to keep the names as short as possible. Fortunately the days when only one or two lettered variables were permissible have long gone. So, if a variable is going to be used to store the length of a room, it makes sense to call it 'LENGTH', and so on.

Let us look at some valid variable names:

Cost	Floating point type
Cost$	String type
COST$	String type, exactly the same as that above.
Cost%	Integer type
Astro1&	Long integer type
P234R678	Floating point type
OutCome&	Long Integer type
Work%(52)	52 integer variables, Work%(1) ... Work%(52)

Remember that each variable can only store the kind of information specified by its identifier. Now here are some variable names that are not valid:

LEN	It's an OPL word
Week	Its an OPL word
4tune	It starts with a number
b2345678%	It's too long
wow*	Bad identifier
dollar$$	Bad character

Using OPL words is a common error, particularly since OPL covers quite a few words that are in common usage!

DECLARING VARIABLES

Having decided what variable names we want to use in our program, and what types of variable they are going to be, we now have to let

Series 3 know. This is done at the very beginning of a program or procedure, by a process called 'declaring the variables'. There are two ways we can declare variables - as LOCALs, and as GLOBALs.

LOCAL variables are used *only* in the procedure in which they are declared. So if every procedure in a program has a variable called 'JUNK', then each one will be quite separate and distinct from the others, and unaffected by any changes made to the others.

GLOBAL variables can be used in any and every procedure called by the procedure they're declared in, and the procedures that *they* call. When a GLOBAL variable has its value changed by a procedure, the new value will be used throughout the program, until it is changed again. GLOBAL variables are, therefore, a useful way of 'passing information' between procedures. However, it is not the only way. When we examine methods of calling other procedures, we shall see that there is another way to pass information back and forth between procedures.

Variables are declared by using the OPL word LOCAL or GLOBAL, followed by the list of variable names, each separated by a comma. For string variables, it is essential to inform Series 3 how many memory boxes must be reserved for storing the characters. So if you want to store eight characters in a LOCAL string variable called Student$, it would have to be declared as

```
LOCAL Student$(8)
```

Yes, this looks like an array: if you want an array of five string variables called Student$, each of which is eight characters long (they must all be the same length), then the *array* dimension comes first in the bracket, and is separated from the number of characters dimension by a comma, thus

```
LOCAL Student$(5,8)
```

The '5' says there are five elements in the array, and the '8' says that each element can store up to 8 characters.

Arrays of other variables simply have the number of elements in the array enclosed in brackets. Thus

```
LOCAL Price(5),Item%(10)
```

will declare an array of five floating point variables called 'Price', and an array of ten integer variables called 'Item%'.

The Basics

Here is an example of what the first lines of a procedure will look like, with the variables declared:

```
PROC Test:
   GLOBAL allover%,lots$(16)
   LOCAL junk,women&(5),t%
   ...
ENDP
```

This declares two GLOBAL variables: the integer 'allover%', and the string 'lots$' which can be used to store up to 16 characters. The three LOCAL variables declared are 'junk' (floating point), women&(5) (an array of 5 long integers), and t% (an integer). All the procedures that this one calls can make use of - and change - the values in the GLOBAL variables 'allover%' and 'lots$', but the values of 'junk', 'women&()' and 't%' can be used and changed only by this procedure.

Note that if a procedure called by 'Test' has a LOCAL variable called 'allover%' declared, then *that* 'allover%' will be unique to that procedure, and any changes made to its value will not affect the GLOBALly declared 'allover%' in the main 'Test' procedure.

Scope of GLOBAL variables

The scope or hierarchy of GLOBAL variables is indicated by the following diagram. In this diagram - which is not a flow chart - PROCedures are assumed to be *calling* only those PROCedures to their right. It shows how PROCedures can use the GLOBAL variables of those PROCedures they are called *by*, but not of those they call. Note that GLOBAL variables don't have to be re-declared in subsequent procedures.

Note how 'PROC One' calls *all* of the other PROCedures, but only has access to GLOBAL variable A. 'PROC Four' on the other hand, when called by 'PROC One' or 'PROC Two', also has access to *their* variables, A and B respectively, as well as its own GLOBAL variable 'D'.

This kind of hierarchy can occur when you start preparing 'libraries' of routines, for use in a number of programs, where a library procedure itself calls other routines.

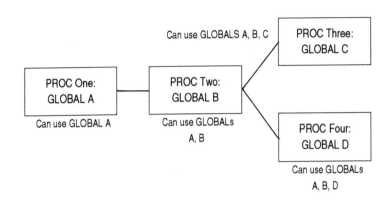

Fig 4.1 The scope of GLOBAL variables

NON-DECLARED VARIABLES

Strictly speaking, there's no such thing as a non-declared variable: Series 3 needs to know all about any variables we may want to store. What we are referring to here are the variables that don't have to be declared by LOCAL or GLOBAL statements. There are three basic types of these. There are values that are passed as arguments. There are variables, or *field names*, that are used when creating or opening files. And there are the Series 3 Calculator memories.

Values passed as arguments

It has already been stated that GLOBAL variables are one way of making variables available to other procedures. It isn't the only way, and it isn't always the neatest way. In fact, for many very short procedures which always act on specific information that's passed to them, GLOBAL variables represent a very clumsy approach.

To explain this, and to demonstrate how values are passed as arguments, let us write a little procedure that gives the remainder left after one number has been divided by another. This is a very handy routine, found in several other programming languages under the name 'MOD', but not in OPL. No problem: we'll create our own.

We will call the procedure 'MOD'. It will need two values to work on. It will need the number to be divided, which we will call 'n', and the divisor, which we will call 'd'. Both will be floating point values. Now, whenever we call this procedure, we want to be able to pass to it values for 'n' and 'd', and we want the answer to be 'returned' to the calling routine.

Incidentally, a procedure which 'returns' a value is known as a *function*. There are numerous *functions* in the OPL language itself: SIN() and UPPER$ are two examples.

Passing values *to* the procedure is done by naming the variables, not as LOCAL or GLOBAL, but as *arguments* in the procedure's name. Like this

```
PROC MOD:(n,d)
```

What we are saying, in effect, is that whenever the procedure 'MOD' is called, the two values that need to be worked on must be included in the calling statement. Series 3 knows that information is being passed from one place to another, by the way we've 'named' our procedure.

We haven't covered how a call to another procedure is made yet, but it won't hurt to let you in on the secret now.

The call is made by simply naming the procedure, as if it were an OPL key word, but followed by a colon. Where arguments have to be passed to the procedure, they are included in brackets, *in the correct order* and *of the correct variable type*. So a call to our 'MOD' procedure could look like this:

```
MOD:(yr,4)
```

'yr' is a floating point variable, which could typically contain a year like 1991 (not a floating point value, but important that the variable *is* floating point). Strictly speaking, the 4 should be written as 4.0, the floating point form, but as it is 'declared' in the MOD procedure as floating point, Series 3 will force the real value 4 into a floating point variable format. If instead of the 4 we had used an integer variable, such as 'v%', then Series 3 would have been very confused, because we've stated we want to pass an integer variable into a floating point variable: the result would be a TYPE MISMATCH error message when the program is translated.

The thing to notice is that the names of the variables in the MOD procedure need *not* be the same as those passed to it: only the *types* must tally. It's a very important point.

Also you should note that the values of the variables passed to a function cannot be changed by the function. For example, in the function MOD(n,d), we can *use* the values of 'n' and 'd' to make calculations or whatever, but we cannot *change* their values.

But back to the plot ...

In the 'MOD' procedure, to calculate the remainder when 'n' is divided by 'd', we can use the following equation

$$rmndr = n-(INT(n/d)*d)$$

INT is an OPL key word, which means 'take the integer of whatever value or expression is in the brackets that immediately follow', in our case, the expression 'n/d'. Briefly, it works is like this (skip this next bit if you don't care how it works). The number 'n' is divided by the divisor 'd', then the decimal part is knocked off completely - by taking the integer. This gives us the whole number of times 'd' divides into 'n'. That whole number is then multiplied by the divisor again, and that gives us the nearest whole number below the original number that is exactly divisible by the divisor. We then deduct this from the original number, and presto, that's the remainder. Try it sometime. (The next Step deals with the way Series 3 handles arithmetic).

Once more, back to the plot.

In the equation above, it looks like we need to store the answer somewhere - in a variable called '*rmndr*', perhaps. But there is no need, because now we come to a way of passing a variable or a result *back* to the routine that called it. And that's with the OPL key word **RETURN**. The format for this word is

RETURN *a variable or result of an expression*

In other words, we can 'return' a variable (which means Series 3 will pass back to the calling routine the *value* held in the variable's memory boxes), or we can return the *result* of an expression. So we don't need to waste space by declaring a local variable to hold the answer. We can 'return' it to the calling routine with the line

RETURN n-(INT(n/d)*d)

And that's it. Our procedure looks like this in full:

```
PROC MOD:(n,d)
   RETURN n-(INT(n/d)*d)
ENDP
```

Pretty impressive, huh? OK, maybe not. But it does demonstrate how to pass values to a function procedure, and how to return a *single* value back to the calling routine.

NOTE: As MOD is a function, you won't be able to run it directly: it needs to be called by another procedure (or used in the Calculator). We'll do this in Step 6.

There are a few things about functions you should note:

1)   Only *one* value can be returned to a calling routine. To return more, you'll have to use GLOBAL variables.

2)   Where a value is being returned, the procedure *name* must be followed by the identifier for the type of value being returned. So if the procedure is to return a string variable, its name must reflect this by being called something like 'ANSWER$:(quest$,part%)'. Note the identifying $ sign to show that, whatever else this function does, it returns a string. Note too that the name, including the identifier, must not be more than eight characters.

3)   You use the functions you write just like OPL functions. That means assigning them to a variable, or using them as part of an another expression. Thus, to use our 'MOD' routine, the calling program might have a line like

```
leapyr = MOD:(yr/4)
```

In this line, the result of the MOD:() routine is passed back and stored in the memory boxes labelled 'leapyr'. We'll come back to this topic again.

Variables used in opening files

This is not the place to tie you up with the file handling capabilities of Series 3. However, you should be aware that, when files are created or opened, certain *field-names* have to be declared amongst other information, and this is *not* done by use of the words LOCAL or GLOBAL. Files, incidentally, are groups of records and so on, that you decide to store in memory, so that you can call them back for perusal/work at a later time. The Diary, Database and Word Processor in your Series 3 all produce files that you can recall. With OPL, you can also create files to do what you want the way you want.

Using the calculator memories

You will no doubt be aware that the calculator in Series 3 has ten memories. These are designated 'M0' to 'M9', and are all of the floating point type. Series 3 knows about them (there's a surprise!), and so if you want to use them, you can without having to declare them first. You simply use their 'name'.

Any information you store in any of the ten calculator memories *remains in that memory* even after the program has finished running. This makes the calculator memories a useful way to store values between programs, and for passing data to the calculator for the calculator's use: you can run OPL *functions* from the calculator. However, you must be aware that the calculator memories could be changed by other programs you may write, or from within the calculator itself.

CONSTANTS (Real values)

Before leaving the subject of variables, real values or *constants* should be mentioned. Constants are those values that actually get written into your program and consequently never change, rather than those entered whilst it is running.

For example, you may have to write a routine that converts degrees Celsius (or Centigrade) to degrees Fahrenheit, which will probably contain a line something like this:

```
fahr=32+(c*9/5)
```

In this, 32, 9 and 5 are constants. Trouble is, the way they're written, they have no decimal point - and Series 3 will take them to be integers and store them accordingly. Integers, remember, can never have a decimal point, and the result of dividing an integer by an integer (as in 9/5 in the example line) will be an integer: which will give you the wrong result. As an integer, 9/5 is '1' not the expected '1.8'.

Consequently it is particularly important when using constants to make sure that they are entered in the correct form. Entering 9.0/5 or 9/5.0 will force *one* of the values into a floating point format, and that, in turn, will force the division result into floating point format. So you'll get the correct answer.

The message is, be careful when using constants, to ensure that they are stored the way you want, to produce the answers you expect.

STEP FIVE

The Maths of Programming

In this Step, you'll learn about
* *Series 3's basic mathematical operators*
* *The order in which calculations are made*
* *Mixing different types of variable in calculations*
* *Making calculations whilst programming*

Don't panic!

You don't have to know any more maths to write a computer program than you need to solve a particular problem using pencil and paper. For those who have never seen a computer program, and who can vaguely remember something about 'algebra' at school, some lines in a program can look downright stupid.

Here's an example:

```
x = x+1
```

Now common sense tells you that x (which we take here to mean 'any number') cannot be equal to the same number *plus one*. No, and this line doesn't mean that: which is why we need to spend just a few moments looking at the way maths works in a computer program.

The line '**x=x+1**', and lines similar to it, are really instructions or statements to the Series 3, and not equations. In an *equation*, what's on the left hand side of the equals sign is said to equal what's on the right hand side. In a computer statement, the *result* of what's on the right hand side is *stored* in the variable name listed on the left hand side. The 'equals' sign represents an *assignment*.

So the line '**x=x+1**' is an instruction to Series 3. It takes the right-hand side first, looks into the memory boxes labelled or addressed as 'x', adds one to the number found there, then *puts the answer into the boxes labelled 'x'*: which, as it happens, are also the boxes Series looked into on the right hand side.

If you could sit there watching the boxes addressed as 'x' while this is going on, you'd see that Series 3 comes along with its strict instructions, looks in the x boxes, adds one to the number it finds there, then, looking at the next part of the instruction, discovers that the answer has to be dropped back into the same boxes.

The value of x has been incremented.

In computer statements, the left hand side of an equals sign denotes *where* any calculation or value that's on the right hand side is to be stored.

So you can 'assign' a value to a variable in a program, with a line something like

    x=42

The maths operators

Series 3 can be programmed to perform all of the operations a calculator offers, and many that a calculator doesn't offer. What can confuse is that there are no apparent multiplication or division symbols. They're there, however, but under a different guise. Here's the list of symbols used for the different mathematical operations:

+	Add
-	Subtract
-	Unary minus (that means 'change the sign')
*	Multiply
/	Divide
**	Raise to a power
%	Percentages

The percentages operator '%' is used in conjunction with any of the four basic mathematical operators, to produce different kinds of result. These are summed up a follows:

100+2% Says 'Add 2% of 100 to 100': the answer is 102 *(100+2)*
100-2% Says 'Deduct 2% of 100 from 100': the answer is 98 *(100-2)*
100*2% Says 'What is 2% of 100?': the answer is 2
100/2 Says 'What is 100 two percent of?': the answer is 5000

Note that if a *variable* were to be used instead of a real or constant value, the '%' would have to be separated from it by a space - otherwise Series 3 would think it was looking at an *integer* variable!. Thus

100+vat %   Says 'Find the value in the *vat* boxes, take *that percentage* of 100, and add it to 100.

There are two other ways the percentage operator can be used, and that's with two the *logical* operators '>' and '<'. We'll be meeting these in some detail when we discuss decision making in a later Step, but essentially they usually mean '*greater than*' and '*less than*' respectively. With the percentage operator, they mean

102>2%   Says 'What number when increased by 2% becomes 102%?: the answer 100
102<2%   Says 'What amount of 102 does a 2% increase represent?' the answer is 2.

These operators are very useful for VAT operations. For example, to find out what a price was before VAT has been added the format would be:

$$price\text{-}with\text{-}VAT \; > \; VAT\text{-}rate \; \%$$

The '*price-with-VAT*' and '*VAT-rate*' are replaced by actual values or variables. Similarly, to find out how much of a total price the VAT part is:

$$price\text{-}with\text{-}VAT \; < \; VAT\text{-}rate \; \%$$

The order of calculation

When Series 3 sees it has something to work out (an 'expression'), it doesn't necessarily work from left to right, but gives priority to certain operators. It looks through the calculation that has to be made, and tackles the operators in this order:

First	**	(*powers*)
	-	(*unary minus or 'sign change*)
	* /	(*multiplication and division*)
	+ -	(*adding and subtraction*)
Last	< >	(*logical operators*)

There are in fact other logical operators as well, which will be dealt with later.

Where an expression has operators of equal precedence, they are worked out from left to right, except for powers, which are worked out from right to left. It is important that you realise this, otherwise you'll get unexpected results.

The Basics

You can force Series 3 to ignore its precedences and perform parts of a calculation in a different order, by enclosing those parts within brackets. Series 3 will look for brackets, and work out what's inside them first following the rules given above. This all looks very complicated, but in fact it is more complicated to explain. Let us look at some examples.

2+3*4	evaluates as 3 times 4, then plus 2	=	14
(2+3)*4	evaluates as 2 plus 3, then times 4	=	20
2+3*4/6	evaluates as 3 times 4, divided by 6, plus 2 =		4
4*(2+3)/5	evaluates as 2 plus 3, times 4, divided by 5 =		4

When in doubt, enclose the parts you want calculated first within brackets.

Mixing variables and constant types

Series 3 follows specific rules when performing calculations on different types of variable and constant. Remember that an integer (or long integer) number doesn't have a decimal point, and an integer variable *can't* have a decimal point.

As a general comment, Series 3 tries to perform the simplest arithmetic possible on an expression. Thus, if all values in the expression are integers, it performs integer arithmetic. This can, however, cause problems. Integer variables have a limited range (-32768 to +32767). If an integer expression produces a result outside this range, you will get an error ('Integer Overflow'). Thus

```
x&=400*400
```

seems legitimate enough: both integer values to be multiplied are within the acceptable range. The result - 160000 - however, is not within the range. Even though the variable that's going to store the result, x&, is a long integer, Series 3 will attempt integer arithmetic. The solution is to convert one of the values to a floating point variable, or better, to a long integer. Thus, either of the next two lines will produce a correct result:

```
x&=400.0*400
x&=INT(400)*400
```

If an integer value is to be added, subtracted, multiplied or divided by a floating point value, Series 3 converts the integer to a floating point value first. The result is stored in a variable according to the *type* declared for that variable. For example, take a typical program line:

```
cost%=30+.175*30
```

First, the 30 is converted to a floating point value (30.0) and is then multiplied by .175. The result, 5.25, is then added to 30.0 to give 35.25. Series 3 then looks at where this answer is to be saved, and discovers that it has to go into the *integer* memory boxes, 'cost%'. So it saves 35.25 as an integer, which is 35.

(*Incidentally, the above program line could also have been written as*

```
cost%=30+17.5 %
```

Notice the space between the value 17.5 and the '%' operator: this is particularly important if you are using variables instead of constants or actual values).

Series 3 obeys its rules implicitly: it is up to you to make sure that the correct instructions are given: in the above example, if you didn't want to lose the decimal part of the answer, *cost%* would have to be a floating point variable, such as *cost*.

Note that when Series 3 converts a floating point value to an integer value, it simply loses everything after the decimal point.

One final point: if the result of a calculation is larger than the variable that's going to hold that result is capable of handling, then you will get an error. So, to give an example:

```
x% = 100.5*1000.2
```

would produce an error, because the result of the calculation is outside the range permitted for integer variables.

Making calculations whilst programming

You will probably be aware that the Program Editor is, in fact, a specially adapted form of the word processor built into Series 3. 'Evaluate', one of the options available in the word processor under 'Edit' menu, is also available in the Program Editor, and this can be an extremely useful tool whilst you are programming to make calculations during the editing process.

The Basics

'Evaluate' (short-cut keys are PSION and 'V') works on *real* values. The procedure is straightforward. You highlight the calculation you want evaluated by holding down the SHIFT key and the left or right arrow keys, and then either select 'Evaluate' from the 'Edit' menu in the Program Editor, or press the short-cut key combination of PSION and 'V'. It is often quicker to make a quick calculation by entering it as a line on its own, rather than going to the calculator section of Series 3 - particularly if you want the result of the calculation as a value in your program. When the calculation is evaluated, the calculation part remains highlighted - so that you can quickly delete it if you wish (using the DELETE key), whilst the answer is not highlighted.

You can use any of the mathematical functions available in the Calculator. Try this example.

1)   Enter any Module that you have saved.
2)   On a line on its own, enter SIN(.2)
3)   Highlight it (SHIFT and arrow keys).
4)   Press the PSION and 'V' keys simultaneously.

The answer will be displayed at the end of the line you have entered. Delete the entire line.

You can set the format for the 'Evaluate' option from the System screen:

1)   Press the 'System' button to get to the System display, then press the MENU key.
2)   Select the 'Special' option, then the 'Evaluate format' option.

You can now set the format for the displayed answer to 'General' (*floating point*), 'Fixed' and hexadecimal. If you select 'Fixed' you will also be able to set the number of decimal places. You can also set whether trigonometric functions act on degrees or radians for evaluations.

The ability to set the format enables you to convert hexadecimal numbers to decimal numbers and vice versa. With the 'General' format for 'Evaluate', enter &A0 on its own line in the Program Editor, highlight it, and press the PSION and 'V' keys: the decimal equivalent, '160' will be displayed. Now set the Evaluate format to hexadecimal, highlight the '160' and evaluate it, and the hexadecimal equivalent of 160 (&A0) will be displayed.

These features can be extremely useful. Remember though that 'Evaluate' works on real values or numbers, not *variables*.

STEP SIX

From Keyboard to Screen

This Step introduces you to the basic methods of
* *Entering information at the keyboard.*
* *Controlling the screen display.*
The keyboard words covered are:
INPUT, EDIT, GET, GET$, KEY, KEY$, *and* KMOD.
The screen words covered are:
SCREEN, PRINT, AT, CLS, *and* CURSOR ON/OFF.

Getting data into a program

We're now in a position to start learning about the basic words in the OPL language, and perhaps the most important of these are the words associated with getting information from the keyboard into the program. There are five different ways that data can be passed into a program when it is running. These are:

* From the keyboard.
* As GLOBAL variables, declared in a calling procedure.
* As arguments, enclosed in brackets after the procedure name when it is called.
* By accessing the calculator memories M0 to M9
* From a *file*.

Information can be passed *out* of a procedure in six different ways:

* Direct to the screen, for you to see.
* By storing it in a GLOBAL variable, declared within the procedure or in a previous 'calling' procedure.
* As a 'returned' value, from a *function* type of procedure.
* By storing it in one of the Series 3 calculator memories (floating point values only).
* Into a *file*.
* Through an external device, such as a printer.

The Basics

In this Step, we're going to concentrate on getting information in via the keyboard, and achieving a reasonable screen display.

Inputs from the keyboard

Almost without exception, the programs you write will need to have information in one form or another entered from the keyboard. Our 'Carpet' program, planned earlier, is a typical example: in this program, each time it is run you will want to enter the relevant measurements and cost from the keyboard.

OPL has a number of 'words' which allow you to find out what is happening at the keyboard. These are now described.

INPUT This word instructs the Series 3 to get an input of characters from the keyboard until the ENTER key is pressed, displaying the characters on the screen as they are entered. The entered information obviously has to be stored by Series 3 for use in the program, and so the format for using INPUT is

INPUT *variable*

The *variable* must have been previously declared, of course, and can be any of the basic variable types - integer, long integer, floating point or string. The type you use will depend on the kind of information you want entered from the keyboard.

If you want only *whole* numbers to be entered from the keyboard, then you'll use an integer or long integer variable (depending on the maximum value of the number). If you want to allow for a decimal entry or for very large numbers outside the range of integer variable, use a floating point variable. If you want characters (including numbers) to be entered from the keyboard, then use a string variable: this must have been declared with sufficient 'space' to allow for the maximum number of characters you're going to allow to be entered. Thus, typical instructions could look like this

INPUT v%	Input an integer value and store it in v%
INPUT v&	Input a long integer and store it in v&
INPUT v	Input a floating point value and store it in v
INPUT v$	Input a string of characters and store them in v$

If an incorrect input is entered, then Series 3 will reject it and give the user the chance to re-enter another input: the cursor is moved to the next line, and Series 3 shows it didn't accept the previous input by displaying a question mark. You can avoid this happening by the use of 'error trapping', but we're not ready for that yet.

EDIT   This is a rather special word enabling the user to 'edit' a 'string of characters' from the keyboard. In some respects it's like INPUT when used for a string. With INPUT, everything that has to be stored is entered at the keyboard. With EDIT, a *previously stored* string can be changed, or 'edited'. Hence the name (!). The format for the instruction is

$$EDIT \ a\$$$

where a$ is any string variable, and holds the string of characters to be edited. The characters are actually displayed on the screen (just as well, really!). So if a$ held the string "Edit me now", then "Edit me now" would be displayed on the screen.

You can use all the usual editing keys - the arrow or cursor keys to move along the line, the DELETE key, and so on. the ESC key will completely clear the line. You can continue editing the string until the ENTER key is pressed. At that point, Series 3 stores the newly edited information in the variable a$. Of course, as with all string variables, a$ must have been declared with sufficient 'boxes' or spaces for the characters: you won't be able to add more characters to the string than has been allowed for in your declaration (using the LOCAL or GLOBAL instruction).

GET   We met this function earlier in Step 2. It waits for a key to be pressed, and 'returns' the character *code* for that key. The character code, remember, is the number which Series 3 uses to convert to the actual character shape. In this instance, however, it returns the *number* and not the shape or character itself.

Series 3 needs to know what to do with the character code, so a complete instruction using GET would look like this:

$$g\%=GET$$

where *g%* is an integer variable that has been previously declared. You can of course use any integer variable - it doesn't have to be *g%*: GET will always return an integer though, so don't use any other type of variable.

There may be times when you're not interested in what key was actually pressed, but merely want to delay anything else happening and leave things on the screen until a key *is* pressed. This was the case in the little routine you entered in Step 2: if we hadn't had a GET, then as soon as the program had finished it would have vanished from the screen!

Note that GET returns special codes or numbers for some of the keys on your keyboard. These are:

DELETE	Returns the value 8
TAB	Returns the value 9
ENTER	Returns the value 13
ESC	Returns the value 27
UP ARROW	Returns the value 256
DOWN ARROW	Returns the value 257
RIGHT ARROW	Returns the value 258
LEFT ARROW	Returns the value 259
PageUp	Returns the value 260
PageDown	Returns the value 261
HOME	Returns the value 262
END	Returns the value 263
MENU	Returns the value 290
HELP	Returns the value 291

If the PSION key is pressed simultaneously with any other key, then 512 is added to the value normally returned by that key. Thus pressing the PSION and HELP keys together will return a value of 803 (291+512).

You can use these values to test whether one of these 'function' keys has been pressed during your programs. The numbers returned by the alphabetic and numeric keys of your keyboard are listed in your Operating Manual.

GET$ This is pretty much the same as GET - Series 3 waits for a key on the keyboard to be pressed. The difference is, in this instance, the actual *character* is returned. The format for using GET$ is

$$g\$=GET\$$$

Notice that this time a *string* variable must be used.

KEY   This too is similar to GET, but in this case, Series 3 *doesn't wait* until a key has been pressed. Instead, it reports the character code of any key that has been pressed since the last time the keyboard was 'polled' or checked for a keypress. You'd use this instruction to find out whether a key had been pressed whilst 'other things' had been going on. As with GET, KEY returns an integer, and it is necessary to tell Series 3 where to store it. So a complete instruction looks like this

$$k\%=\text{KEY}$$

If no key has been pressed, then KEY returns a zero - so the value held by $k\%$ would be '0'. The codes returned by the special keys are the same ass for GET.

KEY$ This is the same as KEY, except that it returns the *character* rather than the character code of any key pressed since the last time the keyboard was 'polled'. The format for the instruction is

$$k\$=\text{KEY}\$$$

If no key has been pressed, then a *null* string is returned. That means the 'string' holds no characters at all: in computer terms, $k\$$ is said to be equal to "" (two quote marks with nothing between them).

KMOD   This instruction returns a code to indicate which *modifier* key was pressed at the time of the last access to the keyboard. There are four modifier keys - SHIFT, CONTROL, PSION and CAPS LOCK. The value returned by KMOD (always an integer) is such that you can tell if any or all of the keys were pressed. It works on the binary system we discussed in Step One. Let us look at the codes for the keys first:

SHIFT	returns 2	(10 in binary)
CONTROL	returns 4	(100 in binary)
PSION	returns 8	(1000 in binary)
CAPS LOCK	returns 16	(10000 in binary)

As before, Series 3 needs to know where to store the information, so the format for the KMOD instruction is

$$km\% = KMOD$$

OK, now let us look at the values that can be returned. First of all, if no modifier key has be pressed, then KMOD returns a zero ($km\%=0$). If any *one* of the modifier keys has been pressed, then the value shown above will be returned. So if, for example, the PSION key had been pressed, then KMOD would return 8. If more than one key has been pressed, then the value returned is the *sum* of the values shown above. Thus, if both the SHIFT key and the CONTROL key had been pressed, then KMOD returns 6 (2+4): $km\%$ will hold the value 6, or 110 in binary.

Later on you will see that there are ways to 'pick out' the information regarding which keys have been pressed, by using 'logical' operators.

Before we put some of these words to use, let us take a look at a few of the instructions available for controlling what happens on the screen.

Basic screen display instructions

Achieving a neat and orderly display on the screen of Series 3 helps to give a program a professional look. At this stage, we're going to look at the most common instructions available for controlling the screen's appearance and display.

SCREEN You will probably be aware that your Series 3 produces its displays in 'windows'. When you run a program that involves only text, Series 3 will assume you want the whole screen to be used as the window area. However, you can define a specific area of the screen for text print-outs with the OPL word SCREEN. There are two ways to use this instruction. The first has the format

SCREEN *width%,height%*

where *width%* is the number of characters wide you want the window to be, and *height%* is the number of rows deep. Whatever your choice, the 'window' is positioned centrally in the display area. You may want the text window to appear in a particular area of the display, in which case the second form of the instruction would be used:

SCREEN *width%, height%, columns%, rows%*

where *width%* and *height%* are the width and height of the window, as before, and *columns%* and *rows%* determine the top left corner of the window. *Columns%* is the number of characters in from the left, and *rows%* is the number of rows down from the top. Note that whichever format is used, the specified screen area does not have a border, nor is the screen area 'cleared': new text is limited to display only within the specified area, until a new area is specified.

PRINT This is probably one of the most important words in OPL, for it enables all of your 'work' to be displayed in the screen window. The general format for the instruction is

PRINT *variable or expression list*

A number of *variables* and/or *expressions* can be included on the same line by separating each of them with a semi-colon or a comma.

A semi-colon between two *variables* and/or *expressions* will result in them being displayed without any spaces between them. A comma will cause a space to be printed between them.

Where it is required to display a message or a string of characters, then that message or string must be enclosed between quotation marks.

A PRINT statement without any variables simply positions the cursor (flashing bar) on the next line: the cursor position marks where the next print-out will occur.

Those are the rules. Now let us have a look at some typical PRINT statements, and examine what the results of them will be. We'll assume some variables have certain values:

a$ = "Hallo"
b% = 1992
c   = 3.147

Here are some examples of PRINT statements:

```
PRINT a$;-b%          display = Hallo-1992
PRINT a$,-b%          display = Hallo -1992
PRINT b%;c            display =  19923.147
```

Notice how a comma causes a space to be introduced between the variable displays. Here are some more examples using 'strings' and 'string variables':

```
PRINT a$;a$           display = HalloHallo
PRINT a$,a$           display = Hallo Hallo
PRINT a$;" all"       display = Hallo all
PRINT a$,"all"        display = Hallo all
PRINT "Hallo","all"   display = Hallo all
```

PRINT can also be used to display the result of *functions* or *expressions*. For example, to display the result of the 'MOD' function we developed in Step 4, you'd have a statement line something like this

```
PRINT Mod:(1991,4)    display = 3
```

What happens here is that Series 3 sees the PRINT statement, then looks at the next bit to see what it has to display. It finds the 'MOD' function (which must, of course, have been written as a part of the same *module*, or *loaded* in with another module). It performs the necessary calculation and displays the result - in this case, 3. One more example:

```
PRINT "2 x 3 =",2*3   display =  2 x 3 = 6
```

If a semi-colon is included at the *end* of a PRINT statement line, then the cursor isn't positioned at the beginning of the next line after the PRINT statement has been executed, but is instead left at the end of the displayed line. So the following two lines in a procedure:

```
PRINT "Hi there";
PRINT " everyone!"
```

would result in a display on the screen of

```
Hi there everyone!
```

Similarly, a comma can be used at the end of a PRINT statement to leave the cursor on the same line, but moved on one space.

You may ask "What happens when the screen is filled up and there's no more room at the bottom to display anything else?". The answer is the screen display *scrolls* upwards, that is to say, every line moves up one, and the top line is lost. The new line to display then appears on the bottom. As we shall see with the next OPL word AT, we can avoid this, if we want.

Finally, PRINT always *overwrites* anything that is already on the screen where the new display is to appear: it doesn't cause other lines to move downwards.

So, as you can see, PRINT is a pretty powerful and important word in the OPL vocabulary.

AT   The display produced by the PRINT statement starts at the current position of the cursor within the window display. But that may not always be what you want. You may want to have the displayed information appear at a specific location in the window. The OPL word that enables you to do this is AT, which has the format

```
AT column%, row%
```

where *column%* represents the number of characters across the screen, from the left, and *row%* represents the number of rows down the screen, from the top, where the cursor is to be positioned ready for the next display.

Thus

```
AT 5,3
```

would position the cursor 5 characters from the left and 3 rows down, and that's where the next item to be displayed on the screen will occur. AT can also be used before an INPUT statement: in this case, the data entered at the keyboard will be positioned at the location determined by the AT statement.

CLS   This OPL word, which stands for CLear Screen, completely clears the contents of the text window. It is very useful for keeping the display nice and tidy between different kinds of operation, and to prevent the display from scrolling all the time. For example, in our Carpet program discussed earlier, once one set of information has been displayed and is finished with, we can perform a CLS to wipe everything out ready for the next display of information. The alternative would be for the text on the screen to scroll up as new information is added, which is unsightly.

CURSOR OFF/ON There may be times when your program is running that you don't want the cursor to be seen on the screen. Well, good news, you can switch it 'off' with the instruction line

CURSOR OFF

The cursor is still positioned where specified in the screen window - by the AT command, for example - but you won't be able to see it. When the time comes for it to be important that the cursor is seen again - for example, during an INPUT instruction, then (you've guessed it) the instruction line

CURSOR ON

will turn it back on again.

EXAMPLE PROGRAMS

We've just covered quite a few important OPL words. Now it's time to put some of them to the test. We are going to create a few procedures and play about with them to see the effects the words have on the display. There is nothing like 'hands on' experience to get the feel of programming your Series 3, so it will be well worth your while to enter these examples.

Test 1: INPUT

Let us start with a simple procedure that will accept an input of data from the keyboard. We'll simply ask the user to enter his or her name and age, and then print the results. In this procedure, we'll also use the CLS command to clear the screen between the input and displayed results. Enter it carefully, the translate and run it.

```
PROC INTEST:
    LOCAL name$(24),age%
    PRINT "What's your name?",
    INPUT name$
    PRINT " How old are you?",
    INPUT age%
    CLS
    PRINT "Hallo, ";name$
    PRINT "I see you're",age%
    GET
ENDP
```

When you're satisfied that this routine works, edit it by entering semi-colons instead of commas at the end of the first two PRINT statements. See what happens too, if you declare name$() to have only, say, 5 characters (name$(5)) - and try to input more than five characters.

Test 2: Calling MOD

In Step 4 we developed a *function* called MOD:(), which returns the remainder after one number is divided by another. You'll remember that we couldn't run it directly, since it needs to be called by another procedure. Here's a procedure to do just that. We are going to enter *both* the calling procedure *and* the MOD:() procedure in this program. You must enter them both in the same *Module*, and both of them must be entered before you translate and run the program, otherwise you'll get an error message when you try to run it.

Notice that the arguments used in the *calling routine*, 'number' and 'denom', are not the same as those in the MOD:() routine itself. They don't have to be. However, the variable *types* must be the same, otherwise you'll get a **'Type violation'** error when the program is run. To demonstrate this point, after you have tested the program as it is written, edit it by entering two integer values, say '12' and '5', in place of 'number' and 'denom' respectively in the line 'PRINT MOD:(number,denom)'.

Incidentally, you'll notice when you're entering the second procedure in this Module that Series 3 doesn't automatically display 'ENDP' for you: you must enter this yourself. Also, you'll notice you have to enter the 'first' indent yourself: Series 3 automatically indents thereafter to your last indented position.

```
PROC MODTEST:
    LOCAL number,denom
    PRINT "Enter a number:",
    INPUT number
    PRINT "Divide it by?",
    INPUT denom
    PRINT "There's a remainder of",
    PRINT MOD:(number,denom)
    GET
ENDP

PROC MOD:(n,d)
    RETURN n-(INT(n/d)*d)
ENDP
```

Test 3:Edit

Here's a program to demonstrate the use of EDIT. You'll be prompted to enter a *string* of characters, and then you'll be asked to change them. Both the original and the changed inputs will be displayed.

```
PROC EDITEST:
    LOCAL new$(32),old$(32)
    PRINT "Enter something now:"
    INPUT new$
    old$=new$
    CLS
    PRINT "Now change it"
    EDIT new$
    CLS
    AT 1,2
    PRINT "You started with"
    PRINT old$
    AT 1,4
    PRINT "...and changed it to"
    PRINT new$
    GET
ENDP
```

STEP SEVEN

Making Decisions

This Step introduces you to the all important task of getting your program to act according to the result of a condition test.
OPL words covered are IF, ELSEIF, ELSE, ENDIF, AND, OR *and the logical operators < and >.*

Putting things to the test

So far, all the procedures that we have discussed have been fairly straightforward in that they simply run from the first instruction through to the last. However, the real power of a computer lies in its ability to make a test and to act according to the result.

For example, we may have a situation in a program which demands a 'Yes' or 'No' input from the user. We can get the user's requirement by displaying the message "Yes or No?", and then testing the keyboard to see whether the 'Y' or 'N' key has been pressed - using INPUT or GET$, for example. We will want Series 3 to act according to the result. How do we do this? With the extremely powerful little OPL word, IF, and its associated words ELSEIF, ELSE and ENDIF.

The general structure or format for these is as follows:

```
IF   first condition test
     . . . do something
ELSEIF   second condition test
     . . . do something else
ELSEIF   third condition test
     . . . do something different
ELSE
     . . . if all other tests fail, do this
ENDIF
```

Now let us look at these words in more detail.

61

The Basics

IF   This tells the Series 3 to make the 'condition' test that immediately follows it on the same line. If the condition is *true* then Series 3 will obey the *next* instruction(s), until it comes to an ELSEIF, an ELSE or an ENDIF instruction, at which point it will jump to the instruction immediately following the ENDIF statement.

If the condition is *not true*, then Series 3 jumps to the next ELSEIF, ELSE or ENDIF instruction (whichever comes first). In other words, it doesn't obey any of the instructions that immediately follow the IF statement. We'll examine the condition tests you can use in detail later on, but so that you get the idea, here is an example. Say we want to know whether the value of a variable *v%* is equal to 100. The test line would look like this

```
IF v%=100
```

Normally, a line such as v%=100 would be an *assignment*: you will recall from an earlier Step that it would mean 'put the value 100 in the memory boxes labelled *x*. Following one of the condition testing words (IF, ELSEIF) however, it is in effect asking the question '*is this true?*'.

So, with the line IF **v%=100**, Series 3 sees the IF command, looks at what follows, and discovers that, in effect, it is being asked 'does v%=100?'. It looks at v%, and if it finds it is in fact 100 (*true*), it obeys the instructions that immediately follow until - as mentioned earlier - it reaches ELSEIF, ELSE or ENDIF. It then jumps to the statement line immediately following the ENDIF statement.

If on the other hand it finds that v% is not equal to 100, then it ignores the following instructions, and jumps straightaway to the next ELSEIF, ELSE or ENDIF, to see what it should do instead.

ELSEIF Is very similar to IF, in that it needs to be followed by a condition test. ELSEIF is never the *first* in a series of tests, always one of the intermediate ones. The results of an ELSEIF test are exactly the same as those described for IF. You can have as many ELSEIF lines in a procedure as you need - or none at all. All you need to bear in mind is that Series 3 starts with an IF statement and continues down through the ELSEIF statements (if any), making the tests until a *true* condition occurs.

ELSE This instruction says to Series 3 "If all of the previous IF and (if they exist) ELSEIF tests have proved to be *not true* then do this...". All the instructions that follow are then obeyed until ENDIF is reached, at which point Series 3 jumps to the instruction following ENDIF.

ELSE can appear only once in an IF...ENDIF series of tests, and it must always be the last one before ENDIF. If you think about it, it would be silly to follow an ELSE with an ELSEIF, since Series 3 obeys only *one set of instructions* in an IF...ENDIF series.

ENDIF Series 3 needs to know where it has to get the next instruction once it has completed all of the tests and any instructions it has to obey as a result of those tests. ENDIF is what it looks for: once the IF series has been completed, it looks for an ENDIF and then obeys the next instruction.

There's nothing like an example to make it all crystal clear. Here's a little procedure that should help: enter it carefully, then run it: it will help to demonstrate the way IF and its associated words work. Notice the indents on lines following IF statements: this is to help when writing and checking procedures, so you can see clearly which instructions are to be obeyed.

```
PROC IFTEST1:
   IF 3=3
      PRINT "Three=three!"
   ELSEIF 4=4
      PRINT "Four=four!"
   ELSE
      PRINT "Nothing=anything!"
   ENDIF
   PRINT "Press a key"
   GET
ENDP
```

If entered properly, when you run the procedure the screen will display "Three=three!". But "Four=four!" won't be displayed, nor will "Nothing=anything!". Can you see why? Having found the result of the first IF test to be *true*, Series 3 obeys the instruction immediately following - to print "Three=three!". The next instruction is an ELSEIF - so it has completed all the instructions it must do on a *true* result, and consequently jumps to the statement after ENDIF, which is our friendly PRINT and GET.

Now edit the program - make the first IF line read

```
IF 3=6
```

and translate and run the procedure again. This time, "Four=four!" should be displayed: the IF statement proved to be *not true*, so the ELSEIF test was made and found to be *true*. One more edit - this time change the ELSEIF line to read

```
ELSEIF 4=1
```

leaving the other changes alone, of course. Now on translating and running the procedure, the display will read "Nothing=anything!". Here, having found both the IF and the ELSEIF tests to be *untrue*, Series 3 sees the ELSE statement, and says to itself "I must obey the next instruction(s) then".

Supposing you didn't want anything to happen if the previous instructions proved to be *not true?* Simple: don't include the ELSE statement or its instruction set.

The only statement that *must* appear after an IF statement is an ENDIF.

Nested IF statements

Series 3 will allow you to include an IF...ENDIF structure within an IF...ENDIF structure. In fact, you can go on *nesting* IF structures quite a few times before Series 3 will complain. Go back to our previous example, and edit it again to read exactly as the following procedure (use the TAB key to indent lines).

When you run this procedure, you should get the message "N doesn't = Y". Notice how indenting the lines makes the program easier to read and to follow what is happening.

Notice too that each IF has an ENDIF at the end of its own little series of statements. This is very important, and is the cause of many a headache when debugging programs. Series 3 won't understand what to do if there's an ENDIF missing, or if there's one too many, or if it is in the wrong place. In fact it will give you a message that something is wrong when you try to translate the procedure prior to running it.

That's one very good reason for using indents. (If you're not already doing so, use the TAB key for indenting).

```
PROC IFTEST1:
   IF 3=3
      IF "N"="Y"
         PRINT "Oh dear!"
      ELSE
         PRINT "N doesn't = Y"
      ENDIF
   ELSEIF 4=4
      PRINT "Four=four!"
   ELSE
      PRINT "Nothing=anything!"
   ENDIF
   PRINT "Press a key"
   GET
ENDP
```

In this last example, we tested the equality of *strings*. It ought to be mentioned here that when strings are tested for equality, Series 3 looks for a perfect match: thus IF "A"="a" would produce a *not true* result.

Now, let us look at the tests that can be made following an IF or an ELSEIF statement.

The logic of it all

The first thing to understand, perhaps, is how Series 3 recognises or 'indicates' a *true* and a *not true* statement. With the lines IF v%=100 or IF 3=3 and so on, when Series 3 makes the condition test it needs to store the result away 'privately' so that it can then use that result for the next part of the instruction. It does this by storing away the value '-1' if the result of a condition test is *true*, and '0' if the result is *not true'*.

However, when Series comes to analyse and act on the result of the test, it takes *any value* to be *true*, and '0' or zero to be *not true*. This is a valuable feature that we can use in our programs, because it means we can make a test for '0' without bothering to use the '=' sign.

For example, let us say that v% is equal to '0'. The line

```
IF v%
```

would result in a *not true* condition, because Series 3 looks at v%, finds it has no condition to test, so takes v% as the result. If v% had any value whatsoever - not just '-1' but 345 say, then it would come up with the answer *true*. This is often useful in programs when we wish to test whether a variable has any value at all. For string variables, such as v$, the *null* string or ' "" ' is the same as zero in numeric strings. So

IF v$

Will be *not true* if v$ = "", and *true* if there are any characters whatsoever in the string.

Series 3 will also make a condition test if the test 'equation' is enclosed in brackets. This is easily demonstrated by the following procedure (enter and run it):

```
PROC IFTEST2:
    PRINT (4=4)
    GET
ENDP
```

The screen will display '-1' - showing that the result of the test is *true*. Now edit the procedure so that the part in brackets is (4=8) and run it again. This time, the screen will display '0', showing that the result of the test is *not true*.

The fact that Series 3 'returns' or saves a value of -1 or zero according to the result of a test is useful in another way. This is best explained by an example. Suppose we want a variable v% to have a value of, say, 5 if a condition is *true*, and a value of zero if the condition is *not true*. We could write it like this:

```
IF condition test
    v%=5
ELSE
    v%=0
ENDIF
```

But as we have just seen, if the condition test is enclosed in brackets, Series 3 will return -1 or zero according to the result of the test. So we could write the line like this:

```
v%=-5 * (condition test)
```

We have made the value we want v% to be *negative*, so that if the condition test turns out to be *true*, it will be multiplied by '-1', and as you know, -5 times -1 gives +5. If on the other hand the result of the condition test is zero (*not true*), -5 will be multiplied by zero - and anything times zero is zero.

This is a slightly more advanced programming technique, but as you can see, it can save a few lines of code. On the 'down' side, it is not as easy to see clearly what the code is doing as the 'IF...ELSE...ENDIF' version.

Logical operators

Now we know how Series 3 makes its condition tests (and stores the result for itself), let us have a look at the various tests at our disposal. The '=' sign on its own wouldn't be adequate for most programming requirements: suppose, for example, you wanted to test whether a variable was *greater than* a certain value, or *less than* the value of another variable. This would hardly be possible if we could only make the 'equals' test.

> This symbol asks the question "Is what's on the left of the symbol *greater than* what's on the right of it?". If it *is* greater, the answer is *true*. If it isn't, the answer is *not true*. Typical statements could be:

```
IF  a>b
IF  a$>b$
IF  a%>b%
IF  "A">"B"
```

If the value of left hand side is greater than the value of the right hand side, then the result is *true* (-1). Otherwise, the result is *not true*.

The last example IF "A">"B" would result in *not true*, because Series 3 looks at the *character codes* when comparing strings. The character code for "A" is less than the character code for "B". As it happens, it's also less than the character code for "a". It's worth looking at a few more examples of string comparisons, because they can be extremely useful in many types of program. Enter the following procedure and run it.

67

```
PROC IFTEST3:
  PRINT ("XYZ">"XYA")
  GET
ENDP
```

Notice the brackets round the part following the PRINT statement: that tells Series 3 it has to evaluate what's in the brackets and to display the result. You should get a display '-1', which indicates that Series 3 has tested along the line and found that "XYZ" is indeed 'greater' than "XYA": in other words, in an alphabetic listing, 'XYZ' would come *after* 'XYA', and so is considered to be 'greater'. Now go back to the procedure and edit "XYZ to read just "XY", and run it again. This time, the result should be '0', meaning *not true*: in an alphabetic listing, "XY" would come *before* "XYA", and so would be less, and the test condition would not be true.

<   This is similar to the symbol above, except that the question this time is "Is what's on the left of the symbol *less than* what's on the right?". Thus

IF 4<6	results in *true* (-1)
IF "B"<"A"	results in *not true* (0)

>=   This combination of the 'greater than' and 'equals' tests produces a *true* result if what's on the left side is equal to *or* greater than what's on the right side, or, another way of saying the same thing, if the left side is *not* less than the right side (it might be equal, but not less). Thus

IF 10>=10	results in *true* (-1)
IF 10>=9	results in *true* (-1)
IF 10>=19	results in *not true* (0)

Note that the 'greater than' sign must come before the 'equals' sign.

<=   This combination produces a *true* result if the left side is equal to *or* less than the right side, or rephrased, if the left **is not** greater than the right side.

< >   This combination produces a *true* result if the left side is either greater than or less than the right side, or, as is more commonly expressed, *if the left side is **not** equal to the right side*. Thus

```
IF 4<>6                          results in true (-1)
IF 4<>4                          results in not true (0)
```

AND   This OPL word can be used in several different ways. Most commonly, it links two conditions in an IF test: if *both* conditions are *true*, then the overall result is *true*. But if either one is *not true*, then the overall result is *not true*.

Supposing, for example, we wish to find out whether the value of a variable v% is the *character code* for a numeral. Character codes, remember, are used by Series 3 to display a pattern on the screen. The numeric character codes run from 48, the code for '0', to 57, the code for '9'. We *could* do this with two IF tests, as follows:

```
IF v%>=48
   IF v%<=57
      Reaching here means v% is the character code for a numeral
   ENDIF
ENDIF
```

With the AND operator, we can make the test in one line, as follows

```
IF (v%>=48) AND (v%<=57)
   Reaching here means v% is the character code for a numeral
ENDIF
```

Notice how the two tests are enclosed within brackets: this is important, as without them, AND will act in a different way, as we shall see a little later on. Incidentally, the above little piece of program could have been written as:

```
IF (v%>47) AND (v%<58)
   Reaching here means v% is the character code for a numeral
ENDIF
```

The first method said "If v% is *equal to or greater than* 48 ..." and so on, whilst the second method said "If *v% is greater than 47* ...": for both methods, '48' is the lowest value to meet the test condition.

You can have as many condition tests on a line as you need - you are not restricted to just two as in the above examples. For example, if for some reason we wanted to know whether v% was any numeric character code *except* that for the numeral '5' (code 53), then the line could read

```
IF (v%>=48) AND (v%<=57) AND (v%<>53)
```

Bearing in mind our earlier discussion on the way Series 3 determines the result of a test, AND can also be used with two values: thus we can write things like

```
(x AND y)
(a% AND b%)
```

However, the way AND works with integer (or long integer) values or variables is different to the way it works with floating point values or variables, although the general principle is the same.

With *floating point variables* (or values), AND works pretty much in the expected way: if both of the two variables are non-zero, then the result is -1. If either of the two variables is zero, then the result is zero (0). To demonstrate this, enter the following procedure:

```
PROC ANDTEST1:
   LOCAL x,y
   x=1.2
   y=2.4
   IF x AND y
      PRINT "True: neither is zero"
   ELSE
      PRINT "Not true: one is zero"
   GET
ENDP
```

When you run this, the screen should display "True: neither is zero". Now edit the procedure, changing the line x=1.2 to read x=0 (that's a zero), and run it again.

This time, the display should read "Not true: one is zero".

With *integer* (or *long integer*) variables, AND compares the two values *bit by bit*, and sets a corresponding *bit* in the returned value to '1' if the two bits tested are '1', and to '0' if either bit is '0'. (Unfortunately, you need to understand a little bit about the binary system to appreciate all this - so if you missed it out in Step 1, now is the time to refresh your memory).

The results of this can look pretty weird if you don't know what's going on. Let's put it to the test: enter the following procedure:

```
PROC ANDTEST2:
    LOCAL x%,y%
    PRINT "Input x%:",
    INPUT x%
    PRINT "Input y%:",
    INPUT y%
    PRINT x%,"AND",y%,"=",(x% AND y%)
    GET
ENDP
```

Run it, and when prompted for x% enter 4 (and press ENTER), and when prompted for y% enter 6 (and press ENTER). The screen should display "4 AND 6 = 4". Strange, huh? OK, run the program again, and this time enter 3 for x% and 6 for y%. This time, the screen should display "3 AND 6 = 2". OK, now let's look to see what's happening.

As mentioned, when used with integers, AND looks at the binary digits of each value. So let's first look at the binary equivalents for '4' and '6'

```
4 =     00100
6 =     00110
```

Now, looking at each column in turn, starting from the right, we see that there is a '0' in each value. So the rightmost column of the result will be '0'.

Result = ...0

In the next column, one value has a '1', and the other a '0': but AND will return a '1' only if both tested values are 1's, so again, the result for this column will be a '0':

Result = ..00

In the next column, the bits of both values are a '1', so the result will have a '1' in that position:

Result = .100

That's as far as we need to go, since the rest of the bits are all 0's. So the result of ANDing 4 and 6 is, in binary, 100. And *that*, in decimal notation, is 4. Hence the first answer. Now let's look at the second example - '3 AND 6'. In binary, it would look like this

3	=	0011
6	=	0110
Result	=	0010

The result, '10' in binary, is '2' in decimal notation.

Now you are probably wondering what's the point of all this. Why do we need to perform such seemingly useless operations? Well, to be quite honest, at the moment we don't. But later on, in slightly more advanced programming, it is useful to be able to *mask out* a value, or to test whether a particular *bit* in a value is equal to '1'. We met such a potential case when we discussed the codes returned by KMOD (Step 6). To recap:

SHIFT	returns 2	(10 in binary)
CONTROL	returns 4	(100 in binary)
PSION	returns 8	(1000 in binary)
CAPS LOCK	returns 16	(10000 in binary)

So if km% holds the value returned by KMOD, we can test whether the PSION key was pressed by a line

```
IF km% AND 8
```

This will return *true* if the bit representing '8' in km% is set - indicating that the PSION key has been pressed. If the result is 0 or *not true*, then the PSION key hasn't been pressed.

You will find it useful to experiment with the procedure ANDTEST2, entering different values for x% and y%, and seeing if you can work out, as we have just done, what the result should be - hopefully, your predictions will be correct!

OR This is very similar to AND in every respect except that, instead of producing a *true* result if *both* conditions are *true*, OR produces a *true* result if *either* condition is *true*. Thus the line

```
IF (a%=4) OR (b%=6)
```

will produce a *true* result if *either* (or *both*) a%=4 or b%=6.

This kind of test is useful if you want 'things to happen' if *any* of certain conditions are met. Compare this kind of test with AND, where *all* conditions have to be met for 'things to happen'.

As with AND, OR can be used on individual values as well as to link two conditional tests. Also, all of the discussion on AND about how it works with integers (or long integers) and floating point variables applies to OR. The difference, remember, is that OR produces a *true* result, or sets a bit to '1', if *either* of the conditions is *true*, or in the case of integers, if *either* of the tested bits is '1'.

Edit the PROC ANDTEST2: program by changing both of the ANDs (on the last PRINT line) to ORs.

NOT This, as it sounds, *negates* a single IF conditional test. In other words, it switches the result of a test - if the result was *true*, NOT makes it *not true*. If the result was *not true*, NOT makes it *true*. Thus,

```
IF v%=4
```

would produce a *true* result if v% equalled 4, whereas

```
IF NOT(v%=4)
```

would produce a *true* result if v% equalled anything but 4.

This example could have been written IF **v%<>4**. As you can see, when programming, there's usually more way than one to achieve what you want. Use of the word **NOT** can sometimes make the logic of a program easier to write or follow.

Unlike **AND** and **OR**, **NOT** cannot be used to link two floating point or integer variables or values: it can only be used on a single variable or value. Used with floating point variables, it returns *true* (-1) if the variable is zero, and *not true* if the variable is non-zero.

Used with integer or long integer variables, **NOT** returns what is called the *one's compliment*. Essentially what that means is it looks at the binary value of the integer, and turns all of the bits set to '1' to a zero, and all of the bits set to zero to a '1'. We won't need to use this feature.

Mixed condition tests

The **AND** and **OR** operators can be used in combination when testing for specific conditions, but it is important that you enclose within brackets the parts you want treated together. For example

```
IF ((Condition 1) AND (Condition 2)) OR (Condition 3)
```

will result in *true* if either

a)   *Both* Condition 1 and Condition 2 are *true*
or b)   Condition 3 is *true*

In this next example,

```
IF (Condition 1) AND ((Condition 2) OR (Condition 3))
```

Condition 1 *must* be true, and *either* Condition 2 *or* Condition 3 (or *both*) must be true for the overall result to be true. As you can see, it is important to get the logic clear in your own mind to achieve the desired results.

STEP EIGHT

Going Round in Circles

In this Step you'll learn
* *How to jump to other sets of instructions according to tested conditions.*
* *How to repeat sequences of instructions in a loop until certain conditions are met.*
* *How to break out of a loop or a program.*
The OPL words discussed are
GOTO, VECTOR, WHILE...ENDWH, DO...UNTIL, REM, BREAK, CONTINUE, STOP.

Repeat performance

Most of the time, you will not want to run your programs through just once: you will want to be able to repeat them, perhaps with new inputs from the keyboard. There will also be many situations where you will want a series of instructions repeated until certain conditions are met: for example, you could accept and act upon inputs from the keyboard until a specific key is pressed.

Series 3 has a variety of words and structures that enable you to do this. A particular program could be written using virtually any of these structures - which structure you pick when writing your program is a matter of style and experience. Indeed, it is in this area that most programmers produce different sections of code to achieve the same result. As mentioned at the beginning of this book, no one way is necessarily right or wrong, but each has its merits for the particular task in hand. Let us first look at the options available.

Jumping around

One of the simplest ways to repeat a series of instructions is to use the OPL word GOTO. It is also considered to be the crudest and most *unstructured* method of transferring the instruction sequence. GOTO is a relic from the very early days of computing, and its use can make code difficult to analyse and change at a later date.

75

Nevertheless, like most programming languages, Series 3 offers the option, and so we will discuss it.

GOTO   This word usually follows a condition test of some kind, and is always followed by a *label*, that is, the name of a 'marker' placed at some point in the *same* procedure. Labels are simply convenient names that you choose, and are always identified as a label to Series 3 by two colons immediately after the name. Typical labels might be 'Start::', 'Repeat::', 'More::' and 'Done::'.

Labels are just that: they appear between statement lines to mark the point where instructions are to return to when directed by a GOTO command. When naming the label in a GOTO command, you can either include or omit the colons, although including them may help you to identify what the procedure is all about at a later date. Here is a procedure using GOTO. It multiplies an *integer* input by 2, until you've had enough. (Enter a number outside the integer range, and you'll get a question mark, denoting an invalid entry).

```
PROC TIMES2A:
   LOCAL y%,q$(1)
   Getnum::
      CLS
      PRINT "Enter a number:",
      INPUT y%
      PRINT y%,"times 2 =",y%*2
      PRINT "Another? (Y or N)"
   Getans::
      q$=GET$
      IF (q$="Y") OR (q$="y")
         GOTO Getnum::
      ELSEIF (q$="n") OR (q$="N")
         GOTO Done::
      ELSE
         GOTO Getans::
      ENDIF
   Done::
      PRINT "Bye now!"
   GET
ENDP
```

The indents in this procedure are there only to help you see the labels clearly. Notice how we loop around according to the answer to the question "Another (Y or N)": if you enter "Y" or "y" at the keyboard, processing will jump back to GETNUM::. If you enter "N" or "n", then processing jumps to DONE::, and continues to the end of the procedure. Press any other key - and that's not good enough: we must have a "Y" or "N" answer - so we loop round to GETANS:: to get another keypress. Notice that we have to test for both the upper or lower case letters (capitals or small letters): we must allow for the fact that the CAPS LOCK may be on.

This is a pretty long procedure for what it does, and as we shall see, it can be shortened without loss of clarity by using the other structures available. Also, later on when we discuss *strings*, you'll find that we won't have to test for both upper and lower case inputs: we will be able to convert the input to one or the other and simply test for *that* condition.

VECTOR This OPL word allows you to jump to any of a number of labels, (which on early models of Series 3 must come after the VECTOR...ENDV structure). The jump is made according to an integer parameter that follows the VECTOR command. The format for VECTOR is

```
VECTOR v%
    label1,label2,label3 ... labeln
ENDV
```

The value of v% must be equal to or less than the number of labels in the list, otherwise processing jumps to the instruction *following* the ENDV statement. When Series 3 meets the VECTOR command, it looks at the value of the integer variable following it, then picks the label in that position in the list, and jumps to that label in the procedure. The label names can be anything you choose, of course, and you can, if you wish, include the two colons after their names in the list. The labels marking positions in the procedure must have the two colons after them, and remember, you can jump only to labels that *follow* the ENDV statement.

One more point about the list of labels in the VECTOR structure: they needn't all be on the same line, but can be spread over a few lines if you wish. However, you must *not* place a comma after a label at the *end* of a line: a comma is used only to separate two labels on the *same* line.

Let us re-write the TIMES2A procedure, this time using the VECTOR command. Since the VECTOR command is not really designed for *string* values, this time we'll have the user input a '1' for 'more' and a '2' to 'end'. Notice the corresponding changes to the variables used (q% instead of q$).

```
PROC TIMES2B:
    LOCAL y%,q%
    Getnum::
        CLS
        PRINT "Enter a number:",
        INPUT y%
        PRINT y%,"times 2 =",y%*2
        PRINT "Another? (1=Yes, 2=No)"
    Getans::
        q%=GET-48
        VECTOR q%
            Goback,Done        REM Try 'Getnum,Done' here
        ENDV
        GOTO Getans
    Goback::                   REM These two lines not needed
        GOTO Getnum::          REM   if the edit above works.
    Done::
        PRINT "Bye now!"
        GET
ENDP
```

Note that in early Series 3 models, VECTOR *only permitted 'forward jumps'. Try the suggested labels for* VECTOR. *If it works, delete the* Goback:: *and* GOTO Getnum:: *statements.*

We have to get an input from the keyboard and break it down to a *real* value of '1' or '2': the GET command, remember, gets the *character code* for the pressed key, and the character codes for the keys '1' and '2' are 49 and 50 respectively. Hence we deduct 48 from whatever was input in order to arrive at a real value of 1 or 2. If neither the '1' or '2' key was pressed, then processing jumps from the VECTOR command to the statement following ENDV, which instructs Series 3 to GOTO Getans, to get another input from the keyboard. Perhaps this highlights the fact that VECTOR is not really suited to acting on keyboard inputs. Nevertheless it *is* useful where a consecutive series of integer values are available: as we shall see later on, selecting from a list of 'menu' of items produces an integer result from '1' to the number of items in the list. VECTOR is perfect for this kind of situation, since it can eliminate a whole series of IF tests.

Looping around

As mentioned at the beginning of this Step, there are numerous occasions when you will want to repeat a series of instructions until a certain condition is met. We saw this with the two procedures TIMES2A and TIMES2B, where we wanted the instructions covering the input of a number and the 'times 2' calculation to be repeated until the user entered "n" or "N". This was just one example: a vast majority of programs that you write will require some instructions to be repeated one way or another. Series 3 provides two 'structures' for doing this: WHILE...ENDWH, and DO...UNTIL.

WHILE...ENDWH The general format for this structure is

```
WHILE  condition test is true
    ...do the necessary operations
ENDWH
```

The test for whether the instructions that follow should be obeyed is made at the beginning of the·'loop'. If the result of the test is *true*, then the instructions that immediately follow are obeyed. On reaching ENDWH, Series 3 'loops' back to the WHILE statement line, *and performs the test again.*

It is *vitally* important, therefore, that during the instruction sequence something is 'done' to *change the possible outcome of the test*, otherwise the loop will go on for ever. Well, until you press the PSION and the ESC keys simultaneously: if that doesn't stop it, and there are certain conditions where it might not, you'll have to remove the batteries. Be warned.

If the result of the condition test following the WHILE statement is *not true*, then the instruction set is not performed at all: processing jumps immediately to the statement following the ENDWH statement. Notice that, like the IF...ENDIF and VECTOR...ENDV structures, Series 3 needs to be told where the WHILE instruction set ends.

Let us now look at the 'times 2' procedure again, this time written using the WHILE structure. Notice the indents between the WHILE and the ENDWH statements: as with the indents we used with the IF...ENDIF structure, this helps to make the procedure easier to read, 'debug' and change, by keeping associated pieces of code in an identifiable 'chunk'. It also helps to ascertain that both parts of the structure - the WHILE and ENDWH statements match up.

```
PROC TIMES2C:
  LOCAL y%,q$(1)
  q$="Y"
  WHILE (q$="Y") OR (q$="y")
    CLS
    PRINT "Enter a number:",
    INPUT y%
    PRINT y%,"times 2 =",y%*2
    PRINT "Another? (Y or N)"
    q$=GET$
  ENDWH
  PRINT "Bye now!"
  GET
ENDP
```

What a difference! Gone are all of those IF tests and labels of the previous two versions of the 'TIMES2' procedure - and see just how much shorter this version is. Admittedly, this time we are testing only for a 'Yes' input: *any* key other than 'Y' or 'y' will result in the procedure ending.

Notice the line q$="Y". Can you see why that is needed? When q$ is declared in the first line, it has no value - it is 'initiated' as a null string, or, put another way, it is made equal to "". If we didn't have the line q$="Y", therefore, the WHILE condition test would give a *not true* result - and the instructions within the loop would not be obeyed at all. Test this for yourself, if you wish, either by deleting the line, or amending it to read

```
REM q$="Y"
```

REM stands for REMark, and it tells Series 3 to ignore the *rest* of the line or statement that follows it. It is a useful word for adding explanatory notes to a procedure, or for temporarily knocking out a statement. After you have checked that without the line q$="Y" the procedure simply ends, you can delete the **REM** word.

As with **IF**, although Series 3 determines a *true* condition as -1, it will recognise *any* value as being *true*. Consequently, one could have a segment of code that looks like this:

```
. . .
c%=4
WHILE c%
   do things
   c%=c%-1
ENDWH
. . .
```

In this example, each time the instructions in the loop are performed, the value of c% is decreased by 1 (it is said to be *decremented*). After four 'passes' through the loop, c% will be equal to zero: the **WHILE** condition test will then give a *not true* result - and processing jumps to the statement following **ENDWH**. This is one useful way of having a loop repeated a specific number of times. For example, suppose for some obscure reason you wanted to produce the first five values in the 13 times multiplication table. Here's a procedure to do it:

```
PROC TIMES13A:
   LOCAL c%
   c%=5
   WHILE c%
      PRINT "13 times",6-c%,"=",13*(6-c%)
      c%=c%-1
   ENDWH
   GET
ENDP
```

We subtract the value of c% from 6 to give 1,2,3,4,5 on each successive pass through the loop, to get an ascending table. Finally, you can use **AND** and **OR** in the condition test.

DO...UNTIL The general format for this structure is

```
DO
    ...do the necessary operations
UNTIL  condition test becomes true
```

Notice that with this structure, the condition test is made at the *end* of the instruction set. If the condition test proves to be *true*, the instruction loop is *not* repeated. If on the other hand the condition test proves to be *not true*, then the instruction set *is* repeated. As with **WHILE...ENDWH** something must be 'done' within the loop to change the possible outcome of the test, or the loop will run for ever.

With the DO...UNTIL structure, the instruction set is *always* obeyed at least once. **WHILE...ENDWH** could miss the instructions set out if the condition test is *not true*.

This distinguishing factor should enable you to pick the appropriate structure for the task in hand: if you definitely want the instructions to be performed at least once, come what may, then choose the DO...UNTIL structure. If you want the instructions to be performed only under a certain condition (or conditions) then choose **WHILE...ENDWH**.

Here's the 'TIMES2' procedure using DO...UNTIL.

```
PROC TIMES2D:
    LOCAL y%,q$(1)
    DO
        CLS
        PRINT "Enter a number:",
        INPUT y%
        PRINT y%,"times 2 =",y%*2
        PRINT "Another? (Y or N)"
        q$=GET$
    UNTIL (q$="N") OR (q$="n")
    PRINT "Bye now!"
    GET
ENDP
```

Notice that, this time, we don't need the line q$="Y": the instructions within the loop will be obeyed once whatever the value of q$ the first time round. Compare PROC TIMES2D: with PROC TIMES2A:, which used a host of IF and GOTO statements: you will agree, it's shorter and neater!

As with IF and WHILE, the condition test following the UNTIL statement can incorporate the logic operators AND and OR. And equally, while Series 3 determines a *true* condition as -1, it will recognise *any* value as being *true*. Our 'TIMES13A' procedure could be re-written like this:

```
PROC TIMES13B:
   LOCAL c%
   DO
      c%=c%+1
      PRINT "13 times",c%,"=",13*c%
   UNTIL c%=5
   GET
ENDP
```

This, too, is marginally shorter than its WHILE...ENDWH counterpart, since we have been able to lose a line (c%=5). It also highlights the fact that, if you want the instructions performed at least once, the DO...UNTIL structure is usually the best choice. Notice the different ordering of the instructions within the loop (as well as the line changes). The first time round, c% will have just been initiated, and will therefore be equal to zero. By making c%=c%+1 the first instruction in the loop (to *increment* it by one), we ensure that 13 won't be multiplied by zero. On the fifth pass through the loop, the instructions are obeyed with c%=5, but then the UNTIL condition will prove to be *true*, and the loop won't be repeated.

Nesting loops

When discussing IF it was stated that IF structures can be 'nested' - that is, you can have IF structures within IF structures. The same is true of WHILE...ENDWH and DO...UNTIL structures. In fact, all of these structures can be 'nested' within each other at will.

The important things to remember when nesting structures, mixed or otherwise, are as follows.

The Basics

a) Each individual structure *must* be terminated properly (with ENDIF, ENDWH or UNTIL, according to the structure)

b) You can have no more than *eight* nested structures, mixed or otherwise. That's Series 3's limit: but it should be more than enough to cope with even the most complex of programs you're ever likely to devise!

Leaving a loop prematurely

We have seen that WHILE...ENDWH and DO...UNTIL loops run until a certain condition is met, as tested at the WHILE or UNTIL statement. There may be times, however, when you want an extra way to leave the loop - another condition that's quite different from that being tested in the normal run of events. Alternatively, you may wish to cancel the current trip through the instruction loop if a particular condition is met. Series 3 has ways of allowing you to do these things. The two OPL words concerned are BREAK and CONTINUE. There is also an instruction which will allow you to break out of the program completely - STOP.

BREAK This statement, which usually follows a condition test of some kind, causes Series 3 to 'break' out of an instruction loop. Program execution continues with the statement following the loop terminator (ENDWH or UNTIL). Let us see how this works by re-writing the TIMES13B: procedure. Instead of going up to just 5 times 13, we'll have the procedure go up to 2000 times 13, and we'll add a way to stop it before it reaches 2000 by simply pressing any key. Here we go:

```
PROC TIMES13C:
  LOCAL c%
  DO
    IF KEY
      BREAK
    ENDIF
    c%=c%+1
    PRINT "13 times",c%,"=",13*c%
  UNTIL c%=2000
  PRINT "Shucks! You stopped me!"
  PRINT "Press a key"
  GET
ENDP
```

When you run this procedure, press a key before it reaches '13 times 2000', and you'll break out of the loop. (The way its written, you get the message "Shucks! You stopped me!" even if you don't break out of the loop). You will recall that the KEY command looks to see if a key has been pressed since the last time the keyboard was 'polled'. If a key hasn't been pressed, it returns a zero - which the IF statement regards as being *not true*. As soon as a key is pressed the IF statement considers it to be *true*, and hence obeys the BREAK instruction.

CONTINUE With BREAK, a 'jump' is made out of the loop to the instruction following the loop terminator. With CONTINUE, however, the 'jump' is made to the condition testing line, WHILE or UNTIL. This means the test is made again - and program execution will either continue round the loop again or not, according to the result of the condition test. It is probably true to say that CONTINUE will always follow its *own* condition test - an IF statement, for example. Let's look at an example, using the DO...UNTIL structure. This procedure will give the '13 times' table up to 12x13, but only if the user decides to see the result of each multiplication displayed. Enter this procedure *very* carefully - making sure that you have the UNTIL line correct!

```
PROC TIMES13D:
   LOCAL c%,q$(1)
   DO
      c%=c%+1
      PRINT c%,"times 13? (Y or any key)",
      q$=GET$
      IF (q$="Y") OR (q$="y")
         PRINT c%*13
      ELSE
         PRINT
         CONTINUE
      ENDIF
   UNTIL c%>11
ENDP
```

For each pass through the loop, you will be asked if you want to see the result. Press any key except 'Y' and processing will jump down to UNTIL, where it will test for the value of c% to determine whether the loop should be repeated or not. Note that this time the test is made for c% being *greater than* 11: this is to prevent any remote possibility of c% becoming greater than 12. Notice too that there is a PRINT statement before the CONTINUE command. This is to keep the display reasonably neat and understandable (try it without that PRINT statement to see the difference!)

STOP   This instruction, which usually follows a condition test of some kind, causes the program to stop running completely.

Unlike BREAK and CONTINUE, which can be used only within DO...UNTIL or WHILE...ENDWH structures, STOP can be used *anywhere* in a program. Here's the 'TIMES13D' procedure, re-written to go up to 100 *unless* the user cries "Enough!". (It's a good example of 'nested' IF statements!)

```
PROC TIMES13E:
  LOCAL c%,q$(1),a$(1)
  DO
     c%=c%+1
     PRINT c%,"times 13? ('Y' or any key)",
     q$=GET$
        IF (q$="Y") OR (q$="y")
           PRINT c%*13
           PRINT "More? ('Y' or any key)"
           a$=GET$
           IF (a$="Y") OR (a$="y")
             CONTINUE
           ELSE
             STOP
           ENDIF
        ELSE
           PRINT
           CONTINUE
        ENDIF
  UNTIL c%>=100
ENDP
```

STEP NINE

Strings and Things

In this Step you will learn how to manipulate the 'string' types of variable, and how to load and unload other Modules into a program.
The OPL words covered are: CHR$, ASC, UPPER$, LOWER$, LEN, LEFT$, RIGHT$, MID$, LOC, REPT$, LOADM, UNLOADM.

What's the character?

Way back in Step One, we saw that *characters* are stored in the Series 3 as *numbers*, and that Series 3 turns these numbers into the 'shapes' we recognise as characters when it knows we want the shape and not the number displayed on the screen. We can also force Series 3 to 'convert' a number into its corresponding character shape by using the OPL function CHR$($n\%$).

CHR$($n\%$) This function 'returns' the character shape or pattern corresponding to the integer value or variable $n\%$, which must be within the range 1 to 255. Some numbers below 32 do not produce character shapes (they are used as 'instructions'), and 255 is the upper limit for a value that can be stored in a single memory box. Because a *character* is returned by CHR$(), it must be stored in a *string* type of variable so that Series 3 knows what to do with it when called upon. The general format for the instruction is:

$$c\$=CHR\$ (n\%)$$

However, since CHR$() is a *function*, it can be used as part of another statement, such as PRINT. Thus,

$$PRINT\ CHR\$(n\%)$$

is equally valid as an instruction. If you look at the complete Character Set, shown in your Operating Manual, you will notice that there are more characters than can be accessed direct from the keyboard. CHR$() gives you a way of accessing the characters that are *not* accessible from the keyboard, should you wish to display them.

Here is a procedure which allows you to enter a number, and which then displays the corresponding character for that number.

```
PROC CHARACTS:
  LOCAL c$(1),num%
  DO
    CLS
    PRINT "Enter 0 (zero) to finish"
    AT 1,3
    PRINT "Which character number?",
    INPUT num%
    IF num%>255
      CONTINUE
    ENDIF
    AT 1,4
    PRINT CHR$(num%)
    GET
  UNTIL num%=0
ENDP
```

Notice a little test is included in this procedure to 'trap' inputs that are too high. You will find when you run this program that some of the numbers below 32 don't display a character at all, while others display characters used by Series 3 for its own displays (a padlock, telephone symbol, and so on). The main non-displayable character codes are

7	This gives a *beep* sound
8	This performs a *backspace*.
9	This performs a *tab* operation.
10	This performs a *line feed* operation.
12	This *clears* the screen or, on printers, gives a *form feed*.
13	This performs a 'carriage return' (*ENTER*) operation.
27	This is the code for an *ESC* operation.

These can be useful in your own programs when providing an output for a printer.

Step 9: *Strings and Things*

What's the character code?

Just as there's an OPL instruction to 'convert' a number into a character, so there's an instruction to convert a character into its equivalent code number. The instruction is ASC(*c$*), where *c$* is the character we want the code for.

ASC(*c$*) is a function that returns the integer number corresponding to the character *c$* (or the first character of a string *c$*), and the general format for the instruction is

$$v\% = ASC(c\$)$$

As with CHR$() and other functions, ASC() can be used as part of another statement without saving the returned value.

Incidentally, if you are wondering why on earth this function is called 'ASC', the answer is it is short for 'ASCII' (bet you wish you hadn't wondered!). Actually, it's not that bad: ASCII stands for 'American Standard Code for Information Interchange', and is the standard used by virtually *all* computers to define the numeric codes for characters. Thus, whatever computer you use, the letter 'A' is the character for the code value '65': '65' is said to be the ASCII code or ASCII value for the letter 'A'.

There is also another method for determining the code for an individual character, and that's by using the '%' sign before the character concerned. Thus:

$$v\% = \%A$$

would return, and store in v%, the character code for the capital letter 'A' (which is 65). The method you use - ASC() or '%' - is really just a matter of choice. However, it must be said that, until you become familiar with programming, use of the '%' symbol could produce confusion. This is because the symbol is capable of being used in three different ways: as the 'terminator' of a variable (or procedure) name to denote an integer, as a 'percentage' operator, and as a way of saying '*the code, not the character of what follows*'.

When using ASC(*a$*), if *a$* is a null string (i.e., it contains no characters, so is equal to ""), then the value returned is zero.

89

The Basics

Joining strings (concatenation)

A *string*, you will recall, is a series of *characters*, all contained in the one string type of variable. There are many, many occasions when you will want to join two or more strings together (which is called *concatenating*). This is done very easily by simply using a '+' sign between the different strings you want to join. The string variable that will hold the concatenation must have been declared large enough to hold the entire string, of course.

You can join string *variables* and string *literals* in any combination. A string literal is where the actual characters are used, between quotation marks. Here are some examples to help make it clear: they all assume that a$ holds the string "Lolly", p$ holds "Pops", and that r$ has been declared of sufficient length.

```
r$=a$+p$              r$ holds "LollyPops"
r$=a$+" "+p$          r$ holds "Lolly Pops"
r$="Green "+a$        r$ holds "Green Lolly"
r$=p$+a$              r$ holds "PopsLolly"
```

You don't need to concatenate strings just to print them out: you can use the PRINT statement for a whole series of variables, remember, by separating them with a semi-colon (no space) or a comma (one space). So to print out the above examples without saving the concatenated strings, you would have:

```
PRINT a$;p$           Displays "LollyPops"
PRINT a$,p$           Displays "Lolly Pops"
PRINT "Green ";a$     Displays "Green Lolly"
PRINT p$;a$           Displays "PopsLolly"
```

Changing the case

You will remember that in Step Eight we had to make tests to see whether or not a particular key had been pressed at the keyboard. We had lines in procedures something like this

```
IF (q$="Y") OR (q$="y")
```

In other words, we had to test for the possibility that the SHIFT key was also pressed, or allow for the fact that the CAPS LOCK may be on. In practice, OPL allows us to avoid this kind of thing, by enabling us to convert a string to all upper case (capitals) or lower case characters. The two functions concerned are UPPER$() and LOWER$().

UPPER$(*str$*)   As you might imagine, this returns the string *str$* as all upper case characters. It only changes *alphabetic* characters of course - numeric characters are left as they are. So if str$ holds the string "abC123", UPPER$(str$) would return the string "ABC123". As with any function, UPPER$() can be used as part of another statement. Thus

```
q$=UPPER$(GET)
```

would return the *upper case* version of whatever alphabetic key had been pressed. So if "y" had been pressed - without the SHIFT key being pressed or without CAPS LOCK set to on - then q$ would hold the character "Y". Similarly,

```
PRINT UPPER$("y")
```

would display 'Y', and if q$ held the characters "n123", then

```
PRINT UPPER$(q$)
```

would display 'N123'.

LOWER$(*str$*)   This does the opposite to UPPER$(): it changes all the capital letters in the string *str$* to lower case letters. Apart from that, its operations are the same.

How long is a string?

Even though you specify how many characters a particular string variable can hold as a maximum when you declare it, what you may not know is exactly how many characters the string actually holds at any time. This information is often required - as we shall see just a little later on - and, fortunately, there is an OPL function to give us the answer.

LEN(*str$*) This function returns the number of characters contained in the string variable represented by *str$*. (Not the number of characters that *str$* has been declared to be able to hold).

The format is

$$n\%=\text{LEN}(str\$)$$

LEN() can also be used as part of other statements. Thus, if str$ holds the string "What a good idea", then

        PRINT LEN(str$)

would display the number '16', which is the number of characters in the string, including the spaces.

Pieces of string

Just as there are times when you will want to join strings together, there will be many occasions when you'll find it useful to snip out a part of a string variable. There are three ways OPL enables you to do this: you can take some characters from the start, some characters from the end, or some characters from the middle. Which just about covers every possibility!

LEFT$(str$,n%) This function returns the leftmost number of characters, as determined by n%, from the string str$. The format, as with other functions is

$$newstr\$=\text{LEFT}\$(str\$,n\%)$$

The function can also be used as part of another statement.

        PRINT LEFT$(str$,n%)

As an example, if str$ held the string "What a good idea", then after the statement

        newstr$=LEFT$(str$,4)

newstr$ would hold the string "What".

RIGHT$(str$,n%) This function returns the rightmost n% number of characters from the string str$. The format is

$$newstr\$=\text{RIGHT}\$(str\$,n\%)$$

and as with LEFT$(), RIGHT$ can be used as part of another statement. If *str$* held the string "What a good idea", then after the statement

$$newstr\$=RIGHT\$(str\$,4)$$

newstr$ would hold the string "idea".

MID$(*str$,start%,n%*) This function returns a string of *n%* number of characters, beginning with the character at the *start%* position in the string *str$*. The format, as before, is

$$newstr\$=MID\$(str\$,start\%,n\%)$$

As you will realise by now, MID$() can also be used as part of another statement such as

$$PRINT\ MID\$(str\$,start\%,n\%)$$

Here is a procedure to demonstrate how MID$() could be used. As we shall see a little later on, there is a way to make this particular routine much shorter.

```
PROC MIDTEST1:
   LOCAL name$(24),monica$(24),m$(1),c%
   PRINT "Enter your full name:",
   INPUT name$
   DO
      c%=c%+1
      m$=MID$(name$,c%,1)
      IF m$=" "
         CONTINUE
      ELSE
         monica$=monica$+m$
      ENDIF
   UNTIL (m$=" ") OR (LEN(monica$)=24)
   PRINT "Your Christian name is",monica$
   GET
ENDP
```

Notice how we use the LEN() function to prevent problems occurring should a name be entered without any spaces!

Where's that string?

In the last example, we had a loop of instructions to find out where the first space occurred in a given string. This helped to demonstrate how the MID$() function worked. In practice, however, there is an easier way to find out where one string occurs within another - and that's with the function LOC().

LOC(*large$,little$*) This function returns an integer value representing the position - number of characters from the start - where the *little$* string occurs within the *large$* string.

The 'search' is not case sensitive: that means if the *large$* string holds "What a good idea" and the *little$* string holds "GOOD", it will be found. If the *little$* string isn't found in the *large$* string, then the value returned is '0' (zero). The format is

$$p\%=\text{LOC}(large\$,little\$)$$

and, yes, you can also use the form

$$\text{PRINT LOC}(large\$,little\$)$$

if you want. The string variable *little$* can be any length from 1 to the length of *large$*, though there's obviously no point in having it the same length!

We'll now re-write that 'MIDTEST' procedure, this time using LOC(): notice the different variables used, and that we use a *literal* string for *little$*.

Also, this time, we shall introduce a test to catch those situations where just one name is entered: in this case, LOC() will return '0' (zero), to indicate that the space between the Christian and Surnames hasn't been found. If we didn't allow for this, there would be an error when the procedure is run, the offending line being 'PRINT LEFT$(name$,p%-1)'. p%, the variable used to hold the position of the space character, would be zero and we would be asking Series 3 to print up to the '-1' character in the string *name$*. It is these types of 'bug' that you have to try to allow for when writing your programs!

```
PROC MIDTEST2:
   LOCAL name$(24),p%
   PRINT "Enter your full name:",
   INPUT name$
   p%=LOC(name$," ")
   IF p%
      PRINT "Your Christian name is",
      PRINT LEFT$(name$,p%-1)
   ELSE
      PRINT "You're just called",name$
   ENDIF
   GET
ENDP
```

Repeating strings

If you wanted to produce a dotted line on the screen, you could have an instruction like

```
PRINT "............................"
```

OPL provides an easier way to repeat characters and strings, and that's with the function REPT$().

REPT$(*str$,num%*)   This returns the string *str$*, the number of times indicated by *num%*. So if *str$* held the string "Good" and *num%* held the value '4', REPT$(str$,num%) would return a string "GoodGoodGoodGood". The format is

```
newstr$=REPT$(str$,num%)
```

and, as indicated above, REPT$() can be used as part of other statements such as PRINT.

Here's a procedure to display 20 dots on the screen.

```
PROC Reptest:
   PRINT REPT$(".",20)
   GET
ENDP
```

The Basics

By the centre - a LIBRARY routine.

It is often desirable to centralise text on the screen. Here is a procedure to achieve it on a full width 'text' screen. This procedure could be worth keeping for future use. So now is the time to start a Library in which to keep all of your 'standard' or stock routines.

Follow these steps.

1) Create a new Module in the Program Editor, called LIBRARY1. (Refer to Step 2).

2) Name the *procedure* 'CNTR'

3) On the *same line*, and after the colon, enter '(msg$,n%)'

4) Enter the rest of the procedure. The complete procedure looks like this:

```
PROC CNTR:(msg$,row%)
   LOCAL w$(40)
   w$=LEFT$(msg$,40)
   AT 1+(40-LEN(msg$))/2,row%
   PRINT w$
ENDP
```

5) Translate the procedure (PSION and 'T' keys), but *don't* run it. (You can't, anyway).

   Note: As MOD: (n, p), (given in Step 4) is also a useful function, you may like to enter this as *another* procedure in the LIBRARY1 Module. You will then have the MOD procedure available for any programs that you write, without having to re-enter it.

Now let us test this Library routine, and at the same time, show how to *load* a module into a program. The OPL command for this is LOADM. Let us have a look at this first.

LOADM *module$*   This command loads a *translated* Module, as specified by *module$* (which can be a literal string or a variable), so that all the procedures in that Module can be used. You can load up to three other Modules at a time (making four in all, with the program Module) - if you need another to be loaded, unload one that is currently not in use first (using UNLOADM *module$*).

If the Module you wish to load isn't in the same directory as the procedure that will use it, you must also specify the *path* in *module$*. Thus, if you keep Library Modules in a directory called '\LIB', and wish to load a Module in that directory called 'Library5', *module$* would be '\LIB\Library5'.

When creating Library Modules, it makes sense to place routines of a similar nature or purpose into the same Module. Thus, you might keep all the string handling utilities you write in one Module, mathematical utilities in another, and so on. You can thus build up several shorter libraries, rather than have just one library - which would be more space consuming when the program calling it is run.

We are now ready to write a test procedure to test our first Library routine.

Create a new Module (PSION and 'N' keys) called 'CNTRTEST', and enter the following test procedure:

```
PROC CNTRTEST:
    LOCAL m$(40),r%
    PRINT "Enter Message"
    INPUT m$
    PRINT "Which row (1 to 8)"
    INPUT r%
    CLS
    IF (r%>0) AND (r%<10)
       LOADM "Library1"
       CNTR:(m$,r%)
       UNLOADM "Library1"
    ELSE
       PRINT "Row out of range".
    ENDIF
    GET
ENDP
```

You can translate and run this procedure: it will load the LIBRARY1 routine you have just written, and call the CNTR:() procedure in that library.

In the CNTRTEST procedure, we unloaded the Library1 Module immediately after it had been used: this isn't absolutely necessary unless you want to load more than three other Modules: it was included to demonstrate how it is done. Note that, if the UNLOADM command had been included at the end of the procedure, after the GET statement for example, an error would occur if you specify a row outside of the permitted range. The reason is that, under this condition, the LIBRARY1 module wouldn't have been loaded - and Series 3 would therefore be unable to 'unload' it.

Useful Tip: When you've written a procedure that accepts inputs, test it thoroughly by entering a wide range of test values. Make unlikely entries - try entering a character when a number input is required, for example, and see what happens to your procedure. This way, you can cater for mistakes that can (and do) happen when the program is running, and adjust your procedure accordingly. Error handling is an important part of programming, and is something we shall discuss at a later Step.

STEP TEN

Converting Variables

In this Step, you will learn how to convert variables from one type to another.

OPL words covered are VAL, EVAL, FIX$, GEN$, NUM$, SCI$, HEX$, INT, INTF, FLT, ABS, *and* IABS

When change is needed

There are numerous occasions when information stored in one type of variable needs to be converted so that it can be used or stored in another type of variable. A typical example is when a number is stored as characters in a string: if you want to make a calculation using that number then it must first be transferred to a numeric type of variable. Similarly, if you want to print or display part of a number - limiting it, perhaps, to just two decimal places - then the easiest way is to convert it to a string.

OPL offers a variety of ways to convert variables from one form to another and there's even a way to perform mathematical operations on values and functions that are stored in strings.

Converting a string to a number

We have already seen that the *code* for a character - its 'ASCII' value - can be obtained by the ASC() function. This is not really of much use, however, if we want make a calculation of some kind on a *value* that's stored as a string - and you'll find there are many occasions when it is preferable to hold numeric values in strings. As just one example, you may keep dates in a 'fixed' type of format within a string - so you could have strings something like "12/02/1992" and 03/11/1993". By using the LEFT$(), RIGHT$() or MID$() functions, you can strip out the day, month and/or year, and convert those values to numeric variables for some possible calculation.

VAL(*str$*) This OPL function returns the *floating point* value of the number stored in the string variable *str$*. Naturally, the number must be valid: strings such as "123-456" or "123A" or "12.234.56" or even "12,345" will produce an error when you try to run the program. The string can, however, use 'scientific notation', so something like "1.23E4" is acceptable. The format is

$$v=\text{VAL}(str\$)$$

If the string *str$* holds an integer value, it is still returned as a floating point value. However, you can force Series 3 to store the value held by *str$* as an integer by using the format:

$$v\%=\text{VAL}(str\$)$$

In this case, if *str$* holds, say, "123.456", the value stored in *v$* will be '123': the decimal part will be lost.

Evaluating a string

Whilst you cannot perform mathematical operations on numbers that are held in string variables, what OPL will allow you to do is to evaluate a valid calculation contained entirely within a string or concatenated strings.

EVAL(*str$*)   If the string *str$* holds a mathematical expression, then EVAL(*str$*) will return the result of evaluating that expression. The format is

$$v=\text{EVAL}(str\$)$$

The expression can contain any mathematical operator or function, such as '+', '/', 'LOG()' or 'SIN()', and *str$* can be a single string variable or a concatenation of string variables. It is possible, therefore, to build up a 'formula' evaluator using this function, where the formula is entered by the user at the keyboard. Here is a very simple example. When the following procedure is run, you will be invited to input a mathematical function (such as 'SIN', 'LOG', 'COS', 'TAN' and so on), and then a value for that function to operate on. The answer is then displayed. So that you can test the operation of this procedure a few times without having to re-run it each time, we'll have it continue accepting inputs until the SPACE key is pressed in place of a function name. Be sure

that when you enter the function name you enter *a valid OPL
mathematical function*, without any brackets at all: the
procedure is written to add the brackets for you.

```
PROC EVALTEST:
   LOCAL func$(6),n$(12),eq$(20)
   DO
      CLS
      PRINT "Enter the function: ",
      INPUT func$
      IF func$=" "
         CONTINUE
      ENDIF
      PRINT "Enter the value: ",
      INPUT n$
      eq$=func$+"("+n$+")"
      PRINT eq$,"=",EVAL(eq$)
      AT 8,5
      PRINT "Press a key to continue"
      GET
   UNTIL func$=" "
ENDP
```

When you translate and run this routine, try it with, say, the 'MEAN'
function, entering not one value when prompted, but a series of
them separated by commas, pressing ENTER only at the end. You can
also try your hand at changing the 'AT 8,5' and 'PRINT "Press a
key..."' lines to load and call the CNTR function in the LIBRARY1
Module (assuming you've entered it and translated it, of course!).

Converting a number to a string
Converting a character *code* to the actual character using the OPL
function CHR$() has already been dealt with. We're now going to look
at the various ways numbers can be converted into strings. The OPL
words available allow you to determine how many decimal places will
be contained in the string, to *position* the number within the string -
that is to say have it at the start or at the end, with preceding spaces
- and so on. In all instances it is essential, of course, that the string
variable that will hold the converted value has been declared of
adequate length.

101

FIX$(*value,dplaces%,length%*)   This function converts the floating point variable *value* into a string. The number of decimal places is determined by *dplaces%*, and the maximum length of the stored value, *including* the decimal place, is determined by *length%*. The *dplaces$* 'argument' enables you to trim the actual number of decimal places in *value*. So if *value* is '123.456' and *dplaces%* is '2', then the returned string will contain the value "123.46". If *value* is '123' and *dplaces%* is '3', then the returned string will contain "123.000". Notice that Series 3 will always 'round up' if there are to be less decimal places in the stored string than in the original value, and it will add spaces if more decimal places are called for than in the original value.

If the value specified by the *length%* argument is insufficient to hold the stored number string, then Series 3 will return a *length%* number of asterisks instead. If *length%* has a *negative* value, then the number will be justified to the *right* of the string: in other words, it will have leading spaces. This probably gives you a clue to the reason for incorporating the *length%* argument: when 'formatting' a column of figures to be displayed, it is neater to have them with all the decimal points lined up. This can be achieved quite easily with the FIX() function. The formats are as follows:

```
f$=FIX$(value,dplaces%,length%)
PRINT FIX$(value,dplaces%,length%)
```

The following examples demonstrate the results achieved with FIX$(). In each instance, *f$* must have been declared to hold at least as many characters as required by the *length%* argument.

```
f$=FIX$(123.456,1,5)        f$ holds  "123.5"
f$=FIX$(123.987,0,5)        f$ holds  "124"
f$=FIX$(123,2,8)            f$ holds  "123.00"
f$=FIX$(123,2,-8)           f$ holds  "   123.00"
f$=FIX$(123.4,2,4)          f$ holds  "****"
```

Notice that in the first two examples Series 3 rounds up the value before storing it in the string f$, since less decimal places are requested than actually exist in the value.

In the third example, two decimal places were requested, and since the value to be converted had none, two trailing zeros are added after the decimal point: this feature is particularly useful when dealing with currency values that have to be displayed.

The fourth example shows what happens when a *negative value* for *length%* is specified: the numeric value is 'justified' to the right hand side of an eight character string. Note that f$ must have been declared toto hold at least eight characters.

Finally, the last example shows what happens when the *length%* argument is inadequate for the conversion. The value to be converted has three *integer* digits, to which must be added two decimal places and a decimal point - 6 characters in all. The *length%* argument specifies only 4, which is not enough. Consequently Series 3 displays asterisks, to show that the number cannot be represented as a string as requested.

GEN$(*value,length%*)   This is very similar to FIX$(), the difference being, as you can see, the number of decimal places is not specified. All the decimal places in the value will be represented in the stored string, and trailing zeros will not be added to 'pad out' the string to a given length.

The *length%* argument can be *negative*, which has the effect of 'justifying' the converted value to the right, filling the left side of the returned string with the appropriate number of spaces. As with FIX$(), if the value of the argument *length%* is inadequate, Series 3 stores asterisks instead.

The formats are

```
g$=GEN$(value,length%)
PRINT GEN$(value,length%)
```

and typical results of using the function are:

```
g$=GEN$(45.6,6)          g$ holds "54.6"
g$=GEN$(45.6,-8)         g$ holds "    45.6"
g$=GEN$(45.678,5)        g$ holds "*****"
```

In the second example, there are four spaces in the string before the first digit.

NUM$(value, length%) This is very similar to GEN$(), only this time the value is converted to an *integer* before being stored as a string. In performing the conversion, Series 3 will 'round up' if necessary. If a *negative* value is specified for *length%*, then the string will be right justified. If the result has more digits than specified by the *length%* argument, then the string will contain just asterisks. The formats are

```
n$=NUM$(value,length%)
PRINT NUM$(value,length%)
```

and typical results are:

```
n$=NUM$(123.456,5)        n$ holds  "123 "
n$=NUM$(123.456,-5)       n$ holds  "  123 "
n$=NUM$(123.9,4)          n$ holds  "124 "
n$=NUM$(12345,4)          n$ holds  "****"
```

SCI$(value, dplaces%, length%) This function is the same as FIX$(), the only difference being that the *value* is changed to scientific notation before being converted to a string. The *length%* argument must be at least *six* greater than the *dplaces%* argument, to allow for the integer part, the decimal point, and the 'E+00' part of the notation. Other wise, a string of asterisks will be returned. If a negative value for *length%* is used, the resulting representation is right justified within the string. Here are some examples:

```
s$=SCI$(123456,2,8)       s$ holds  "1.23E+05"
s$=SCI$(12,3,12)          s$ holds  "1.200E+01"
s$=SCI$(12,3,-12)         s$ holds  "   1.200E+01"
s$=SCI$(1,2,3)            s$ holds  "***"
```

HEX$(decimal&) This one is really more for the more experienced programmer. It returns a string containing the *hexadecimal* equivalent of the value *decimal&*, which although indicated here as a long integer, can also be an integer. Where the binary system has 2 digits (0 and 1), and the decimal system has 10 digits (0 to 9), the hexadecimal system has 16 digits -

0 to 9, followed by A to F. So A is 10, B is 11, C is 12 and so on, up to F which has the value 15.

The hexadecimal system is important in computing, since it provides an easier way to understand what's happening in the computer (believe it or not), and in fact the system has a very close relationship with the binary system. It is not necessary for you to understand any more about hexadecimal, so you can skip this next bit if you wish.

The reason why hexadecimal is so attractive to programmers is that the maximum decimal value that can be stored in one eight-bit memory box, 255 in decimal, or 11111111 in binary, is 'FF' in hexadecimal. Four bits store up to 15 in decimal - which is 'F' in hexadecimal. So each four bits in a series of memory boxes can represent an increase of 'F' in the hexadecimal system.

The counting process in hexadecimal is just like the decimal system: when you've run out of single characters to represent a value, you add '1' to the column to the left and start again. So after 'F' comes 10 (which is equal to 16 in decimal), and then the next 'change' occurs after 1F - 20, which is 32 in decimal.

Here's a little procedure that will help you to explore the hexadecimal values of decimal numbers.

```
PROC HEXTEST:
   LOCAL h&
   DO
      PRINT "Enter 0 to finish"
      PRINT "Decimal value?",
      INPUT h&
      IF h&
         PRINT "In HEX that's",
         PRINT HEX$(h&)
         GET
         CLS
      ENDIF
   UNTIL h&=0
ENDP
```

105

The Basics

Converting number types

There are several ways that numeric variables can be converted from one type to another. In assignments, it is possible to force a floating point result to an integer or a long integer by using the appropriate assigned variable, thus

```
i%=12.5*3.6
l&=123.456*.123
```

In both of these cases, only the integer part of the result will be stored. However, this method will not always be adequate, for there will be occasions when you will want to convert a value to an integer *in the middle* of an expression. It would be cumbersome (and unnecessary) to first make an assignment to an integer variable, and then use that integer in the expression. OPL provides the alternative.

INT(*fltexp*)   We have met this one before: INT() converts the expression or floating point value *fltexp* into a *long* integer. Thus, the two lines

```
a%=12.345
v=4.5*a%
```

can be replaced by

```
v=4.5*INT(12.345)
```

thus saving use of an extra variable. Notice that while an integer variable *a%* was used in the two line example, in the one line example INT(12.345) would actually be converted to a long integer.

It can sometimes happen that you want the integer of a floating point value - but still wish to retain the number as a floating point value: the 'range' of values a floating point variable can have is considerably greater than the range provided by long integers, remember. OPL caters for this situation as well.

INTF(*fltexp*)   This function is used the same way as INT(), the only difference being that the value returned is a *floating point* integer. Thus, after

106

```
i=INTF(1234.567)
```

the floating point variable *i* will hold the number '1234' as a floating point value.

This brings us to the conversion of *any* integer variable to a floating point value.

FLT(*integer&*) As you might expect, this converts the value of *integer&* to a floating point value. The format is

$$v=FLT(integer\&).$$

or

$$v=FLT(integer\%)$$

Knowing the way that Series 3 works when evaluating expressions (if one value is floating point, then floating point arithmetic is performed prior to the actual assignment), you may be wondering why **FLT()** is needed. If you have a procedure that expects a floating point value as an 'argument' and you wish to pass to it the value in an *integer* variable, then you would use **FLT()** to convert that variable first. Similarly, if the value you wish to pass is already a floating point value, but you wish to have only the integer part of it passed as the argument, then you would use **INTF()**.

There are two functions which allow the *absolute* value of a number to be returned. The absolute value is simply the 'positive' value, whether the number is negative or not.

ABS(*v*) Here, *v* can be a value or an expression. Whatever the value of *v* (or the result), the returned value is '+*v*' - where *v* is a floating point variable. This is useful when you have to deduct one number from another to find the difference, but don't know (and perhaps don't care) which of the two numbers is the larger. The format is

$$a=ABS(v)$$

Here's a little demonstration procedure to explain this: when you run it, enter two numbers as and when prompted, and irrespective of whether you enter the larger number first or last, you will be given the difference between those two values.

As with other test procedures, `ABSTEST` allows you to continue putting the theory to the test until you've had enough, at which point, simply enter a zero for the *first* value.

```
PROC ABSTEST:
   LOCAL n1,n2
   DO
      CLS
      PRINT "Enter 0 for to stop"
      PRINT "Enter first number",
      INPUT n1
      IF n1=0
         STOP
      ENDIF
      PRINT "Enter second number",
      INPUT n2
      PRINT "The difference is:",ABS(n1-n2)
      GET
   UNTIL n1=0
ENDP
```

`IABS(v&)` This similar to `ABS()`, the difference being that `IABS()` operates on integer values or expressions and returns an integer value. The integer can be normal or long. The formats are, therefore:

$$a\% = IABS(v\%), \text{ and } a\& = IABS(v\&)$$

Hexadecimal to decimal
Series 3 will allow you to enter hexadecimal values as constants, by *prefixing* them with a '$' if they're 16-bit (up to 'FFFF' hex), or with a '&' if they're 32 bit (up to 'FFFFFFFF' hex). Thus you could enter $1F (equivalent to 31 decimal), or &FFFFF (equivalent to 983040 decimal). You can also use these 'converters' to assign values to integer or long integer variables (such as d%=$FF, and d&=&FFFFF).

The Carpet Program

We now have all the programming tools we need to write the 'Carpet' program discussed in Step 3. This will be written as one Module. Start by creating a new file in the Program Editor, called 'CARPET', then enter the following program in its entirety before translating and running it.

```
PROC CARPET:
   LOCAL area,ppyard,tcost,q$(1)
   area=getarea:
   ppyard=getcost:
   DO
      tcost=area*ppyard
      cls
      AT 1,2
      PRINT "You need",area,"sq yards"
      AT 1,3
      PRINT "Which will cost £";
      PRINT FIX$(tcost,2,8)
      AT 1,4
      PRINT "at £";ppyard,"per sq. yard"
      AT 1,6
      PRINT "Another (C)ost, (A)rea, or (E)nd"
      q$=UPPER$(GET$)
      IF q$="C"
         ppyard=getcost:
      ELSEIF q$="A"
         area=getarea:
      ENDIF
   UNTIL q$="E"
ENDP

PROC getcost:
   LOCAL cpsy
   CLS
   PRINT "Cost per sq. yard:",
   INPUT cpsy
   RETURN cpsy
ENDP
```

Continues overleaf...

109

```
PROC getarea:
   LOCAL w,h,area
   CLS
   PRINT "Room Width (in feet:",
   INPUT w
   PRINT "Room Length (in feet):",
   INPUT h
   area=w*h/9
   IF area>intf(area)
      area=INTF(area)+1
   ENDIF
   RETURN area
ENDP
```

This program follows the structure discussed in Step 3. We start by getting in the room dimensions and cost of the carpet per square yard, then enter a loop which enables the user to 'test' out other carpet prices or room areas.

Notice how we check whether an extra square yard is needed (getarea: procedure): if the *area* is not the same as the *integer* of the *area*, then we must round up to the next square yard above. This is done in the line area=INTF(area)+1. Notice, too, how we use the FIX() function to limit the number of decimal places to two, for the 'pence' figure.

The options offered after the cost of a carpet has been displayed are for another cost (enter 'C'), another area (enter 'A'), or to end altogether (enter 'E'). If any other key is pressed, the loop is repeated, re-displaying the original information.

STEP ELEVEN

Mathematical Functions

In this Step we take a look at the mathematical functions available when programming. You'll find out about
* *Using the logarithmic functions.*
* *Evaluating roots.*
* *Using trigonometric functions.*
* *Getting random sequences of numbers.*
* *Working on lists of numbers*

The OPL words covered are LOG, LN, SQR, EXP, COS, SIN, TAN, ACOS, ASIN, ATAN, DEG, RAD, RND, RANDOMIZE, MAX, MIN, MEAN, SUM, STD, VAR

Calculator functions, at the ready

Many of today's calculators are blessed with a range of engineering and scientific functions, to help simplify problem solving. Series 3 has such functions too, for inclusion in your programs. Whilst these functions are also available in the Series 3's calculator mode, for lengthy, repeated calculations it is quicker to prepare a program: the user can be prompted for the inputs required, and the rest of the calculation can then be performed under program control, displaying the answer with no further ado.

Remember that functions can be used in an assignment, or as a part of other statements or expressions, where the value returned by the function is used for further calculation or display. Only the assignment formats will be given in this Step: previous Steps will have given you an idea on the other ways that functions can be used.

We'll start by looking at the basic mathematical functions.

Logarithms

Series 3 covers logarithms to the base 10 and *natural* logarithms to the base e. The functions are:

LOG(x) This returns the logarithm of x to the base 10. The format is

$$a = LOG(x)$$

where a is a floating point variable that will hold the returned value, and x is the value for which the logarithm is required. If a is made an integer variable, then only the *exponent* of the logarithm will be returned, and the *mantissa* will be lost.

LN(*x*)   This returns the natural logarithm - that is, the logarithm to the base e (2.71828...). The format is

a=LN(*x*)

where a holds the natural logarithm of x.

Roots and powers

Series 3 has a prepared function for finding the square root of any number:

SQR(*x*) This returns the square root of x, and has the format

$$s = SQR(x)$$

However, other roots are easily obtained by using the 'power' operator. For example, to find the cube root of a value x, you can use the format

$$c = x**(1/3.0)$$

which is the programming way to write '*x raised to the power one third*'. Note particularly that it is important to force Series 3 to perform a *floating point* calculation, by the inclusion of a decimal point in the value of either the '3' or the '1' (ie, '(1.0/3)' will also produce the desired result). If you don't - that is, if you simply use '(1/3)' as the power, then integer arithmetic will be performed, producing an incorrect result.

EXP(*x*) This function enables you to raise the natural constant e to the power x, saving the need to remember the value of e. The format is

$$v = EXP(x)$$

Step 11: *Mathematical Functions*

Trigonometric functions

There are six trigonometric functions available - COS(radians), SIN(radians), TAN(radians), ACOS(x), ASIN(x) and ATAN(x). You'll notice that the angle for the COS, SIN and TAN must be given in *radians*. However, the OPL function RAD(*degrees*) allows you to convert from degrees to radians. The formats for these three functions, therefore, are

$$v=COS(radians) \qquad v=COS(RAD(degrees))$$
$$v=SIN(radians) \qquad v=SIN(RAD(degrees))$$
$$v=TAN(radians) \qquad v=TAN(RAD(degrees))$$

To refresh your memory, in a right-angled triangle,

1) The cosine is given by the dividing the side adjacent to the angle by the hypotenuse.

2) The sine is given by dividing the side opposite the angle by the hypotenuse.

3) The tangent is given by dividing the side opposite the angle by the side adjacent to the angle.

ACOS(x), ASIN(x), and ATAN(x) are the *inverse* of the COS, SIN and TAN respectively (i.e. ACOS = (COS^{-1})), and the value returned will be an angle in *radians*. This can however be converted to degrees, using the OPL DEG() function. The formats for these three functions, therefore are

$$radians=ACOS(x) \qquad degrees=DEG(ACOS(x))$$
$$radians=ASIN(x) \qquad degrees=DEG(ACOS(x))$$
$$radians=ATAN(x) \qquad degrees=DEG(ACOS(x))$$

Note that, for ACOS(x) and ATAN(x), the value of x must lie within the range -1 to +1, otherwise you will get an error.

There is one other OPL word that should be covered here, and that is PI. This simply returns the value of pi (π) as a constant (3.14159265358979) and saves you from having to remember it. You use it just like any other floating point variable except, of course, you cannot change its value! Thus

$$v=4*PI/180$$

113

The Basics

Numbers at random

For programs involving an element of 'chance' - such as games programs - one often needs a *random* number. For example, to represent the throw of a die, you'd want a random number between 1 and 6, and to represent the throw of two dice, you'd want a random number between 2 and 12.

RND   returns a value from zero to 0.9999999... to 15 significant figures, and the value returned is different every time it is used within one program. This value can be used to provide a random number between *any* two specific limits. For example, multiplying the random number by 6 will produce a value within the range 0 to 5.99999999999994. If we take only the *integer* part of this value, we have a range of random numbers from zero to 5 - six possibilities in all. If we want to make these six possibilities simulate the throw of a die, then we need to add '1' to the generated random number. Thus

```
throw%=1+INT(RND*6)
```

or, more simply - since assigning a floating point value to an integer variable will force that value into an integer:

```
throw%=1+RND*6
```

As another example, to generate a random number between 10 and 20 inclusive, we require a range of 11 random numbers starting with 10. Hence:

```
n%=10+RND*11
```

Note that, if a program uses RND, the sequence of random numbers provided will be the same each time the program is run. You can avoid this by use of the command RANDOMIZE.

RANDOMIZE *x&* This sets a 'start' point for the RND function, which will then produce a specific sequence of random numbers. On its own, RND will produce the same sequence each time a program using it is run. So if you designed a game, say, that used RND, then the random sequence during play would be the same each time the game is run. This can be useful for testing out the game, but not when you want some variety!

RANDOMIZE sets a new random number sequence, which depends on the value of the argument x& (which can be an integer or a long integer). If you use a constant value for x&, then again, the sequence for RND will be repeated each time the program is run.

To ensure a *different* sequence is used each time, x& needs to have a different value whenever the program is run, and the easiest way to do this is to use one or two of the built-in functions (yet to be discussed), SECOND and or MINUTE. These return the number of seconds or minutes, respectively, from the system clock. By using

```
RANDOMIZE MINUTE
```

you will produce one of 60 random number sequences, depending on the minute past the hour that the program is started. Similarly,

```
RANDOMIZE SECOND
```

will produce one of 60 random sequences, depending on the particular second within the minute that the program is started. To get one of 3600 different sequences - with less chance of a repeat, you can use

```
RANDOMIZE SECOND*MINUTE
```

In this case, you'd have to start the program at exactly the same minute and second past the hour to have a repeated sequence. You can also use HOUR (which returns the hour of the day): however, to use RANDOMIZE SECOND*MINUTE*HOUR could produce an error, since the result of the multiplication could be outside the permitted integer range. (SECOND, MINUTE and HOUR return simple integer values). You can get round this easily:

```
h&=HOUR
RANDOMIZE SECOND*MINUTE*H&
```

This will force the result of the multiplication to be a long integer, and will give a range of 86400 different sequences, with far less chance of a specific sequence being repeated.

Calculations on lists of numbers

OPL has a number of functions that enable you to perform specific operations on a series of numeric values. (These functions are also available to you in the Calculator section of your Series 3).

MAX (*list*)   This looks at a list of values, and returns the highest value in that list. The list can be included in one of two different ways. It can either be a straight list of real values, variables or expressions, each separated by a comma, thus:

```
bignum=MAX(5,9,v,4*x)
```

or it can be the elements of a floating point array. In this instance, two 'arguments' are required: the array name (which must include the brackets), and the number of array elements to be examined. Thus:

```
bignum=MAX(arry(),n)
```

where arry() is the name of the array you wish to have examined, and *n* is the number of elements in the array to be examined, starting with the first. Here is a procedure to demonstrate this last example:

```
PROC maxtest:
   LOCAL a(5),c%
   DO
      c%=c%+1
      PRINT "Enter number",c%,":",
      INPUT a(c%)
   UNTIL c%=5
   CLS
   PRINT "The highest number entered =",
   PRINT MAX(a(),5)
   GET
ENDP
```

This procedure will also give you an idea on how arrays are used to store values. The *elements* of the array are a(1), a(2)...a(5), and each of these is, in effect, a different variable. As you can see, by having an array, we can enter the values in a DO...UNTIL loop, rather than have a lengthy repetition of input requests for each individual variable.

MIN(*list*)   This is similar to MAX(), the difference being that, surprise, surprise, MIN() returns the smallest value. You can edit the maxtest procedure to show the smallest number entered, by changing the PRINT MAX(a(),5) line to PRINT MIN(a(),5). You must also change 'highest' to read 'lowest' in the message line for the displayed answer of course! (And don't forget to *translate* the procedure before running it).

MEAN(*list*)   This returns the *mean* value of the list. The formats for MEAN() are the same as for MAX() and MIN(): the arguments can be a list of values, variables or expressions, each separated by a comma, or an array. In the case of the array, the number of elements to be examined must be the second argument. You can edit the maxtest procedure by simply changing the PRINT MAX(a(),5) line to read PRINT MEAN(a(),5), to show the mean of a series of five entered numbers. (Don't forget the message line!)

SUM(*list*)   This returns the *sum* of the list. The formats are the same as for MAX(), and you can put the function to the test by editing the maxtest procedure, changing the PRINT MAX(a(),5) line to PRINT SUM(a(),5), (and the message line to read 'sum' instead of highest') to show the sum of a series of five entered numbers.

STD(*list*)   This returns the *sample standard deviation* of the list. The formats are the same as for MAX(), and you can put the function to the test by editing the maxtest procedure, changing the PRINT MAX(a(),5) line to PRINT STD(a(),5), (and the message line to read 'standard deviation' instead of 'highest') to show the standard deviation of a series of five entered numbers.

VAR(*list*)   This returns the *sample variance* of the list. The formats are the same as for MAX(), and you can put the function to the test by editing the `maxtest` procedure, changing the `PRINT MAX(a(),5)` line to `PRINT VAR(a(),5)`, (and the message line to read 'variance' instead of highest') to show the variance of a series of five entered numbers.

STEP TWELVE

Dates and Times

In this Step, we take a brief look at the date and time functions available for use in your programs. The OPL words covered are DATIM$, YEAR, MONTH, MONTH$, DAY, DAYS, DAYNAME$, HOUR, MINUTE, SECOND, DOW, WEEK, DATETOSECS, SECSTODATE.

Using the System Clock

You will be well aware that Series 3 keeps tabs on the time and date. This information - and information based on it - is available for use in your programs. You will also have noticed that, generally speaking, OPL words indicate the particular function they perform - HOUR, for example, returns the current hour in the System clock. Tempting though it may be, you cannot use the names of the OPL words as the names of *variables* in your programs. Thus, you cannot write a program with a variable called 'hour'. This is true of all OPL words, of course, but for those associated with time, naming one of the OPL words as a variable is a very common error. You *can* however use one of the OPL reserved words if you give it a different identifier. 'Hour', for example, would produce errors as a floating point variable, but 'hour%' would be perfectly acceptable. Now let us examine the OPL words related to the time and date.

Accessing the System clock

A series of OPL words can be used to return 'simple' data from the system clock. These are:

DATIM$ This returns the current day of the week, date and time - including the seconds - as a string. If the entire string returned by DATIM$ is assigned to a string variable, that variable must have been declared to hold at least 24 characters. Using the string handling functions, (Step 9), you can 'pick off' various elements of the string, if you wish. The format for the function is

```
dt$=DATIM$
```

and you can naturally use it in statements such as PRINT DATIM$. The string returned by DATIM$ has the form

```
Mon 16 Sep 1991 11:00:15
```

Remember that DATIM$ returns the current time and date - and is being updated every second.

YEAR   This returns as an integer value the current year from the system clock. Years from 1900 to the year 2155 are covered. The format is

```
y%=YEAR
```

MONTH   This returns as an integer value the current month from the system clock. Naturally, the range of values returned is 1 to 12. The format is

```
m%=MONTH
```

DAY   This returns as an integer value the current day of the month from the system clock. The range of values is 1 to 31. The format is

```
d%=DAY
```

HOUR   This returns as an integer value the current hour of the day, using a 24-hour clock, from the system clock. The format is

```
h%=HOUR
```

MINUTE   This returns as an integer value the current minute from the system clock. The format is

```
m%=MINUTE
```

SECOND   This returns the current second, according to the system clock, as an integer value.

Converting time and date data

Very often you will be working on 'month' and 'day' information in
the form of numeric values, rather than the names of the months or
days of the week. Nevertheless, you may well wish to display the
name of the day or month rather than its number. OPL has two
functions which make the conversion for you.

MONTH$ (*mn%*)   This function converts the month number,
represented by *mn%*, into the corresponding three-letter
name. Obviously *mn%* must have a value from 1 to 12. The
format is

m$=MONTH$ (*mn%*)

or PRINT MONTH$ (*mn%*)

DAYNAME$ (*dn%*) This function converts a day number, represented
by *dn%*, into the corresponding three-letter day of the week,
The format is

dn%=DAYNAME$ (*dn%*)

or PRINT DAYNAME$ (*dn%*)

Date calculations

Most programming languages leave it to the programmer to write
routines that will enable him to evaluate, for example, the number of
days between two dates. OPL has functions to help achieve this and
similar tasks for you.

DAYS (*dy%,mn%,yr%*)   This function returns as a long integer the
number of days between January 1st 1900 and the date
specified by *dy%*, *mn%*, *yr%*, which represent the required
day, month number and year respectively.

d&=DAYS (*dy%,mn%,yr%*)

To find the number of days between two dates, all that is
needed is to enter the two dates in a suitable form, use the
'DAYS()' function for each of the dates, then subtract one
from the other. Here's a short(ish) program to evaluate the
number of days between any specified date (your Birthday,
perhaps) and the current date as determined by the system

clock. You could enter a date some time in the future: the ABS() function ensures that a positive result is always given.

```
PROC NUMDAYS:
   LOCAL dy%,mn%,yr%
   PRINT "Enter year:",
   INPUT yr%
   IF yr%<100
      yr%=yr%+1900
   ENDIF
   PRINT "Enter Month number:",
   INPUT mn%
   PRINT "Enter day of month:",
   INPUT dy%
   CLS
   PRINT "There are",
   PRINT ABS(DAYS(dy%,mn%,yr%)-DAYS
line continues             (DAY,MONTH,YEAR)),
   PRINT "days between",dy%,month(mn%),yr%,
   PRINT "and today"
   GET
ENDP
```

You'll see that this procedure allows you to enter a two-figure number for the year: if you do, then the '1900' is added to prevent an error occurring.

WEEK(*dy%,mn%,yr%*)   This function returns, as an integer, the week of the year in which a particular date falls, the date being specified by *dy%*, *mn%*, and *yr%*. The value of *dy%* must be sensible for the specified month, *mn%* must be a valid month number, and *yr%* must have a value between 1900 and 2155, otherwise an **'Invalid arguments'** error will occur when the program is run.

The starting day for each week is taken from the 'Start of the Week' setting in your Series 3 (under the 'Time' utility). There must be four or more days in the 'first week' for it to count as 'Week 1': if there are less, it is returned as Week 52.

```
wn%=WEEK(dy%,mn%,yr%)
```

DOW(`dy%,mn%,yr%`)   This   function   returns   an   integer representing the number of the day in the week, with '1' representing Monday through to '7' representing Sunday. As before, the arguments dy%, mn% and yr% must be valid, otherwise an error will occur. The format is

$$\text{daynum\%=DOW}(dy\%,mn\%,yr\%)$$

If you want the actual name of the day, rather than its number, you can use the DAYNAME$() function, thus:

```
PRINT DAYNAME$(DOW(dy%,mn%,yr%))
```

This is a good example, in fact, of how functions can be used as part of other functions: here we are using DOW() to obtain the day of the week as an *argument* for DAYNAME$(), to return the name of the day, which in turn is an expression for PRINT to operate on in order to display the answer. Notice how each function requires its arguments to be contained within its own set of brackets. Hence the double brackets at the end of the line given above.

DATETOSECS(`yr%,mon%,dy%,hr%,min%,sec%`)   This function goes the whole hog: it returns as a long integer the number of *seconds* between the turn of the year 1970 (00:00 on Jan 1st, 1970) and the date and time specified by the arguments yr%, mon%, dy%, hr%, min%, sec%. The value returned is positive up to +2,147,583,647, and then becomes *negative*, starting from -2,147,583,647, and going on until -1.

SECSTODATE(`s&, yr%, mon%, dy%, hr%, min%, sec%, dayinyr%`) This   does the 'opposite' to DATETOSECS(): it converts the long integer s& into its component parts - year (*yr%*), month (*mon%*), day (*dy%*), hours (*hr%*), minutes (*min%*) and seconds (*sec%*), plus the number of the day within the year, *dayinyr%*. The variables must have been declared: this function assigns the appropriate values to them, so that you can subsequently use them, for printing out, perhaps. As with DAYTOSECS(), s& can have a positive value up to +2,147,483,647. For a value higher than that, you must subtract 4,294,967,296 from the value.

STEP THIRTEEN

The Sound of Music

Time for a little 'light relief': in this Step, we take a look at the Series 3's capability to produce 'music'. The OPL word covered is BEEP.

Your own *Beep show*

By now, you will undoubtedly have heard some of the sounds that your Series 3 can create - the chimes and 'ringing' for the alarms, and the tones used for DTMF dialling. OPL has a command - BEEP - which enables you to create sounds other than a simple 'bleep' for use in your own programs.

The format for the command is

```
BEEP length%,pitch%
```

The *length%* value determines how many thirty-seconds of a second the sound will last. So for a one second sound, *length%* will have a value of 32.

The *frequency* of the sound is determined by the value of *pitch%*, as follows:

$$frequency = 512000/(pitch\% + 1)$$

which can be re-written as

$$pitch\% = (512000/frequency) - 1$$

This enables us to determine what value we should give to *pitch%* in order to produce a note of a specified frequency. Thus to play a note that has a frequency of 800 Hz for a quarter of a second, you would write

```
BEEP 8,512000/800-1
```

Note that brackets aren't needed round the '512000/800' part, since Series 3 performs the division first anyway (Step 5).

125

The Basics

If you make *length%* negative (eg BEEP -8,500) then Series 3 first checks whether the sound system is already in use. If it is, then BEEP simply returns without making any sound at all. Otherwise, BEEP waits until the sound system is free, then plays the note.

Keyboard music-maker

As a programming exercise, we will use BEEP to turn your Series 3 into a musical (?) instrument. Of sorts. This program uses many of the aspects of OPL we have discussed so far but not yet implemented, so although it is fairly crude in what it achieves, you may find it useful to enter it, if only temporarily.

The Internationally accepted frequency for the note 'A' is 440Hz. To find the frequency of a note one octave higher, the frequency is doubled. So 'A' in the next scale is 880Hz. Armed with this scant information, a formula can be devised to determine the frequency of any note in the scale.

If we say that 'A' is the first note in a scale, then 'A sharp' is the second note, 'B' is the third, and so on. Calling this the note *number*, the formula is

$$\text{note frequency} = 440 \times 2^{(\text{note number}/12)}$$

which in computer-write is

$$\text{note frequency} = 440 * 2^{**}(\text{note number}/12)$$

Thus, for 'C', the 'fourth note' from 'A', the frequency is 440*2**(4/12), or 554.365.

We now have the information we need to convert your Series 3 keyboard into a musical keyboard.

There are two ways to approach the actual playing of a note. The first is to calculate the required frequency each time a key is pressed, and then calculate the value required for the BEEP command. The second is to calculate the necessary values first and store them in an array. As this is an exercise, it will be useful to demonstrate the use of arrays, and so that's the method we shall adopt.

Ideally, each note would sound only while a key is being depressed. However, it is the nature of computer keyboards that there is a short delay before the key 'auto-repeats'. This means there would be a break in the note before it repeats for the duration of the keypress. The alternative is to arrange for the note to play continuously until another key is pressed - and to use the SPACE key to turn the sound off. Also, we shall use the ESC key to terminate the program when it is running.

Whilst the Series 3 keyboard doesn't resemble a piano keyboard, we can get some measure of similarity by using one row for the 'white keys', and appropriate keys from the row above it for the 'black keys'. The 'qwerty' row will give us our 'white keys'.

It will be useful to know the name of the note being played at any particular time - and which Series 3 key produced it, so we will arrange for this to be displayed on the screen whilst a note is being played.

The BEEP part of the program will be placed in a separate procedure, so that it can be called from various places: this saves us from having to repeat the command in the program.

The variables used are as follows:

n%(18) This is an array holds the calculated *pitch%* for 18 notes. It is a **GLOBAL** variable, since it will need to be used in the second procedure.

k$(18) This string of 18 characters holds the keyboard letters for the notes, in ascending sequence of played note.

c$(1) This will hold the character of the pressed key when the program is running.

nn$(36) This string holds the musical names of each of the eighteen notes, in ascending order. To allow for the fact that some notes require two characters (A#, for example), a space will be added to those only having a single character, so that all notes are defined by two characters.

c% This integer variable is used first as a 'counter' during the initial set up, then it is used to determine the position of a pressed key from the 18 valid key names in the k$() string. Thus we don't 'waste' a declared variable, or take up space by declaring another.

f This floating point variable is used in the calculation of the frequency for each note.

p% This holds the value of the last key that was pressed, so that we can avoid the gap in the note due to the keyboard's delay in auto-repeating.

You must enter both of the procedures in the same Module, before translating and running the program. Take care when entering it to ensure the variables have the correct identifiers throughout, that you have the right number of spaces in the appropriate places, and so on.

127

```
PROC music:
  GLOBAL n%(18)
  LOCAL k$(18),c$(1),nn$(36)
  LOCAL c%,f,p%
  k$="q2we4r5ty7u8i9op+-"
  c%=1
  DO
     f=440*2**(c%/12.0)
     n%(c%)=51200/f-1
     c%=c%+1
  UNTIL c%=18
  nn$="A A#B C C#D D#E F F#G G#"
  nn$=nn$+LEFT$(nn$,12)
  DO
     c$=LOWER$(KEY$)
     IF (C$="") AND p%
        Playit:(p%)
     ELSEIF c$=""
        CONTINUE
     ELSEIF c$=" "
        p%=0
        AT 18,4
        PRINT "Play        "
     ELSE
        c%=LOC(k$,c$)
        IF c%
           AT 18,4
           PRINT c$,"=",
           PRINT MID$(nn$,c%*2-1,2)
           Playit:(c%)
        ENDIF
     ENDIF
  UNTIL c$=CHR$(27)
ENDP


PROC Playit:(a%)
  BEEP 1,n%(a%)
ENDP
```

Now for the explanation on how this program works. First, as always, the variables are declared. Note that you can use more than one line to declare a specific type of variable: here we have used one line for the LOCAL string variables, and one for the LOCAL numeric variables.

The program starts by initialising the necessary variables and arrays. k$ is loaded with the key letter characters, in the correct sequence for the ascending notes. Then, in a loop, the frequency and pitch for each note is calculated and loaded into the array n%(). This is followed by loading the note names in the string variable nn$. Note how this is done: we enter all of the note names once, then simply add the necessary extra notes using the string function 'LEFT$()'.

Then comes the part of the program that plays the notes. This is contained within a DO...UNTIL loop, which will terminate when ESC is pressed (CHR$(27) - see Page 88).

We start by checking whether a key has been pressed - storing it in c$ if it has. Then, if a key hasn't been pressed since the last keyboard 'poll', but there *is* a previous valid keypress, we call the Playit:() procedure, using the previous keypress as the required *pitch.*

If there is neither a previous valid keypress, or a current keypress, then we jump to the UNTIL statement, to repeat the loop until something relevant *does* happen.

We then check to see whether the SPACE key has been pressed: if it has, we want to stop the note from playing, and clear the screen display. We stop the note from playing be assigning zero to p%.

Failing all that, another key must have been pressed, and so we must check whether it is a valid note-playing key. We do this by checking for its location in the string of valid notes. At the same time, we will find out which key or note of the eighteen has been pressed: this will be returned in c%. If the key isn't valid, c% will hold zero.

If it is valid, the IF c% statement is *true*, and so we set about displaying the appropriate keyboard key and the corresponding note on the screen before calling the Playit:() routine to actually create the sound. Notice how we pick out the *two* appropriate characters from the 36 character string nn$. We multiply the note's position (in the range of 18) by 2, because this string is double length. Then, we subtract 1, to get to the *start* of a relevant pair of characters. Thus, if the note's position is '3', multiplying by 2 gives 6, which would 'point' to the second character of the pair: subtracting 1 moves us back to the first character of the pair.

And that's it. You may not have created a wonderful keyboard instrument. But you will have learned a bit more about the basic operation of your Series 3!

Finally, here is a short routine to provide an alarm tone until a key is pressed.

```
PROC alarm:
  DO
     BEEP 1,400
     BEEP 1,200
  UNTIL KEY
ENDP
```

STEP FOURTEEN

Errors and Bugs

In this Step, we review the things that can go wrong when writing a program, and what to do about them. OPL words covered are TRAP, ERR, ERR$, ONERR and RAISE.

When things go wrong

The programmer who has never made a mistake doesn't exist. So if one of your programs doesn't run properly - or even fails to 'translate', don't despair - you've joined the club!

There are three areas where things can go wrong.

a)   Typing errors when entering the program.

b)   Incorrect use of the programming language.

c)   The program 'logic'.

You have to become a 'detective' to resolve any of these, examining every possible clue, and studying Series 3's analysis of the problem, when it is given.

Errors when entering

The easiest problems to detect are those caused through typing errors when entering your program. These will be revealed as soon as you try to translate it, for if Series 3 finds it doesn't understand the actual instructions, it will stop the translation process, report the nature of the problem and, in most instances, place the cursor at the point where the problem occurred. You can put this to the test for yourself by entering the following procedure exactly as it is written:

```
PROC bugs:
   PRINT (4*5
ENDP
```

There are actually two problems with this procedure. The first one you will discover when you try to translate it: Series 3 will stop, briefly report a '**Mismatched (or)**', and will leave the cursor at the end of the PRINT line. It is telling you that it found one bracket, but can't find the other. Hence the mismatched '(or)'.

The Basics

If you want to review the error message again, you can do so by selecting 'Show error' from the 'Prog' option on the MENU, or by pressing the PSION and 'E' keys at the same time.

Spelling errors in OPL words and errors of 'construction' are reported as a '**Syntax error**'. Typical errors of this nature are entering 'PRINY' instead of 'PRINT', missing out a space or a comma where a space or a comma is expected, or missing out the colon after a procedure name. What Series 3 cannot do when *translating* your program is detect errors in the spelling of your variables. You may have called a variable 'COST' in one place, and 'CAST' in another. Similarly, you may have given a variable a different identifier in one place. This type of error will show up, however, when you try to run the program - usually as an '**Undefined external**'.

During the translation process Series 3 will also report structural errors - finishing a 'WHILE...' loop with 'UNTIL', for example. In fact, it will report quite an extensive range of error types, to help you identify the mistake that you have made.

Generally speaking, the error message provided will give you an excellent clue to what has gone wrong, and the positioning of the cursor will often help you to locate where it has gone wrong. There are times, however, when Series 3 is unable to position the cursor near to the point of the error, so be prepared for a little searching through your program.

If you have more than one procedure in your Module, Series 3 will tell you which procedure caused the trouble when it reports the error. Again, in all but a few instances, this is where the problem actually lies.

The list of error messages that can occur during the translation process is given in your manual in the Error Handling Chapter. Hopefully, you won't see too many of them.

Run-time errors
The second type of problem that can occur - usually involving incorrect use of the language in some way or other - doesn't reveal itself until you attempt to *run* the program. Series 3 will find it is faced with a situation which prevents it from obeying your instructions. In such circumstances the program stops running, and a message relating to the nature of the problem will be displayed. As with all errors that cause Series 3 to stop whatever it is doing for you, program-wise, you can review the error message with the PSION and 'E' short-cut keys.

A typical - and very common - error of this kind is '**Undefined externals**'. In the 'bugs' program, if you edit ' (4*5 ' to read ' **x** ', you will find that it translates ok, but when you run it, the message

Error in BUGS\BUGS,X
Undefined externals

will be displayed. This is telling you that in the Module '**bugs**', the procedure '*bugs*' has an 'external' called 'x' which it cannot resolve. When you press ESC to return to the Program Editor, the cursor, in this instance will be placed at the beginning of the 'offending' procedure - that is, the procedure where it had the problem.

You may wonder why it is called an 'external', and not 'variable'. The reason is, as far as Series 3 is concerned, the 'variable' hasn't been declared in the *current* procedure, and therefore perhaps should have been declared in another external procedure, or should be included as a parameter or argument.

Whatever it is, it is something that Series 3 needs to know about - either through a LOCAL or GLOBAL declaration, or as a defined argument. Series 3 is telling you it has found something, in this case 'x', and it doesn't know what it is or where to look for it. In many instances, you will find that you have made a simple typing error, or failed to declare the variable concerned.

'**Undefined external**' is just one of a whole range of messages that Series 3 will report when it has a problem. The messages relate to specific situations, and will usually give you an excellent clue as to what you must do to correct the situation.

To give two more examples, a '**String too long**' message means that you have tried to assign too many characters to a string variable - more than it was declared to be able to hold. Thus:

```
PROC bugs:
   LOCAL a$(4)
   a$="abcdefg"
PRINT a$
ENDP
```

This procedure will translate without problem, but when run, it will stop, give the '**String too long**' message and, on re-entering the Program Editor, will place the cursor at the offending assignment line. You won't need much detective work to put that one right: however, if the assignment is of the form 'a$=b$', then you'll have to examine the declarations for both variables.

The Basics

A '**Subscript or dimension error**' message means that you are trying
to use an array element that hasn't been allowed for in the array
definition. Here's 'bugs' procedure edited yet again to demonstrate
this:

```
PROC bugs:
    LOCAL a%(4),c%
    PRINT a%(c%)
ENDP
```

On the face of it, everything looks fine: however, although all of the
variables have been declared, c% hasn't been assigned a value and
so it is equal to zero. We are therefore asking Series 3 to print the
value of the array element a%(0) - which doesn't exist. Array
subscripts start from '1' when the declaration is made, remember, so
a declaration of a%(4) means 'set up variables a%() to have a range
or 'dimension' of a%(1), a%(2), a%(3) and a%(4). Four variables in all.
When you attempt to run the procedure, the error message will be
displayed and on re-entering the Program Editor, the cursor will be
positioned at the offending 'c%'.

This particular kind of situation needs a little more detective
work on your part. You must ascertain *why* the value of the variable
c% has caused the subscript error. In the '**bugs**' example, it isn't too
difficult to spot, once you realise that declared variables are zero
until they are assigned a value. In different circumstances the error
could equally well be that c% has been assigned a value greater than
'4' or less than '1' somewhere in the program. You need to find out
where, and why, and correct for the situation from occurring again.

Errors of logic

We now come to the programmer's nightmare: errors in the logic of a
program. This type of error varies considerably in its degree of
complexity and the ease with which it can be resolved. Sometimes,
the error is fairly easy to detect. On other occasions it can take hours
of work - and possibly a great deal of re-writing to detect the error
and put it right.

The problem is, unless the error causes the program to stop
running, it can be difficult to detect. Furthermore, the error may
become apparent only under very specific running conditions.

The very first '**bugs**' program in this Step of the book had a very
simple error of logic. If you clear the intended bug and run it,
nothing will seem to happen. The program clearly states (when

134

corrected) 'PRINT (4*5)', yet nothing appears on the screen: you will be returned to the Program Editor almost as soon as you run it. What has gone wrong? Nothing as far as Series 3 is concerned: it has obeyed your instructions perfectly. Trouble is, after displaying the result of 4*5 - '20' - it went onto the next instruction, which is ENDP. So it finished running the program, before you had a chance to see the display. You need to 'hold' the screen display whilst you see the result, and for that you need another instruction such as GET.

A common error occurs when one variable is being divided by another. As long as the second variable has a value, the program will run perfectly. But for just one value of the second variable - when it is zero (equals '0') a '**Divide by zero**' error will occur.

This particular error will be detected by Series 3 since it cannot perform such an operation: it will stop the program. But there are many times when errors aren't revealed. And that's when you need to put your Sherlock Holmes hat on and winkle out the problem, carefully and methodically.

The first thing to do, always, is to examine your code very carefully, and ensure that there are no obvious mistakes - such as a missing GET. Examine your 'flow-chart' and see that *its* logic makes sense. (If your program is of any length and you *haven't* prepared a flow-chart, then you are asking for trouble).

There are several techniques you can employ when trying to locate errors of logic. The objective is to create 'clues' where clues don't exist, and this can usually be achieved by adding lines of code on a temporary basis.

For example, you can insert statement lines to PRINT out the name and values of suspect variables at various points in the program (followed by GET of course!), and then run the program observing what happens to the values of those variables under specific running conditions.

Where programs have a number of individual *function* procedures, you can copy each of them in turn to another Module, and then write a *test* procedure (as the first one in the Module) to call the function and test it out thoroughly, allowing for various types of input.

If you can get a print-out of your program, try to follow it through, step by step, for different conditions: run the program 'in your mind' as though you are the Series 3! Check that each OPL instruction does what you think it does: if in doubt, write a short procedure to test the instruction out (as indeed we have been doing in this Book).

Finally, if you can identify the particular area of the program that is causing the trouble, try writing it in a different way, perhaps using different OPL instructions altogether. This may give you a clue to the problem, and then you can either go back and correct the original coding, or simply use the new instructions.

Trapping detectable errors individually

It has already been stated that with a number of 'run-time' errors, Series 3 will stop and inform you it has a problem, and will spell out the nature of the problem. Errors that Series 3 can detect *you* can also detect, and prevent from stopping the program from running. OPL has instructions specifically designed for this purpose.

The range of instructions which, if used incorrectly, will cause a 'program stopping' error is quite large: most of the instructions however are concerned with *Graphics* and *File Handling* operations, neither of which we have dealt with yet: to do so now would only confuse. However, there is one instruction that we have dealt with, INPUT, which although doesn't actually stop the program from running, will enable us to examine the 'trapping' method.

You may have noticed that, where there is an INPUT statement, an incorrect entry for the variable type concerned will cause a question mark to appear on the next line of the display. Series 3 has in effect said "What you have entered at the keyboard is of the wrong *type* for the variable I've been told to use. Try again". Enter the following procedure, then when you run it, enter anything you like *except* a number. Then, when the question mark appears, enter a small integer number.

```
PROC Traptest:
    LOCAL a%
    PRINT "Enter a number"
    AT 18,1
    INPUT a%
    PRINT "You entered",a%
    GET
ENDP
```

Although the program doesn't stop running, the question mark that appears on incorrect entries can be a pain if you have carefully arranged for a neat display. You can avoid it with the OPL instruction TRAP. Before we show how it can be used to solve this particular problem, let us look at the instruction itself.

TRAP   This instruction can precede a number of the OPL
commands, to 'trap' any error that occurs when that
command is executed. Such errors would normally stop the
program running completely, with a relevant message
displayed on the screen. When TRAP is used, however, any
error that occurs *is handled under your control.* It is very
important to remember this: the Series 3's mechanism for
dealing with the error - which is short and curt - is
effectively switched off. It is up to *you* to deal with the error
in your program. The benefit, of course, is that you can
anticipate what might go wrong and prevent it from stopping
the program from running. How you handle the error is up
to you, but usually you will want to correct the error in some
way and perhaps display a message, so that the program can
continue to perform the way you intended.

When TRAP is used, any error resulting from the
execution of the associated command will not stop the
program running. Series 3 will register the fact that an error
has occurred, by storing an identifying 'number' for that
error in an OPL variable called ERR. Execution will then
continue with the next statement in your program. *This is
where your 'action on an error' routine should be.* You can
detect the nature of the error by examining the value held by
ERR, and then act accordingly.

ERR on its own simply holds a value. There is also an OPL
function that will return the relevant message for a
particular error number, and that's ERR$(en%), where *en%*
is the error number. The format normally used would be
PRINT ERR$(ERR).

Note that although it doesn't have an identifier, ERR
stores a (negative) integer value for Series 3's error codes.

The commands that TRAP can be used with are (most of
these are dealt with in Parts 2 and 3 of this Book):

Data Entry: INPUT, EDIT
Data File Handling: APPEND, BACK, CLOSE, CREATE,
    DELETE, FIRST, LAST, NEXT, OPEN, OPENR, POSITION,
    UPDATE, USE.
Directory File Handling: COMPRESS, COPY, ERASE,
    LCLOSE, LOADM, LOPEN, MKDIR, RENAME, RMDIR,
    UNLOADM.
Graphics: gCLOSE, gCOPY, gFONT, gPATT, gSAVEBIT,
    gUNLOADFONT, gUSE.

The Basics

Now let us take a look at how TRAP can be used with INPUT, to demonstrate the usage of this command. We are going to precede the INPUT command in the Traptest program with a TRAP command, and then follow this statement line with our own error handling routine. Edit Traptest as follows:

```
PROC Traptest:
   LOCAL a%
   PRINT "Enter a number"
   DO
      AT 18,1
      TRAP INPUT a%
      IF ERR
         AT 3,3
         PRINT "Bad input"
         GET
         AT 3,3
         PRINT "           "
      ENDIF
   UNTIL ERR=0
   PRINT "You entered",a%
   GET
ENDP
```

You'll see that the input routine is contained within a DO loop which will run until an error free input has been obtained (UNTIL ERR=0). Following the TRAP INPUT line, we are simply testing for *any* error - although in practice there are probably only two that can occur - 'General failure' (-1) and 'Escape key pressed' (-114). If no error occurs with the input, ERR is zero, IF ERR is *not true*, and execution jumps to the UNTIL ERR=0 (which is *true*). The program will then continue the way you planned, with an acceptable input, and with the screen display entirely under your control.

Since the ESC key produces an error number when pressed during an INPUT operation, you can use it to escape from the routine altogether. To show this, delete the IF ERR line in Traptest, and insert the following in its place:

```
IF ERR=-114
   STOP
ELSEIF ERR
```

Now when the procedure is run, pressing the ESC key will simply break out of the program. This gives you an easy way to terminate a program without going through the rigmarole of having statements such as "Press 0 to exit", and then testing for a zero input.

Trapping any program-stopping error

TRAP gives us control over errors that occur with specific OPL commands. But there is also a universal way to trap any *program stopping* error, irrespective of the command that caused it. (This universal method won't trap errors occurring with INPUT, for example, since they don't actually stop the program from running).

Trapping any program-stopping error takes a little more care and thought, for whereas you can be fairly sure of the type of error that is likely to be produced by one of the OPL commands, when spreading a broad net over a procedure, module or even an entire program, you cannot be too certain of which error is going to occur. Consequently, you will have to test for the nature of the error. The OPL command for 'overall trapping' is ONERR.

ONERR   This command (which stands for 'ON ERROR'), must be followed by a label name, indicating where Series 3 is to continue to execute the program should an error occur. The label can be positioned anywhere in the current procedure (even before the ONERR command, so that processing will 'jump back').

ONERR switches off the Series 3's handling of errors on all the instructions that follow it, including instructions in *called* procedures. You could, therefore, protect an entire program by having ONERR as one of the first statements. This, however, is not recommended since it can result in endless loops, and it makes the handling of specific errors difficult - and prone to mistakes.

You can have more than one ONERR in a procedure, but only the last one to be executed is obeyed. You can also 'switch off' all ONERRs in one procedure, with the line

```
ONERR OFF
```

Note that this affects only the action of the ONERR commands in the current procedure: those in procedures that call the current procedure are unaffected.

It is important to note that, since ONERR covers all possible 'reportable' errors, it should be *switched off* as the first instruction in the error handling routine. If it isn't, and an error occurs within the routine, your program will wind up with the error handling routine calling the error handling routine calling the error handling routine calling the ... you get the idea.

If you use ONERR and TRAP, the TRAP command takes precedence: the error handling routine you write following TRAP will be executed, rather than the ONERR error handling routine.

The format for using ONERR is

```
ONERR label or
ONERR label::
```

When protecting an entire procedure with ONERR, it is usual but not necessary for the error handling routine to be placed either at the start or the end of the procedure. When at the start, you would probably want to have an 'IF ERR' as one of the early statements, to prevent the program from executing the routine during the normal sequence of events. Similarly, when the error handling routine is placed at the end of a procedure, to prevent it from being executed you would most likely place a statement such as 'RETURN' before the routine's label.

We'll demonstrate both of these methods with programs that divide 10 by an integer number. Whilst *any* error will be trapped, it is unlikely that anything other than a 'Divide by zero' will occur. Nevertheless, these programs serve our purpose in showing how the ONERR command can be used.

Here's the procedure with the error handling routine 'up front'. You'll see that we start the error handling routine (Fixit::) with an ONERR OFF, even though so far we haven't apparently switched it on yet. Point is, should an error occur later on in the program, ONERR *will* be 'on', and it is important to make sure it is switched off within the error handling routine itself. The TRAP command is used with INPUT, to show how both error handling techniques can be included within the one procedure. Remember that TRAP takes precedence over ONERR for all *program stopping* errors. When you run this program, first enter a letter instead of a number, then, next time you're asked for a value, enter zero, and then finally, enter a small(ish) integer number.

```
PROC Traptest:
   LOCAL a%
   Fixit::
      ONERR OFF
      IF ERR
         AT 1,4
         PRINT "Divide by 0 trapped by ONERR"
         PRINT ERR$(ERR)
         GET
         AT 1,4
         PRINT "                          "
         PRINT "                          "
      ENDIF
   ONERR Fixit::
      CLS
      PRINT "Divide 10 by?:"
      DO
         AT 18,1
         TRAP INPUT a%
         IF ERR
            AT 1,4
            PRINT "TRAPped input error"
            GET
            AT 1,4
            PRINT "                    "
         ENDIF
      UNTIL ERR=0
   PRINT 10.0/a%
   GET
ENDP
```

Notice how we avoid the error handling routine from being executed when the program is initially started, by checking OPL's ERR variable.

Now let us look at a program with the error handling routine at the end. This time, we've used RETURN to prevent the error handling routine 'Fixit::' from being executed during the normal running of the program (in this case, you could also use STOP). Also, you'll see that in order to give the user a chance to enter another value, we've used the dreaded GOTO to jump back to the start of the program in the event of an error. Without this, the program would end after the error had been announced.

```
PROC Traptest:
   LOCAL a%
   Redo::
   ONERR Fixit::
   CLS
   PRINT "Divide 10 by?:"
   DO
      AT 18,1
      TRAP INPUT a%
      IF ERR
         AT 1,4
         PRINT "TRAPped input error"
         GET
         AT 1,4
         PRINT "                        "
      ENDIF
   UNTIL ERR=0
   PRINT 10.0/a%
   GET
   RETURN   : REM or STOP will do here

Fixit::
   ONERR OFF
   AT 1,4
   PRINT "Divide by 0 trapped by ONERR"
   PRINT ERR$(ERR)
   GET
   AT 1,4
   PRINT "                              "
   PRINT "                            "
   GOTO Redo::
ENDP
```

The ONERR command is fairly powerful, in that it will also trap the program stoppers you hadn't bargained for. Remember that you can detect the nature of the error through the ERR variable, and print it out with PRINT ERR$(ERR).

As a general strategy, in an ONERR handling routine you can use 'IF ERR=*en1%*' and 'ELSEIF ERR=*en2%*' statements to deal with the errors you're catering for (where *en1%* and *en2%* represent error code values), and an ELSE statement to deal with anything unexpected.

Raising errors

To help when testing or debugging a program, OPL allows you to generate an error. The effect is exactly the same as if an error had actually occurred: the requested error code is stored in the OPL variable ERR, and acted on accordingly. If you don't have an ONERR command preceding the RAISE statement, Series 3 will stop the program and report the 'raised' error just as if it had really occurred.

RAISE   The format is

$$RAISE\ errcode\%$$

where *errcode%* is the negative code value for the error type you wish to generate.

You must be a little careful when using RAISE where loops in the program structure are involved. For example, if in the previous Traptest program you include a line 'RAISE -8' (for 'Divide by zero') after the ONERR Fixit:: statement, the program would go into a perpetual loop. The error would be generated, dealt with by the error handling routine Fixit::, then program execution returned to the point a little before the error is generated again. Wheels will spin. You can break out of such a loop, so that you can happily continue using your Series 3, by pressing the PSION and ESC keys.

Nevertheless, RAISE can be useful in generating a message for you. Say, for example, that at some point in your program the user is required to enter an input from 1 to 10 inclusive. Anything else is not acceptable. Rather than use a DO...UNTIL loop, we'll write a procedure using RAISE to handle it. We'll use RAISE to generate an "Invalid arguments" message, which is quite appropriate for the circumstances. But notice how the RAISE instruction is obeyed *only* if the user makes what we deem to be an incorrect entry. Any valid entry, and the error message is not generated, so perpetual loops are avoided. When you've entered the program, run it and enter a value over 10 before entering a value between 1 and 10.

```
PROC raistest:
  LOCAL a%
  Fixit::
    ONERR off
    IF ERR
      PRINT "Naughty you"
      PRINT ERR$(ERR)
      GET
    ENDIF
  CLS
  PRINT "Enter a number (1-10)",
  INPUT a$
  ONERR Fixit::
    IF (a%<1) OR (a%>10)
      RAISE -2
    ENDIF
  PRINT "Thank you!"
  GET
ENDP
```

Finally you can use **RAISE** to generate your own error messages for particular circumstances by raising a *new* error code, different from those used by OPL. Psion strongly recommend that, when raising your own numbers, you avoid any negative values like the plague: they may wish to add to the list themselves.

In the **raistest** procedure, first edit '**RAISE -2**' to read '**RAISE 1**', and run the program. With an entry of over 10, the error message reported will be 'Unknown error [2]". Then edit the 'IF ERR' line to read 'IF ERR=1', and the 'PRINT ERR$(ERR)' line to read 'PRINT "My error message". That shows how you can 'catch' errors of your own choosing and display a message accordingly.

PART 2

The Graphics

This Part of the Book deals
with the very powerful
Graphics capabilities of OPL,
enabling the creation of
Windows, Menus, Dialogs,
Icons and drawings.

STEP FIFTEEN

Putting You In The Picture

This Step introduces the powerful Graphics capabilities of Series 3, and then looks at simple ways to get special messages displayed on the screen. OPL words covered are BUSY and GIPRINT.

Now comes the power...

All the OPL commands and functions we have discussed so far will enable you to write *text* programs: that is, programs which use no graphics at all. But you will have realised, from the way Series 3 presents its own built-in facilities (such as the World Map or Agenda) that it is capable of far more than simple textual displays. Clocks, pull-down menus, dialog boxes, little button displays that 'press down' when the appropriate key is pressed, brief on-screen messages tucked away in a corner - all these and more are available for you to use. They'll add life to your programs, give them a professional feel and help to make them easier to use, or as they say, 'user friendly'.

Why didn't we start off with all of the Graphics commands and functions, so that the programs written so far could have benefited? Quite simply, instructions involving the graphics capabilities can *appear* fairly complex at first, entail a good working knowledge of the language and an understanding of the various techniques involved. To have combined learning the essential basic commands and functions of OPL, the various techniques, *and* the graphics commands would have made it very difficult to build up a clear background of knowledge.

But now you should be ready to assimilate the principles of the extensive range of graphics commands and functions available. If you found the very first program you entered an exciting achievement (and most people do), then, to paraphrase that well known saying, "You ain't seen nuthin' yet!".

The capabilities of the graphics are vast: consequently it must be stated at the outset that, in this Book, we can do no more than explain how to use them and give demonstration examples where practical. It will then be up to you, armed with an understanding of how they 'work', to incorporate them into your own programs. But

147

The Graphics

bear in mind that almost anything is possible, even a Chess game with properly designed pieces...

Text and Graphics screens

When dealing with text only displays, the screen area your programs can occupy could be considered as a grid 40 characters wide by nine rows deep. In the Program Editor, this is reduced by the border line. You can set the location where characters are printed by use of the AT command. Also, you may recall, there is a command (SCREEN) which enables the 'text' screen to be reduced to a smaller size, and positioned at a specific location on the actual screen. You may have wondered why this command could be needed. In this part of the book, we shall see that you can have 'windows' - defined areas of the screen - where specific displays are portrayed: the text screen, either the 'whole' display area or that defined by the SCREEN command - is, in effect, one of those windows. In a text 'window', the characters available are all from one 'font' - monospaced.

For graphics, the whole screen is made up not of 40 by 9 blocks, which can each take one character, but rather of 240 by 80 'points' or, as they're known, *pixels*.

The blocks are 'referenced', as in the AT command, by their column and row positions. Thus, with text screens, AT 1,1 defines the position of the first block to the left of the first row of the screen or window.

The *pixels* are also referenced by two numbers, representing the column across the screen, and the row down the screen. For these, however, the *pixel* in the very top left position is not '1,1', but '0,0'. So a *pixel* that has its position identified as '2,3' is actually the *third* pixel across, and the *fourth* pixel down. The pixel in the bottom right hand corner of the whole screen is identified as '239,79'.

Just as Series 3 keeps a 'note' of which of the 40 by 9 blocks the next PRINT command will act from, so it also keeps track of the current *pixel* location for *graphics* commands. Only one command, AT, allows you to position the 'cursor' or set the screen location for text displays. There are several graphics commands that will re-position the current *pixel* location, depending on what you are doing.

The overall graphics display screen can be divided up into 'windows' using special OPL commands - and these windows can overlap and cover each other. Windows to the rear - the displays on which are therefore hidden from view - can be brought to the front for display, then pushed back to the rear again. This 'windowing' capability opens an incredible variety of possibilities for programs.

We shall be dealing with windows in a later Step in the Part of the book.

The Graphics commands

The graphics commands can be divided into three groups:

a)   Those dealing with the creation of *menus* which look just like menus in the Series 3 applications. These commands are identified by an initial letter 'm'.

b)   Those dealing with the creation of *dialog boxes* which look like those offered by Series 3 applications. These are identified by an initial letter 'd'.

c)   Those dealing with *drawing shapes*, displaying *specially formatted text* and *clocks*, and working with *windows* and *bitmaps*. These, collectively, are the *true* graphics commands, and are identified by an initial letter 'g'.

To identify and help differentiate all these commands from others dealt with so far, the initial letters will be shown as lower case. You can type them in as capitals or lower case.

There are also commands for displaying the 'Status window' (the one with the clock that can be set to appear to the right of Series 3's display), for displaying the name of an icon against your own program when it is installed on the main System display of Series 3, and for displaying those 'information' and 'Busy' messages that can appear on the screen to inform the user that 'something' is happening.

Brief screen messages

We'll start this Graphics part of the Book with a look at the two commands available for displaying 'program' messages on the screen.

BUSY   This command produces a reversed out, 'flashing' message in one corner of the screen, similar to the 'Busy' message you sometimes see when Series 3 is running one program whilst you are doing something else - 'multitasking'. The command has four possible formats:

> BUSY *msg$*, corner%, delay%
> BUSY *msg$*, corner%
> BUSY *msg$*
>
> BUSY OFF

where

msg$ is the message to be displayed, and can either be a variable or a string literal of no more than 19 characters.

corner% is a value from 0 to 3, representing the corner of the screen that you want the message to be displayed:

0   the top left corner
1   the bottom left corner (*default* location)
2   the top right corner
3   the bottom right corner.

delay% is a delay, in half-seconds, before the message is displayed. Thus, to prevent the message appearing for two seconds, *delay* would have a value of 4.

In some programs, Series 3 will spin its wheels for a while whilst it is making complex calculations. For example, in a game program, you may have written routines for Series 3 to assess the best of the possible moves. During the period of this assessment, nothing will appear to be happening at the screen, and so to assure the user that Series 3 hasn't in fact 'seized up' or gone into hibernation, you can use the BUSY command. The *delay%* argument can be used to prevent the message appearing too quickly - if the assessment periods are short, then the messages will appear very briefly. If you don't specify a delay period, then the message *msg$* will be displayed immediately the command is met.

If you don't specify which corner of the screen you want the message to appear, then by default it will appear in the bottom left hand corner.

This command must be 'turned off' with the BUSY OFF command at a suitable point in your program: in the case of the 'next move assessment' period discussed above, you'd turn BUSY off when the next move had been evaluated.

Note that you can have only one 'Busy' message on the screen at a time. If you issue another BUSY command whilst one is being displayed, the new one replaces the original.

GIPRINT   This is very similar to BUSY, except that the message doesn't 'flash', and it automatically switches off after about two seconds, or sooner if a key is pressed. The formats are

```
GIPRINT msg$,corner%
GIPRINT msg$
```

where

msg$ is the message to be displayed, and can be a string
variable or literal up to 63 characters long, although if
it is too long for the screen display, it will be 'clipped'.

corner% is a value from 0 to 3, representing the corner of the
screen that you want the message to be displayed:

0   the top left corner
1   the bottom left corner
2   the top right corner
3   the bottom right corner (*default* location).

Note that the default location, if you don't have a value for
corner%, is the bottom right corner.

This command is useful for printing brief messages on
the screen - such as those like 'Syntax error' that Series 3
displays when you have an error during the 'translation' of a
program. (Surely, you *must* have seen it?!).

Like BUSY, only one GIPRINT message can be on the
screen at a time, although you can have both a BUSY
message and a GIPRINT message on display at the same
time.

Here is a program that makes use of both of these words:

```
PROC msgtest:
    LOCAL c%
    BUSY "I'm working!",0
    DO
        c%=c%+1
        PRINT c%;
        PAUSE 3
        IF c%=120
            BUSY "Nearly done!",2
        ENDIF
    UNTIL c$=40*4-4              (C% = 40 x 4 - 4
    BUSY OFF
    GIPRINT "All done! (Press a key)",1
    GET
ENDP
```

The Graphics

In this program, the message "I'm working!" is flashed in the top left corner whilst the screen is filled slowly (the PAUSE command slows it up) with a range of numbers. Towards the end of this task, the BUSY message is switched to the top right corner, to inform you that it is "Nearly done!".

The BUSY message is then switched off, and the "All done..." message displayed for about two seconds, *unless* you have pressed a key whilst the program is running. GIPRINT, like the KEY command, doesn't wait for a keypress, but rather examines a *buffer* in Series 3 where keypresses are stored. So if a key has been pressed whilst the program is running, GIPRINT sees that keypress - but does nothing with it: program execution jumps to the next statement, GET, which also sees the keypress, removes the keypress information from the *buffer*, and so the end of the program is reached.

It's worth running this program a few times - testing it with and without a keypress, and removing the BUSY OFF statement, to see how it all works.

It is also worth trying another little test whilst the program is running: press the PROGRAM button. You will be returned to the Program Editor, with the Series 3 'Busy' message displayed at the bottom left corner. This is telling you that whilst you are looking at your program entry, Series 3 is still carrying out your program instructions. If you then press the SYSTEM button, and select the program under the RUNOPL icon, you will be returned to the running program - which by then may well have finished, and be waiting for your final keypress.

You have seen 'multitasking' at work: Series 3 has the powerful capability of handling more than one job at a time. So if you have a program performing lengthy computations, you don't have to wait until they're finished before you use one of the other facilities available. You could, for example, dial out a telephone number whilst your program is running, and whilst *that* is happening, you could examine your Agenda. There are very few desk-top machines that offer that as a built-in capability!

As with the other explanatory programs in this book, once you are satisfied that you understand the principles involved, you can delete both the *source* code file and the *translated* code file.

STEP SIXTEEN

Creating Menus

In this Step, we examine the process of creating menus like those Series 3 uses. The new OPL words discussed are mINIT, mCARD *and* MENU.

Making the choice easy

Menus make choosing from a variety of functions and operations a simple process. You can write menus with the same look and feel as those provided by the Series 3 menus. You can make your menu 'active' as part of the natural running of a program, or arrange for it to 'pop up' when the MENU key is pressed. When a menu is displayed, the options can be selected by using the arrow keys and pressing ENTER or by pressing a short-cut key combination (which you must define). You can also arrange for your program to act on the short-cut keys even when the menu isn't being displayed. Clearing a menu from the display without selecting an option is achieved by pressing the ESC key.

Menu displays appear 'over the top' or in front of any other display on the screen at the time. When they are cleared, the original display is restored (this is, in fact, an example of 'windowing').

The menu comprises a list of main 'subject' headings across the top of the screen, rather like the 'tabs' on a card filing system. Each tab has its own 'drop-down' options, which appear when the tab is selected. In fact it's all the same as the menus provided by Series 3 applications.

There are three steps to creating a menu:

a)   Get the Series 3 ready to receive a new menu operation, using the mINIT command. Only one menu 'set' can be used at a time.

b)   Define the menu options using mCARD commands: a separate command is needed for each 'subject' option you want at the top of the screen.

c)   'Switch on' the menu display, using the MENU function.

The Graphics

Naturally, you would group associated options under one 'subject' heading at the top of the screen. Now let us have a look at the commands concerned in detail.

mINIT   Series 3 needs a section of memory devoted to the creation and display of menu items. You have to tell it to abandon the current information, and prepare for new information: mINIT is the command that does this. It cancels any existing menu, and prepares Series 3 to receive information about your new menu.

mCARD *subject$,item1$,sck1%,item2$,skc2%...item6$,sck6%*
    This command is less complicated than it looks! The first item, *subject$*, is a string variable or literal that gives the name of *a single* menu option on the top line of the display. You need an mCARD command for each option you want displayed at the top of the screen. You can have as many mCARD commands as *subject$* names will fit across the top of the screen: if the names you choose are, together, greater than the width of the screen, you will get '**Too wide**' error.
    You can have up to six items named on the drop-down part of the menu, specified by the string variables or literals *item1$, item2$,* and so on. Each item *must* be associated with the *character code* for a short-cut key, defined by the variables *sck1%* and so on. The short-cut key is the one that can be pressed, together with the PSION key, to select the particular menu option (without having to use the MENU key, if you program for it!).
    Thus, if you want the short-cut key for the first item to be the letter 'A', *sck1%* would be '65'. You could also write this as ASC("A"), or %A, as explained in Step 9, to save looking up the *character code*, and to make your program easier to understand when checking it through. You should be aware that 'A' and 'a' are the same *as far as short-cut keys* are concerned: either will select the associated option. In fact, if you select 'a' (%a or ASC("a")), the capital letter will actually appear as the short-cut key on the drop-down menu. However, the *lower case* letter is returned when the option is selected, irrespective of whether you use an upper or lower case letter. (This may change in future models of Series 3).
    In most instances, you will be able to choose a short-cut key related to the function it selects. Thus, if the option is 'Edit', you would probably choose the short-cut key 'E'.

However, you must be careful that you don't use the same letter twice in the complete menu - only one of the two actions will be performed. Also, although almost the entire keyboard is available for use as short-cut keys, those that can be used with the PSION key to produce a character (indicated by the yellow letters or symbols above the keys) are best avoided.

MENU   This function 'switches' the menu display on. All of the 'subject' options appear along the top of the screen, and the 'drop-down' options for the first 'subject' will also be shown. The arrow and return keys are used to make a selection.

When a selection is made using the arrow and ENTER keys, *the lower case character code for the short-cut you selected* is returned. It is important to remember this. For example, if you choose 'A' as your short-cut key (%A), the character code actually *returned* will be that for 'a' ('97') when that particular item is selected. Remember, if you use 'a' (%a) as your short cut key, 'A' appears on the menu. The format for the function is

$$m\% = MENU$$

Note that the short-cut key combinations won't select an option item when the menu is *not* being displayed unless you specifically program for it to happen.

You should also be aware that, when the menu is displayed, *any* short-cut key combination will clear the menu and return the code for the key you pressed with the PSION key. If your program doesn't cater for this, an error could occur. (*Note: This may be changed in later models*).

A simple menu example

A menu can become the main core of your program. You can arrange for it to be displayed as soon the program starts to run, to act on the selected option, and then return to the menu for further action. One of the options, of course, would be to quit the program.

This is the simplest way to use a menu: more complex would be to have the menu 'pop up' whenever the MENU key is pressed, and arranging for your program to 'react' when the short-cut key combinations are pressed even though the menu *isn't* being displayed at the time. We'll come to these later.

Enter the following program 'MENU1' carefully. There are several points that are worth noting. First, the three menu instructions must

be kept together: you cannot, for example, set up the menu with
mINIT and mCARD instructions, and place the MENU function within a
DO or WHILE loop. Series 3 will report a '**General failure**' error when
the program is run.

```
PROC MENU1:
   LOCAL k%
   DO
      mINIT
      mCARD "Program","Run",%r,"Quit",%q
      mCARD "Action","Multiply",%m,"Add",%a
      k%=MENU
      IF k%=%r
         PRINT "I'm running!"
      ELSEIF k%=%m
         PRINT "5*5=25!"
      ELSEIF k%=%a
         PRINT "5+5=10!"
      ELSEIF k%=%q
         PRINT "OK, I'll quit"
      ENDIF
      GET
   UNTIL k%=%q
ENDP
```

The program is terminated by selecting 'Quit' from the 'Program'
option list (if two items can be called a list!). If you press the ESC key
whilst the menu is displayed, the 'returned' value is zero: in this
program a message is displayed accordingly, so that you can test out
all the operations possible. When you have entered the program and
tested it out a few times, try editing one or two of the short-cut key
definitions to be the upper case letter (eg '%R' instead of '%r'), then
translate and run the program again: you will find that, whilst the
MENU function responds to either the upper or lower case version of
the short-cut key, the action required on such a key *won't* (for
example, the IF k%=%R will be *not true* and so the PRINT statement
won't be executed). This shows it is important to keep your short-cut
keys *lower case when using* 'IF' *tests to assess the keypress*.

You'll also find when running this program that nothing happens
if you use the short-cut keys when the menu isn't on display. The
program must be written to cater for the short-cut keypresses.

In the MENU1 program we used a series of IF statements to test which particular action has been selected: in each case the 'action' is to simply display a relevant message. You would, of course, write program instructions to handle the relevant action required. In order to break the program into smaller, easily tested 'chunks', it is better for the 'action' to be written as *another* procedure, which is called when the IF statement proves to be true. For example, instead of having 'PRINT "5*5=25!' after the test 'IF k%=%M', you could call a procedure called 'Mult'. Try this for yourself by editing the 'PRINT "5*5=25!" line to read 'Mult:', then add the following 'procedure' after MENU1:

```
PROC Mult:
    PRINT "Multiply procedure"
ENDP
```

You don't need a GET statement in this procedure, since execution will return to the main procedure which has a GET covering all of the PRINT statements, (between the ENDIF and UNTIL lines).

Series 3 actually offers another way to call procedures, which can save having to use a whole string of IF statements.

Another way to call procedures

If your overall menu has a large number of options, then you will be faced with an equally large number of 'IF' statements in order to cater for the action required for each. Good programming practice would require that each IF statement would simply call a relevant procedure.

However, OPL allows you to call a procedure whose name is stored in a string variable. If the variable is called *procnam$*, and *procnam$* holds the string 'Mult' - *without* the colon, note - then you can call it with a statement line such as

$$@(procnam\$):$$

The '@' sign is in effect saying "Call the procedure named in the following brackets". Notice that the colon comes *after* the brackets. It's as if you had written 'Mult:' in your program. The advantage, of course, is that the string can be assigned a 'name' according to the operation of the program, without necessarily having to make a whole series of tests. We'll see how this works in a moment.

The Graphics

The technique can also be used for functions which 'return' values, and for passing values to the functions. The formats under these circumstances are as follows:

$$r\% = @\%(procnam\$):(\quad argument\ list \quad)$$
$$r\& = @\&(procnam\$):(\quad argument\ list \quad)$$
$$r\$ = @\$(procnam\$):(\quad argument\ list \quad)$$
$$r = @(procnam\$):(\quad argument\ list \quad)$$

Note the use of the 'identifier' following the '@' symbol in each case - as well as in the variable that will hold the 'returned' value. The identifier must *not* be included as part of the *procnam$* variable.

Obviously any variables used must have been declared as LOCALs or GLOBALs, and string variables must have been declared sufficiently large to hold any information they're likely to carry.

You may wonder how this technique can help: it looks fairly complicated at first sight, and let's face of it, one has to somehow or other create the 'contents' of the *procnam$* variable for each procedure that is likely to be called.

In practice, this is not so difficult as you might imagine. You just need to be clear about what is happening. In the MENU1 procedure, we tested for which option had been selected by examining the integer value returned: this is always the *character code*, remember, that you associated with the option. Thus, the IF statements tested for the codes of each character in our short-cut key list.

Supposing, however, we don't test for the *character code*, but instead convert it to a character, and then use *that character as all or part of the relevant procedure's name*. In one line we can cover all of the options provided by a string of IF statements. However, you must remember that if a short-cut key combination that hasn't been catered for is used whilst the menu is on display, the code returned will be for a key for which you won't have a procedure. So you must allow for such cases, if you don't want a **'Procedure not found'** error to stop the program from running.

There are (at least) two ways to do this. One is to use the ONERR command to trap any error. The other is to ensure, *before* any 'option' procedure is called, that the returned character code is one that you have catered for.

We'll start with a program using the ONERR technique. You'll notice that this program has a number of procedures - all of which should be entered in the same Module, with the MENU2 procedure first.

```
PROC MENU2:
  LOCAL k%,k$(1)
  DO
MORE::
    ONERR Noproc::
    mINIT
    mCARD "Program","Run",%R,"Quit",%Q
    mCARD "Action","Multiply",%M,"Add",%A
    k%=MENU
    IF k%
      k$=CHR$(k%)
      @(k$):
    ELSE PRINT "ESCape was pressed"
    ENDIF
    GET
  UNTIL k%=%q
  RETURN
Noproc::
  ONERR OFF
  PRINT "Bad short-cut key!"
  GET
  GOTO MORE::
ENDP

PROC A:
  PRINT "Add procedure"
ENDP

PROC M:
  PRINT "Multiply procedure"
ENDP

PROC R:
  PRINT "Yes, I am running still!"
ENDP

PROC Q:
  PRINT "OK, I quit."
ENDP
```

As you can see, we have given the simplest possible names to the procedures that are called when an option is selected. You can however use the 'string concatenation' technique to build the names up into something else, although the difference between the procedure names will always be in the one character. For example, the line 'k$=CHR$(k%)' could read

$$k\$=CHR\$(k\%)+"job"$$

and the procedures named accordingly - PROC Ajob, PROC Mjob, PROC Rjob and PROC Qjob. This could be useful if there is a possibility of having two procedures with the same name in your program, which might be the case if you have more than one menu, and there is a duplication of the short-cut key letters between the menus.

When you run MENU2, test it out using the arrow and ENTER keys, and also using the PSION and short-cut key combinations whilst the menu is on display. Try it with non-valid short-cut key combinations, and you'll find that the ONERR error trapping routine will 'catch' the error and prevent the program from stopping as a result.

Now here's the same procedure again, but this time using a different technique to check that a valid short-cut key has been pressed: the four 'action' procedures, *which must be entered*, are the same as for the MENU2 program, so aren't repeated here.

```
PROC MENU3 :
    LOCAL k%,k$(1),sck$(4)
    sck$="AMRQ"           REM Our valid keys
    DO
        mINIT
        mCARD "Program","Run",%R,"Quit",%Q
        mCARD "Action","Multiply",%M,"Add",%A
        k%=MENU
        IF k%               REM i.e., not ESC key
            k$=CHR$(k%)
            k%=LOC(sck$,k$)
            IF k%           REM is it valid?
                @(k$):
            ELSE
                PRINT "Wrong short-cut key"
```

```
        ENDIF
    ELSE
        PRINT "ESCape means no action"
    ENDIF
    GET
    UNTIL k%=4          REM 'Q' is fourth in sck$
    ENDP
```

Don't forget to also include in MENU3 the four 'action' procedures from the MENU2 Module. Note the change in the UNTIL line: the value of k% is altered when we use it to check whether the pressed short-cut key is among our permitted keys. If it isn't, k% is zero - and the appropriate procedure isn't called. However if it is - and it's the code for 'Quit', we need to use the corresponding new value of k% to terminate the loop.

MENU2 and MENU3 demonstrate two techniques for ensuring the program doesn't stop running if an invalid key combination is used. There are undoubtedly other ways - and other ways to use these techniques. The ONERR method is perhaps a little less 'rigid' in trapping invalid key errors - since it will trap *any* program-stopping error that may occur in your program, and as written now, will report such an error as a 'Bad short-cut key'. You can test this for yourself by adding to the PRINT line of PROC M in the *MENU2* program, ',4/0'. This creates a deliberate 'Divide by zero' error: but when translated and run, the program will report it as a 'Bad short-cut key'. In the method used in the MENU3 program we know what keys we're using and test for them accordingly, but you have to be a little more careful if, at a later stage, you add options to your menu: you'll have to make changes at various points throughout the program - in the declared length of the string holding the key list and the key list itself, for example.

Direct short-cut key selection

So far, we have seen how to write menus that enable a choice to be made whilst the menu is displayed. And we have seen how, even when the menu is displayed, the short-cut key combination can be used instead of the arrow and ENTER key method.

If your program is structured to display the menu as part of its normal running process (as indeed are the MENU1, MENU2 and MENU3 programs), then that's as far as you need to go. However, for a greater degree of sophistication, you can arrange your program to act on short-cut key presses even when a menu isn't being displayed,

The Graphics

and for the menu to 'pop-up', just as Series 3 menus, when the MENU key is pressed.

The programming necessary for this is a little more advanced: we can demonstrate it here easily enough, but for large programs you must arrange your 'flow-charts' very carefully or allow short-cut key or MENU key operations only at specific points or times while the program is running, otherwise the actual flow of the program can get itself in a tangle.

To demonstrate the processes involved, we'll arrange for the short-cut or MENU keys to be effective only during the main 'controlling' part of the program.

The first step, after 'initialising' the program is, obviously, to test the keyboard for a keypress. We need to know whether this keypress is a short-cut key, the MENU key, or something else. For the purposes of our demonstration, 'something else' will print the key's character to the screen.

We have two basic ways to test for a keypress. GET (and GET$), which actually waits for a key to be pressed, and KEY (or KEY$), which looks to see if a key has been pressed, but doesn't wait: program execution continues with the next statements. Since our purpose is to show that your program can be actually 'doing things' whilst waiting for a keypress, we'll use the more dynamic 'KEY' function. If your program has 'nothing' to do except wait for a keypress, you would probably use GET: however, in this case you may as well display the menu straight away!

To make things a little interesting, we'll have a sideways scrolling display of a message whilst waiting for a keypress.

The MENU key button returns the value '290' in decimal (represented by $122 in hexadecimal), so that's one test we need to make. For other key presses, we need to test whether the PSION key has also been pressed. There are two ways to do this: we can use the KMOD function (Step 6) - which will return '8' if it has, or we can simply see whether '512' (represented by $200 in hexadecimal) has been added to the returned value of the keypress. Either way, since '512' is added to a keypress combination involving the PSION key, this must be deducted from the returned value.

So that the menu or short cut-keys *could* be used from any of the various 'action' procedures that make up the program, we'll write them as a separate procedures.

With this program, we'll also use the GIPRINT command for the 'action' procedures, to indicate that the relevant procedure has been selected. Your programs would, of course, have proper routines in these procedures. Note that you don't have to enter the 'REMarks'

```
PROC MENU4:
  LOCAL msg$(14),k%,c%
  GLOBAL sck$(4)
  sck$="AMRQ"              REM Valid short-cut keys
  msg$=" I'm working! "    REM Note: 14 chrs in all
  DO
     k%=KEY
     IF k%                 REM Key pressed?
        IF k%=290          REM Yes. MENU key?
           DoMenu:         REM Yes. So do it.
        ELSEIF KMOD AND 8  REM PSION key then? (Note 1)
           Dosck:(k%-512)  REM Yes: see Note 2.
        ELSE               REM Display what was pressed
           AT 12,6
           PRINT "You pressed",CHR$(k%)
        ENDIF
     ENDIF
     c%=c%+1+14*(c%=14)    REM Wow! See Note 3!
     at 12,4
     PRINT MID$(msg$,c%,15-c%); REM See Note 4
     PRINT MID$(msg$,1,c%)
     PAUSE 4               REM To slow things down!
  UNTIL k%=27             REM ESCape route
ENDP

PROC DoMenu:
  LOCAL m%,m$(1)
  mINIT
  mCARD "Program","Run",%R,"Quit",%Q
  mCARD "Action","Multiply",%M,"Add",%A
  m%=MENU
  IF m%                   REM i.e. not ESC key
     m$=CHR$(m%)          REM Get the character
     m%=LOC(sck$,m$)      REM Check against valid keys
     IF m%                REM If it's valid...
        @(m$):            REM ...do it
     ENDIF
  ENDIF
ENDP
```

Continues overleaf...

163

```
PROC Dosck:(kv%)
   LOCAL sk%                    REM See Note 5.
   sk%=kv%
   sk%=sk% AND $FFDF            REM See Note 6.
   sk%=LOC(sck$,CHR$(sk%))
   IF sk%                       REM If it's valid...
      @(MID$(sck$,sk%,1)) :     REM See Note 7.
   ENDIF
ENDP

PROC A:
   GIPRINT "Add routine",0
ENDP

PROC M:
   GIPRINT "Multiply routine",0
ENDP

PROC R:
   GIPRINT "Running OK!",0
ENDP

PROC Q:
   GIPRINT "OK, I quit!",0
   BUSY "Press a key",1         REM See Note 8.
   GET
   BUSY OFF
   STOP
ENDP
```

Please make sure you enter this program carefully: it does work! The REMarks will help you to understand how most of it functions, but there are some lines, identified by 'See Note...' which may require further explanation.

Note 1: You could use 'ELSEIF KMOD=8' here. However, if the SHIFT key, say, is also pressed (making three keys altogether if you include the character key), then KMOD will not be equal to 8, but to 10 (See the KMOD discussion in Step 6, Page 53). We're only interested in the PSION key, and want to exclude any other *modifier* keypress. Hence the use of AND.

Note 2: When the PSION key is pressed with another, it adds 512 to the returned value. We have to subtract that 512 in order to find out which 'other' key was pressed. We also need to pass the actual key press through to the Dosck: procedure handling the short-cut keypress action (otherwise it won't know which key was pressed!). In this line, we combine both operations: the expression k%-512 is evaluated, and the result passed on as the argument. This demonstrates how *expressions* can be used in place of simple variables.

Note 3: This line is not quite as complicated as it may look, and is an example of the use of the logic capabilities discussed in Step 7. We need to define a 'print' position for the scrolling message display (discussed in Note 4), and to do this, we simply add 1 to the counter variable, c%, each time this part of the program is executed. When c% reaches the maximum number of characters in the message (14), it needs to be reset to '1' again. Now we could do this with the lines:

```
c%=c%+1
IF c%=14
   c%=1
ENDIF
```

However, we can use the fact that (c%=14) will be *true*, and hence 'return' a value of *minus* one, when c% is equal to 14. For any other value of c%, (c%=14) is *not true*, and a value of zero will be returned. Now if you examine the program line with this in mind, you will see that for any value of c% *except* 14, it looks like this

```
c%=c%+1+14*0
```

14*0 is 0, so the line resolves to c%=c%+1. Which is what we want, until c% is equal to 14. Then the line looks like this:

```
c%=c%+1+14*(-1)
```

14*(-1) is -14, so as c% is equal to 14, the line now resolves to

$$c\% = 14 + 1 - 14$$

which is equal to 1. It has saved us three lines of code, and valuable memory space.

Note 4: We want to print a message that's scrolling horizontally - the message stored in *msg$*. To do this, we can repeatedly print the entire message, but starting from the next character along each time. This would give a message of decreasing length, so we add to that the chunk from beginning of the message up to the first print's start point. That's why we needed the counter variable c%. In practice, you could enter both of the PRINT statements on one line - ignoring the second use of 'PRINT', thus PRINT *first$;second$*. It was written in two lines in the program as the page isn't wide enough to cater for such a long line of text!

Note 5: You may recall that when a value is passed to a procedure, it cannot be changed. We need to change the value of the keypress code, *kv%* in this procedure, and hence we must declare a LOCAL variable and assign it the value of *kv%*. You will recall from Note 2 that *kv%* holds the keypress minus 512.

Note 6: Tests made when running this program show that, in fact, this line isn't necessary: LOC ignores 'case' when searching for a letter, so 'a' and 'A', for example, both produce the desired result. However, there may be occasions when you need to convert the character code for a lower case letter to the character code for an upper case letter. This line shows how it is done. It is also a good example of using a *mask*, as discussed in Step 7

If you examine the list of character codes in your User Manual, you will see that the lower case letters all have character codes exactly 32 greater than their upper case counterparts. So if we want to convert the character code for a lower case letter to the code for an upper case letter, we need to deduct 32. But first, we have to check that it is in fact a character code for a *lower case* letter: if we deduct 32 from the code for an *upper* case letter, we'll get the wrong result. We can do the check by using IF statements and so on, but that's a long winded way to do it.

32 (or $20 hexadecimal) looks like this in binary:

```
00000000 00100000
```

So if that particular bit of a character code is set, it means it's a lower case letter. Now, to make it an *upper case* letter, we simply need to remove that 'bit' (which is what would happen if you deducted 32, or $20 hexadecimal). We can remove it without actually *deducting* 32 and without any tests as to whether it exists or not. We simply prepare a *mask* which *excludes* the crucial 'bit'. In binary, our mask will look like this:

$$11111111 \quad 11011111$$

All the 'bits' are set, except for the one we want to exclude. If we **AND** this value with *any* character code value, the result will be the character code *less* 32 if that bit is set, and without any change if it isn't. The hexadecimal value of binary 11111111 11011111 is 'FFDF' - which is the value we need for our mask.

Note 7: Here's another example of using an *expression* instead of a variable: Series 3 will examine the **MID$** function, and return the appropriate letter, which is then used as the name of the procedure to be called. We've already checked that a valid key has been pressed, in the preceding line of the program.

Note 8: In this program, we're using **PROC Q:** to terminate everything, rather than return to the main routine. The 'BUSY' message, which continues flashing until it's 'cancelled', is a handy way to remind the user to press a key.

You'll notice that, in the main procedure (the actual procedure called **MENU4**), pressing the **ESC** key is an alternative way to stop the program from running. When you have thoroughly checked the program out - trying every key combination - you can try it with an extra line between **UNTIL k%=27** and **ENDP**, which simply says ' **Q:** '. When the **ESC** key is pressed, the main loop terminates, and processing will jump to **PROC Q:** for the 'standard' program ending.

Menus or short-cuts from anywhere

Should you wish to have a menu - or its options - selectable from *anywhere* in your program, the process is very similar to that given for the **MENU4** program. You would make the relevant part of the **DO** loop in the **MENU4** program - from '**k%=GET**' through to the **ENDIF** before '**c%=c%+1+14** ...' a separate procedure - called, say, 'Checkey', and then simply call that procedure as required from the 'Action' procedures.

You would have to declare the k% variable in the Checkey procedure, and check through any other declarations you may have in case of conflict.

More importantly, you must ensure that, when a menu or menu action is 'requested', the routine that it is called from is 'terminated' properly, otherwise all kinds of trouble can develop when the program is run. It would be virtually impossible to test for every situation that is likely to occur when one series of actions is by-passed to perform another: as mentioned earlier, the result could be one enormous programming tangle.

You must remember, for example, that program execution will return to the point where the menu/menu action was requested, once that action has been completed - and this could be within a procedure, other than the 'main' controlling procedure, which was itself called from another procedure. (If that sounds like a tangle - it adequately reflects the tangle your program could get into!). There may well be a limitation on the number of times such a calling action can be taken: in particular, you may run out of memory.

STEP SEVENTEEN

Time for a Dialog

This Step deals with 'Alert' and Dialog Boxes.
The OPL words covered are: ALERT, dINIT, dPOSITION, dTEXT, dEDIT, dXINPUT, dFLOAT, DLONG, dFILE, dDATE, dTIME, dCHOICE, dBUTTONS and DIALOG

The 'friendly' way to get an input

Just as menus offer the user an easy way to select a function or operation, *Dialog boxes* offer an easy way for options to be selected or edits to be made. A Dialog box can, in fact, be used to provide the same choice of functions or operations as a *menu.* You can even arrange for a Dialog box to appear when the MENU key is pressed, if you wish, just as we made the menu display appear in the MENU4 procedure. However, Dialog boxes offer many more facilities, and cater for a greater variety of different types of input.

For example, with a Dialog box, the user can be given the facility to input and 'edit' specific types information, with the display formatted to suit that information. You can also provide a display of 'buttons', suitably labelled, to help the user make a choice by pressing particular keys.

As well as this type of Dialog box, there is a simple box which gives the user from one to three options to choose from - the choice being made by a single keypress. This is actually called an '*Alert box*', since it is most often used to alert the user to something with a simple message. We'll examine this type first.

Creating Alert boxes

Alert boxes have a variety of useful applications. For example, you can use them just to inform that an error has occurred. Or you can give the user a choice of two or three options, with defined keys to press to make those options. The defined keys used by ALERT are ESC, ENTER and SPACE, and are displayed as 'buttons', suitably labelled with words of your choice.

Unlike *Dialog boxes*, the Alert box completely fills the screen. It appears 'over' anything else you have on the screen, the previous display being restored when the Alert box is cleared.

169

The Graphics

The formats for `ALERT` are as follows

```
a%=ALERT(line1$)
a%=ALERT(line1$,line2$)
a%=ALERT(line1$,line2$,escbt$)
a%=ALERT(line1$,line2$,escbt$,entbt$)
a%=ALERT(line1$,line2$,escbt$,entbt$,spbt$)
```

where

line1$ is the message you want displayed on the top line.

line2$ is the message you want displayed on the second line.

escbt$ is the annotation you want to appear over the ESC button display.

entbt$ is the annotation you want to appear over the ENTER button display.

spbt$ is the annotation you want to appear over the SPACE button display.

Note the permissible formats: if you want to use one or more button displays at the bottom with your own annotations, the strings *line1$* and *line2$* (either as literals or as variables) *must* be present.

If you choose to use one or two lines of message, without annotating any buttons (the first two formats listed), then Series 3 automatically creates a single, centred button marked as the ESC key, and annotated '**Continue**'. The messages are centred, and the lines can be as long as you like: if the message is too long for the screen width, then only the *central* part of the message is displayed - so there's no point in having overlength messages.

When the buttons are displayed, the value returned by this function when one of the displayed keys is pressed is as follows:

ESC key	returns '1'
ENTER key	returns '2'
SPACE key	returns '3'

To make life easy for the user, you should make your annotations appropriate for the keys displayed. For example, if you wish to provide two options 'Cancel' and 'Continue', then it makes more sense to annotate the ESC button with 'Cancel' and the ENTER button with 'Continue', rather than the other way round.

Here is a short procedure to demonstrate the use of the **ALERT** function with three options. It also demonstrates the use of a string array, and how an element of the array can be selected by use of a variable.

```
PROC ALERT1:
    LOCAL a%,but$(3,10)
    but$(1)="Cancel"
    but$(2)="Go forward"
    but$(3)="Go back"
    a%=ALERT("Top line","2nd line",
        same line continues    but$(1)$,but$(2),but$(3))
    PRINT "OK. I'll",but$(a%)
    GET
ENDP
```

You may like to experiment by editing this program - first deleting but$(3), then but$(2) and finally but$(1) from the ALERT statement - translating and running it each time.

Using Dialog Boxes

Unlike ALERT boxes, Dialog boxes are automatically sized to take the messages and lines they contain. In other words, they don't necessarily fill the screen. Furthermore, you can within reason determine the location on the screen that the Dialog box is displayed, so that you can avoid overprinting an important part of the background display

As well as the 'Dialogs' that can be displayed, you can, like ALERT, have up to three 'exit' buttons - or none at all. Unlike ALERT, *you* can define which keys are used: they are not pre-defined, but under your control.

Generally speaking, the use of a Dialog box therefore makes for a more versatile and neater display on the screen, and you will probably find that you prefer its use.

Creating Dialog boxes

The procedure for creating a Dialog box is very similar to that for creating a Menu. However, you have many more options available to you. Fortunately, much of the formatting and display 'work' is done for you automatically by the Series 3. Nevertheless, the number of possibilities available can make the process look a little forbidding at first. The entire Dialog must be created in one 'chunk': it must be in one procedure.

The steps involved are as follows.

The Graphics

a)   Get the Series 3 ready to receive a Dialog operation, using the dINIT command.

b)   If you don't want the Dialog to appear in the absolute centre of the screen, use the dPOSITION command to re-position it. Actually, this command can be used *anywhere* between the dINIT and DIALOG statements, but for convenience, we'll take it to be our second step.

c)   Set up each line of the Dialog with the functions you want. These cover: the display of text in various ways - as messages or options; the input or editing of string data; the input of numeric data; the input of date or time data; the input of a *file* name; and the selection from a range of listed options. Which just about covers every possibility! However, there is a limitation: the entire Dialog must not exceed seven lines. This number includes the three lines necessary for displaying 'exit' buttons, if you choose to use them, and the 'title'. You should also note that, unlike ALERT which prints the central part of any overlength line, if a line is too long for the screen you will get a '**Too wide**' error when the program is running.

d)   If you want 'exit' buttons - and you can have up to three - they must be defined as the penultimate step, using the dBUTTONS function.

e)   Finally, switch on the Dialog display using the DIALOG function.

We will now examine in detail the commands and functions that are available for each of these steps.

Initialising the Dialog

Series 3 has to be prepared for the fact that it is about to display a Dialog, and this is achieved quite simply by the single statement dINIT.

dINIT *title$*   Only one Dialog box can appear on the screen at a time. The formats are

          dINIT
          dINIT *title$*

Use the title$ format if you choose to give your Dialog box a title. The string literal or variable will be displayed at the top of the box, centred, and with a line beneath it across the entire box: however, Dialog boxes can have only one horizontal line in them, so if you choose to add a horizontal line elsewhere in the box, then the title will not be underlined. If you choose to include a title, remember that it counts as one of the seven lines which are the maximum permissible for a Dialog box.

Positioning a Dialog

The 'default' location for a Dialog is the dead centre of the screen. However, you may not want the Dialog in this position: you may wish to position it so that it doesn't cover other vital information on display. You can do this with the dPOSITION command. Note that, irrespective of how your screen display is made up (ie. whether you're using 'windows' and specified display areas), the Dialog will always appear 'on top'. When the Dialog is cleared, the original screen display is restored for you.

dPOSITION hp%,vp%   where *hp%* and *vp%* represent the horizontal and vertical positions respectively. These can have one of three values, as follows:

	-1	0	1
hp%	Left	Centre	Right
vp%	Top	Centre	Bottom

Thus, the statement dPOSITION -1,1 would position the Dialog box at the bottom left corner of the screen. Remember that the default position is the centre of the screen (equivalent to the statement dPOSITION 0,0), so if that's where you want the Dialog box to appear, you don't need to use the dPOSITION statement at all.

The Dialog 'action' lines

As previously noted, there is a variety of different 'action' lines you can have in your Dialog box. For *some* of them, you *must* use a variable declared previously as LOCAL or GLOBAL: using a string literal or an actual value is not permissible for these. Neither can you use a variable that has been passed to the procedure as an argument, or a *field* variable (these are special variables used when creating data files). The reason is that, when the Dialog is actuated, certain information will be entered by the user, and this information must be stored in a variable: if you have a string literal or a value instead of a variable, there will be nowhere for Series 3 to store the entered information, and a '**Function argument**' error will occur when you try to translate the program.

Where *only* variables can be used, they will be identified by the use of a sans-serif face and a preceding 'v', thus: *vfloat*.

The 'action lines' commands and functions are as follows.

Displaying text. Apart from any title you may give the Dialog box when using the dINIT command, you can have lines of text as messages, or as 'selectable items'.

dTEXT *prompt$*,*body$*,*type%* This command is extremely versatile and very flexible: it can be used to simply display a text message in various ways, and it can also be used to provide one of a series of options for selection, as on a drop-down menu. You need one dTEXT statement for every line of text you wish to include in the Dialog box, except for the 'title' - which can be provided by the dINIT statement. The formats are:

> dTEXT *prompt$*,*body$*
>
> dTEXT *prompt$*,*body$*,*type%*

where

prompt$ provides the message that will appear on the left side of the text line as a 'prompt'. This can be a null string ("") if you don't want a prompt.

body$* This is the main part of the message that will be displayed on the line. If *prompt$ is a null string, then *body$* will assume the whole width of the line for itself - its position within the line being centred or determined by *type%*, if present. Otherwise, if *prompt$* is not a null string, the text of *body$* is positioned on the right side of the Dialog box, either left-aligned, or as specified by the *type%* variable. Note that you cannot have a null string for *body$*.

type% This determines the *position* of the *body$* text within the line, and also what *type* of display the line is to use. There are three options for the *position* of *body$*:

Type%	Effect
0	Aligns *body$* to the left.
1	Aligns *body$* to the right.
2	Centralises *body$*.

Any unit values for *type%* outside of this range will result in an '**Invalid arguments**' error when translating the program. You can also use *type%* to select a combination from three *styles* for the way that *body$* will appear. These are best considered as their *hexadecimal* values, and are as follows:

Type%	Effect
$100	Displays *body$* in bold text.
$200	Draws a line below this item, across the Dialog box.
$400	Places a 'bullet point in front of *prompt$*, provided that it is *not* a null string.

You can use all, any or none of these three, by simply adding the effects you want to the value of *type%*. For example, if you want a bullet point and bold lettering for *body%*, then *title%* would be '$500'. If you also wanted *body%* to be aligned to the right, then *title$* would have the value '$501'.

Note that there can be only one horizontal line across the Dialog box: the last one to be specified is the one that takes effect.

When you give a line a bullet point, it can be selected by using the arrow keys. Lines that aren't given a bullet point cannot be selected in this way. The following demonstration procedure simply shows the type of Dialog produced by dTEXT statements using some of the *type%* values discussed.

```
PROC Dialog1:
  dINIT
  dTEXT "Line 1","Can't choose",$200
  dTEXT "Line 2","Can Choose this",$400
  dTEXT "Line 3","Ditto",$402
  dTEXT "Line 4","Can't select",$100
  DIALOG
ENDP
```

When you translate and run this demonstration, you'll see that two of the lines have a bullet point to the left, and that you can use the up or down arrow keys to switch between them: the other lines are not selectable. When you exit the Dialog, provided you haven't used the 'buttons' as a means

175

of exiting (or pressed ESC), the *line number* for the highlighted line is returned by the DIALOG function. If ESC is pressed, then '0' is returned.

Entering or editing text. Three commands facilitate the entry of text within the Dialog: dEDIT covers plain text, dXINPUT covers 'secret' information, and dFILE covers the entry of a file name.

dEDIT *vedit$, prompt$, len%*   This function will display the string variable or literal *prompt$* to the left of the line, and the initial contents of *vedit$* (which *must* be a previously declared variable) to the right of the line. The contents of *vedit$* can then be edited or entered, as the case may be, using the usual editing keys. The number of characters that can be entered is determined when the variable is declared.

The variable *len%* can be ignored, if you wish, in which case the editing area is made wide enough to cope with the number of characters declared for *vedit$*, allowing for the widest character in the font (proportionally spaced characters are used).

If you specify a value for *len%*, then that's the number of characters wide the editing area will have. If the value of *len%* is less than the declared length for *vedit$*, then the *vedit$* string will scroll sideways within the editing area as you edit. If *len%* is made greater than the number of characters declared for *vedit$*, then all that will happen is you get extra width to the editing box - it doesn't mean you can add extra letters.

If your *prompt$* and edit width are such that the line would have more characters than the maximum possible width of a Dialog box, you will get a '**Too wide**' error.

The formats for the function are

> dEDIT *vedit$, prompt$*
> dEDIT *vedit$, prompt$, len%*

When you exit the Dialog box, *vedit$* will contain the newly entered or edited string, *unless* the ESC key is used to make the exit. In this case, *vedit$* is left unchanged.

Here's a short demonstration procedure to show how dEDIT works. When you've entered and translated it, run it a few times to see the effects of editing, and test what happens when you press ESC to exit instead of ENTER.

```
PROC Dialog2:
  LOCAL str$(12)
  str$="Series 3"
  dINIT "Editing Box"
  dEDIT str$,"Change it:",8
  DIALOG
  PRINT "You changed it to",str$
  GET
ENDP
```

dXINPUT **vedit$,prompt$** This function enables you to enter eight characters of 'secret' information, such as a password. The *prompt$* string is displayed to the left of the line.

vedit$ *must* be a variable declared to hold *at least eight characters*. Declaring less than eight characters won't produce any error messages, but could cause problems in your program. Anything previously assigned to *vedit$* is *not* displayed when dXINPUT is used. The edit area *always* has eight blank 'spaces' for *character* entry *irrespective of the number of characters defined for vedit$ when it was declared.* You can thus enter up to eight characters only, even though *vedit$* may have been declared to hold more. Remember, because eight characters can be entered, *vedit$* must be declared to hold *at least* eight characters.

As the entry is being made, special 'lock' characters appear instead of the actual characters, to preserve the secrecy. When you exit the Dialog box, the newly entered information will be stored in *vedit$, unless* you use the ESC key to exit. In this case, the original contents of *vedit$* remain unchanged. Here is a simple demonstration procedure that will enable you to put this function to the test.

```
PROC Dialog3:
  LOCAL str$(8)
  dINIT "Secret Edit"
  dXINPUT str$,"Password:"
  DIALOG
  PRINT "You entered",str$
  GET
ENDP
```

When you run this, try it a few times, using both ESC and ENTER to exit the Dialog. Note that, whilst the entry is kept 'secret', your program can access the information. This is obviously necessary, to enable you to compare the entered string with another.

dFILE *vedit$,prompt$,fedtype%* This powerful function is generally for use in *file handling* situations, and offers a wide variety of options for entering or selecting a file name, or examining *directories*. The actual display and the way it 'operates' depends on the options - and combinations of options - that you select. All the features which by now may be familiar to you when using the Series 3's file handling features, are available for you to use: the good news is, they are provided automatically.

Note that although the actions of dFILE are programmed in just one statement, the screen display occupies *two* lines (as you will see with the demonstration program given later). Both of these lines count towards the maximum number of seven permitted for a Dialog box.

fedtype%   determines the way the line is going to operate - that is, the type of display, and the inputs allowed. There is a range of options - and these can be used in any combination by simply adding together the appropriate values. You can therefore tailor the actions to suit the needs of the program.

The options are:

fedtype% value	Function
0	Simply allows the *selection* of (matching) files in the file path defined by *vedit$*. The TAB key can be used to list all the selectable files. The name of the selected file, with its path, is stored in *vedit$* on leaving the Dialog (unless ESC is pressed).
1	Enables the contents of *vedit$* to be *edited*, as well as permitting file name selection as in '0' above. The name of the selected file, with its path, is stored in *vedit$* on leaving the Dialog (unless ESC is pressed).
2	Allows directory names to be used.

4	Allows *only* directory names to be edited into *vedit$*. This is useful if you're getting in the directory for a file-copying operation.
8	Stops an *existing* file from being used when editing the contents of *vedit$*. This is useful when creating a new file - to prevent the name of an existing file from being used again. A warning is given if an existing file is named, and re-entry of the name requested.
16	*Queries* when the file specified or edited in *vedit$* is the same as an existing file: you are asked if you want to 'overwrite' the existing file, on the assumption the file name being entered will be used to create a new file.
32	Allows a null string to be entered for *vedit$* (ie, when the edit area is being used).

One of the first two options (0 or 1) will, of course, always be applicable. The other options you 'add' as required: note that the last three options, 8, 16 and 32, only have relevance when option 1 is also selected.

As an example, if you're creating a new file and are asking the user to supply a name for the file, you might choose options 1, 2 and 8, or 1, 2 and 16 - making *fedtype%* '11' or '19': this would either prevent the use of an existing file name, or warn the user and allow him to overwrite an existing file name.

vedit$ must have been declared as a LOCAL or GLOBAL variable, and dimensioned to hold *at least* 128 characters: you will get an '**Invalid arguments**' error when the program is run with any less. If *vedit$* is assigned a string before the dFILE statement, that string is displayed: if the number of characters is too great for the display, it will sideways scroll as required.

The contents of *vedit$* in fact define the *path* to the files you're interested in, or to a file you may wish to create or open. This *path* can include the 'drive' and directories. If *vedit$* is a null string, then the path set by another OPL command SETPATH is used: failing that, the '\OPD' directory on the default drive (usually the 'internal drive', 'M:') is used.

**prompt$** holds a 'prompt' message that will be displayed to the left of the line: but note, the word 'Name' is automatically added to your message (so you don't need to include it). For example, if you want the prompt to be 'File Name', all that *prompt$* needs to be assigned is 'File'.

The following program will allow you to experiment a little with this Dialog function, and will display the results so that you can see what is happening. It will also allow you to check the size of each of your OPL source ('*.OPL' files), compared with the corresponding translated files ('*.OPO' files).

```
PROC Dialog4:
   LOCAL fnopl$(128),fnopo$(128)
   fnopl$="\opl\*.opl"
   fnopo$="\opo\*.opo"
   dINIT "File Name Edits"
   dFILE fnopl$,"Source file",0
   dFILE fnopo$,"Coded file",0
   DIALOG
   PRINT fnopl$
   PRINT fnopo$
   GET
ENDP
```

When you translate and run this program for the first time, perform the following operations: they will help you to understand the facilities and actions involved. (It is assumed that you have a number of Module files saved, and a number of translated files saved).

1) Notice that each line has a 'bullet' point to the left, indicating that it can be 'selected'. The up and down arrow keys will allow you to run up and down through each line - except for the 'Title' line, of course.

2) With the flashing cursor on the top line, press the left or right arrow keys to run through the saved Module files in your Series 3.

3) With the flashing cursor still on the top line, press the TAB key: you will see a list of all the files as a table, with the size of each file and the date it was last changed. (This is much the same as the operations you can perform from the 'File' option on the System display menu). Press TAB *again*, and you'll be asked for a 'Filename pattern': you can at this point obtain a *selective* display of filenames. For example, if you want to see all the files you have that begin with the letter 'm', enter 'm*.*' as the Filename pattern, and press ENTER. Now all the files that begin with the letter 'm' (and 'M') will be shown. (In case you're wondering, the '*' stands for *all letters and numbers here*, and is called a 'wild-card' in computer jargon).

4) Whilst still in the listing display, use the arrow keys to move the highlight bar up to the top line - which will have a '\' symbol on the left side - and press ENTER. You will now see a list of all the *directory* names in your Series 3: typically '\OPL\', '\OPO\', '\WDR\' and so on. Use the up and down arrow keys to select one of them - say '\DAT\' and press ENTER. If no files are shown, press TAB, and set the 'Filename pattern' to ' *.* ' and press ENTER: you will now see the name, size and the 'last changed' date of your Database files. Notice that heading the list is the name of the current directory, and above that, the directory selector symbol '\'. Select this symbol again, choose the '\OPL\' directory and press ENTER. Notice that at the top of the Dialog there is a line which will be saying 'Disk Internal, ???k free', with arrows at each side. Press the right or left arrow keys, and you'll cycle through the drives available: 'Internal' is in the RAM area, 'A' and 'B' are the two slots, and 'C' is for the expansion socket. Unless you have Solid State Disk(s) fitted, these drives will be marked as 'Absent!'.

5) Return to the files listed under '\OPL\', select one and press ENTER. You will now be returned to *your* Dialog box, with the selected file name (excluding the 'extension - the bit that comes after the 'dot') between the two selector arrows.

6) Now 'arrow' down to the 'Coded file name' line, and press TAB again. This time you will see a list of the *translated* file names you have in Series 3. Note that this listing was selected by the assignment of the appropriate path to the *fnopo$* variable in the program. Browse through the list as before: note how, for most Modules, the *translated* length of

a program is less than its source code - the program Module you actually entered.

7) Select a file name from the list, and press ENTER: you'll now be back at *your* Dialog box again. Press ENTER once more, and the screen will display the names of the two files that you have selected, together with their complete 'paths' and the full extension names. The 'LOC::' at the beginning stands for 'LOCal' - meaning within the Series 3: you could equally well be accessing files on a computer connected to your Series 3, in which case instead of 'LOC::' you will see 'REM::', which is short for 'REMote'. In other words, your Series 3 can create access files on other computers too, provided they follow the MS-DOS file format.

8) Press any key to return to the Program Editor and your program listing.

Having completed that exercise - a good demonstration of the power behind the dFILE function - edit the dFILE lines of the program by changing the '0' at the end of the lines to a '1'. Now when you translate and run the program, in addition to all of the features mentioned in the explorations (1) to (8) just given, you will be able to actually type in a file name - or a 'pattern', using the '*' as before. The TAB key works as before, so you can continue browsing and experimenting.

Now return to the Program Editor and edit the end of the dFILE lines to read '9' instead of '1'. We are now saying we want to be able to input a file name as well as select it ('1'), and we want to prevent an existing file name from being selected or entered ('+8'). Translate and run the program as before, and using the TAB key, select an existing file name and press ENTER to return to your Dialog. When you press enter again, to say 'that's the information I want stored in the *fnopl%* and *fnopo$* variables', a warning will be given that the **'File already exists'**, and instead of leaving the Dialog box, it will remain on display for you to make another choice - that is, enter the name of a file that *doesn't* exist. This is the effect of having '8' as part of the *fedtype%* value: selection of an existing file name has been prevented.

Press the ESC key to abandon the Dialog box.

It is left to you to experiment with the other *fedtype%* options available - in particular, try '17'. Note that values of 8, 16 and 32 are only effective when '1' has also been selected. Note too that if you use the 'prevent existing files' option (8), the 'query overwriting an existing file' option (16), is ignored so there's not much point in using these two in combination.

Entering numbers. Two functions are available for entering numeric values: one covers *floating points*, and one covers *long integers*. With both functions the minimum and maximum acceptable values are defined, so the input can be restricted to any range you wish.

dFLOAT *vfp,prompt$,minimum,maximum* This permits the entry of floating point numbers - with a decimal point in them somewhere.

vfp must have been defined as a LOCAL or GLOBAL variable, and will store the input value when you exit the Dialog, *unless* the ESC key is used for the exit.

prompt$ displays a prompt message, to the left of the edit area in the Dialog box.

minimum and ***maximum*** define the minimum and maximum values for the entered value, and can have a decimal point in them. Both must be specified, and the *minimum* value must be less than the *maximum* value, otherwise you'll get an error. If a value *outside* of the minimum-maximum range is entered, a warning is given when an attempt is made to exit the Dialog - with the specified minimum or maximum figure to guide the user.

dLONG *vlng&,prompt$,minimum&,maximum&* This is the same as dFLOAT, except that only integer values are allowed.

Here is a short program to demonstrate the use of these two functions.

```
PROC Dialog5:
  LOCAL fl,lng&
  dINIT "Entering numbers"
  dFLOAT fl,"Enter decimal",1,100
  dLONG lng&,"Enter integer",2,10
  DIALOG
  PRINT fl,lng&
  GET
ENDP
```

Entering the time or date. The two functions that enable you to enter a date or a time both work on the 'time since' principle used within Series 3. The entry can be made in the same way that you set the date and time on your Series 3. However, the values actually stored on leaving the Dialog box are 'days since 1st January 1900' for the date, and 'seconds since 00:00 on the same day' for the time. In other words, once you have the stored values, you'll have to convert them (using the appropriate OPL words) for 'conventional' displays of the date and time.

dDATE *vdt&, prompt$, minimum&, maximum&* The three numeric arguments required for this function are all *long integers*, and relate to the number of days since 1/1/1900. *vdt&* must be a variable: it will hold the value representing the chosen date.

prompt$ provides a prompt message that will be displayed on the left side of the line.

minimum& and *maximum&* give the limits of the date entry - entries of dates before the *minimum&* date or after the *maximum&* date will be rejected by Series 3, and the user invited to re-enter. Note that the statement line requires these to be long integer *values*: this is no problem, since the DAYS() function will convert an actual date into the long integer value required. No function is provided (Version 1.58F) for converting a value back to the equivalent date, but as we shall see, this is quite achievable using existing functions.

When the Dialog box is displayed, the *minimum&* date appears in the edit area, in whatever format you chose when you set up your Series 3.

Here's a routine that will allow you to calculate what the date will be (or was) a given number of days from a specified date. You enter a date (from 1st Jan 1970 onwards), and the number of days - either as a positive value or, for days previous, a negative value. On pressing ENTER, the appropriate date is displayed. This program uses the built-in capability of Series 3 to display a date from a given value, using the dDATE function. Note that the value for the maximum date is set as 73413.0 (the decimal point is important): this is 31st December 2100, which should be far enough ahead for most people! Note that the display of the actual date is within an 'edit' area: the program as written won't allow you to change the date. Exit by pressing the ESC key.

```
PROC Datefind:
    LOCAL d1&,nd&,fd&
    fd&=DAYS(1,1,1970)
    dINIT "Date Finder"
    dDATE d1&,"Start Date:",fd&,73413.0
    dLONG nd&,"Days ahead/back:",-30000,30000
    dTEXT "","(Negative for days previous)",2
    IF DIALOG
        d1&=d1&+nd&
        dINIT "Date Finder"
        IF d1&>fd&
            dDATE d1&,"The Date is:",d1&,d1&
            dTEXT "","Press ESC to exit",2
        ELSE
            dTEXT "","Date out of range",2
        ENDIF
        DIALOG
    ENDIF
ENDP
```

Notice how a different Dialog is set up if the number of days takes the date outside the permitted range allowed by Series 3.

dTIME *vtm&,prompt$,type%,minimum&,maximum&*   This function allows the user to enter a particular time of day, between the limits set by *minimum&* and *maximum&*. Note that the values of *maximum&* and *minimum&* represent the number of seconds from midnight to the specified time. This should not be confused with the value returned by DATETOSECS - which gives the number of seconds since 00:00 on Jan 1st, 1970.

vtm&   must be a LOCAL or GLOBAL declared variable. Any value assigned to this variable - as a number of seconds since 00:00 - will be displayed as an actual time, for editing. The time that is entered will be stored in this variable on exiting the Dialog.

minimum& and *maximum&* are the minimum and maximum values that you are going to allow: again, these must be expressed as a number of seconds from 00:00.
type% determines the nature of the displayed time, as follows

Type% value	Time Display
0	Absolute time, without seconds.
1	Absolute time, with seconds
2	Duration period, without seconds
3	Duration period, with seconds.

Absolute time here means a specific time of day display, such as 10:35. Duration period means just so many hours, minutes and (if requested), seconds. In terms of the display, absolute time will appear according to the format you set for your Series 3: for example, if you've set Series 3 for a 12 hour clock, 'am' or 'pm' will appear after the time period, but not after a duration period. Here's a program to add up to 23 hours 59 minutes to a specified time: the result will show if this runs into 'tomorrow'.

```
PROC Timeadd:
   LOCAL tm&,pd&,d$(8)
   dINIT "Time Adder"
   dTIME tm&,"What time?",1,0,&1517F
   dTIME pd&," How long?",2,0,&1517F
   IF DIALOG
      tm&=tm&+pd&
      IF tm&>=&1517F
         tm&=tm&-&15180
         d$="Tomorrow"
      ENDIF
      dINIT "Time Adder"
      dTIME tm&,"Time will be:",1,tm&,tm&
      IF d$<>""
         dTEXT "",d$,2
      ENDIF
      DIALOG
   ENDIF
ENDP
```

Offering a choice. Series 3 enables you to offer a variety of options
in one line of a Dialog box - selection of the required option being
made by using the left and right arrow keys, or the TAB key and up
and down arrow keys. The same way, in fact, that Series 3 offers
such options when selecting a file name, for example.

dCHOICE *vchoice%,prompt$,list$*   In this function:

  prompt$ is a prompt message that will be displayed to the
  left of the line.

  list$ is your list of options, each of which must be
  separated by commas. The entire list must be enclosed by a
  single set of quotation marks.

  vchoice% must be a LOCAL or GLOBAL declared variable. On
  leaving the Dialog, the option that has been selected will be
  stored in *vchoice%* as a number - '1' for the first item in the
  list, '2' for the second, and so on. If you assign a value to
  vchoice% before the dCHOICE command, the relevant option
  item will be the one that is displayed within the selector
  arrows. If you don't assign a value, the last option is
  displayed (this may be changed in future models of Series 3).
  Here is an example of the use of dCHOICE: in this program,
  the Dialog part is in a separate procedure, to show how it
  can be called from other procedures which set up the
  necessary lists.

```
PROC Choice:
  LOCAL d%,item$(4,12),list$(52)
  item$(1)="Drive A,"
  item$(2)="Drive B,"
  item$(3)="External,"
  item$(4)="Internal RAM"
  DO
    d%=d%+1
    list$=list$+item$(d%)
  UNTIL d%=4
  d%=Listqry:(list$)
  IF d%
    PRINT "You selected",item$(d%)
  ELSE
    PRINT "You ESCaped!"
  ENDIF
```

Continues overleaf

```
        GET
ENDP

PROC Listqry:(list$)
    LOCAL ch%
    dINIT
    dCHOICE ch%,"Choose:",list$
    DIALOG
    RETURN ch%
ENDP
```

Notice how the list is constructed in this program: the commas, essential for the dCHOICE function, are made a part of each *item$()* string assignment. In practice, your programs would operate on the numeric value returned, and so you could simply assign the string to a variable such as *list$*.

Providing exit buttons. So far, all of the Dialog functions that we have discussed have used either the ENTER or ESC key as the means of leaving the Dialog box. When the ENTER key is pressed, the entries that have been made are assigned to the appropriate variables, and the line number for the highlighted line is returned by the DIALOG function. The ESC cancels the operation, leaves the various variables unchanged, and returns '0' or zero.

You can however define up to three of your own exit keys, thus offering another range of options. In fact, you could use simply the 'exit buttons' as the main purpose of your Dialog box. DIALOG doesn't return the highlighted line number when exit buttons are used, but rather a code related to the button.

When you use buttons as the means of leaving the Dialog, you define which key on the keyboard must be pressed to activate the button, and the annotation or message that goes above it. The keyboard character (or key name) appears on the button itself.

Only the keys that you have defined will permit an exit, plus, if you *haven't* defined it, the ESC key. You can if you wish include both the ESC or ENTER keys as buttons. The ENTER key works only if you define it. If you don't define the ESC key as one of your exit buttons, you can have four different ways to terminate the Dialog - your three buttons and the ESC key.

dBUTTONS *text1$,key1%,text2$,key2%,text3$,key3%*   This command *must* be the last item to appear in your Dialog program set up before the DIALOG function itself, and there can be only one dBUTTONS command per Dialog box. Also, you should remember that it takes up three of the permitted seven lines maximum for a Dialog (which includes the Title line).

You can use one, two or all three of the button pairs *text?$,key?%*.

text?$ This variable in each pair defines the annotation that is to appear over the associated button.

key?% This specifies the character code for the key that must be pressed to 'activate' the button. It also specifies the character (or key name) that will appear on the key itself, and, apart from ESC, *determines the value returned by* DIALOG *on exit*. This means that you cannot use dTEXT to have a highlighted line number returned. As well as the letter (or number) keys, the following can be used:

Character code	Appearing on Button
9	Tab
13	Enter
27	Esc
32	Space

Note that ESC will *always* return zero, whether you define it as a key or not. Note too that it is the character *code* that must be used: the easiest way to do this is to use the form '%A' - which gives the character code for the letter 'A' without you having to look it up. When using letters, the actual value returned is *always* for the *lower case letter*. It is important that you realise this: for example, if you use '%A', the character code for which is 65, the actual code returned is 97 - the code for the lower case 'a'. The character code for numerals is returned as expected: '%1' for example will return '49' if that key is pressed.

You should also note that, if you use the character code for a *lower case* letter, such as '%a', the *capital* letter ('A') will actually appear on the button.

If you want to use a key *other* than ESC to cancel the Dialog - and disregard any input entries that may have been made, then use a *negative* value for the character code. Thus, to have the letter 'c' cancel any inputs, use '-%c'.

The buttons can be used to provide a simple 'what next' type of Dialog: here for example is how they *could* be used to provide the options in the Carpet program:

```
PROC Whatnext:
    LOCAL wn%
    dINIT "What next?"
    dTEXT "","Another...",2
    dBUTTONS Price",%c,"Area",%a,"Quit",27
    wn%=DIALOG
    PRINT "You selected",wn%
    GET
ENDP
```

This procedure simply shows which button was pressed: you would of course use the returned value to determine the next step to take in the program.

Completing the Dialog

As you will have realised by now, the Dialog you have prepared is displayed when you use the DIALOG function.

DIALOG This completes the Dialog box set-up, displays it, and waits for an *exit* key or button to be pressed.

The information returned on leaving a Dialog is as follows.

Pressing the ESC key - or any 'button' that is given a *negative* character code value, such as '-%a', simply exits the Dialog box, leaving everything as it was. DIALOG returns zero ('0').

Pressing ENTER when not using 'buttons'   If you have used 'action' lines involving a declared variable (such as dEDIT), any information entered in those lines will be stored in the appropriate variable. Since such variables must be either LOCAL or GLOBAL, their contents can therefore be used by the rest of your program.

DIALOG 'returns' the *row number* of a highlighted line (if any) when ENTER is pressed. If there is no highlighted line, then DIALOG returns '1'. If you have used dTEXT lines with the '$400' option for the *type*, the line can be highlighted, and its row position returned. Note that rows are counted from the top, and that if you have included a 'Title' (with the dINIT command), the title line is row 1. All visible lines have a row number: only those selectable by the up and down arrow keys can be highlighted and returned by DIALOG.

Pressing* ENTER *when using buttons. If you have used 'action' lines involving a declared variable (such as dEDIT), any information entered in those lines will be stored in the appropriate variable.

In this instance, however, DIALOG itself returns the *lower case* of the *character code* associated with the pressed key.

Since DIALOG is a function, the value it returns can be used in a variety of ways. The following program demonstrates how it could be used to provide a Library function that simply asks a question for a 'Yes' or 'No' response:

```
PROC Qrytest:
   LOCAL q%
   DO
      PRINT "Clever stuff!"
      PAUSE -20
      q%=Yornqry:("Again?")
   UNTIL NOT q%
END


PROC Yornqry:(msg$)
   dINIT msg$
   dBUTTONS "No",%n,"Yes",%y
   RETURN DIALOG=%y
ENDP
```

Notice how DIALOG is used in 'Yornqry' to return a *true* condition only if the 'Y' key is pressed: pressing the 'N' *or* ESC keys will produce a *not true* condition. Notice too how the 'title' for the displayed Dialog can be passed to the Yornqry procedure. The function Yornqry could be a useful routine for your Library Module.

Here's the Carpet program again - this time using Dialogs. Note that the program prevents 'zero' values from being entered. Note too that some lines include several statements, to keep the entire program on one page.

```
PROC Carpet2:
   LOCAL a,ppy,q%
   a=getarea:
   ppy=getcost:
   DO
      dINIT "Carpet Prices"
      dTEXT "Sq Yards needed: ",num$(a,3)
      dTEXT "Cost:£",fix$(a*ppy,2,7)
      dBUTTONS "New Cost",%c,
         same line continues    "New Area,%a,"Quit",27
      q%=DIALOG
      IF q%=%c        :ppy=getcost:
      ELSEIF q%=%a    :a=getarea:
      ENDIF
   UNTIL q%=0
ENDP

PROC getcost:
   LOCAL cpsy
   DO
      dINIT "Cost of Carpeting"
      dFLOAT cpsy,"Per sq.yd:£",1,100
      DIALOG
   UNTIL cpsy
   RETURN cpsy
ENDP

PROC getarea:
   LOCAL w,h,a
   DO
      dINIT "Enter Room Dimensions"
      dFLOAT w,"Width (feet):",1,100
      dFLOAT h,"Length (feet):",1,100
      DIALOG
      a=w*h/9
      IF a>INTF(a)   :a=INTF(a)+1    :ENDIF
      UNTIL a
      RETURN a
ENDP
```

STEP EIGHTEEN

Formatted Text

In this Step, we examine how you can display text in different styles.
OPL words covered are gAT, gMOVE, gPRINT, gPRINTB, gTWIDTH, gPRINTCLIP, gTMODE, gSTYLE, gXPRINT *and* CURSOR.

A different way to PRINT

In the first part of this book, we discussed how you produce *monospaced* text on the screen using PRINT. Characters can be positioned in any of 40 columns and 9 rows. This is the text screen. The location of the next print position can be identified by a flashing cursor (when it is on), and can be set by using the AT command, or by comma or semi-colon separators between the items in a PRINT statement.

By using *graphics* commands, you can produce a display of text that can be emboldened, italicized or underlined, and in a choice of styles. The start of this text can be at any of about 230 by 70 screen locations or *pixels*. This is graphics text. You can use the CURSOR command to display a cursor on the current screen window (this is discussed at the end of this Step), and there are functions that will tell you the column and row of the pixel where the next graphics operation will take effect from: these are discussed in a later Step. CURSOR OFF turns off all cursor displays, including the text cursor.

Setting a Graphics location

There are two basic ways to reset the current pixel location on the graphics screen, ready for the next graphics operation.

gAT x%,y% This is very similar to the text-screen command, AT. It operates on the *current* graphics screen or window (in a later Step, you will see you can define up to seven different graphics windows in addition to the 'default' window). x% can have values from 0 and 239, and y% can have values from 0 to 79 for a full-screen sized window. Pixels beyond the range of a window's dimensions will not be 'visible'.

You'll notice that the minimum values for *x%* and *y%* are '0' (not '1', as with AT). Thus gAT 0,0 determines the top left-most pixel in the current window. For the moment, we will ignore the fact that you can have a number of windows, and deal with the whole screen area. The position set by gAT is absolute: whatever the current location, the new location will be defined by the *x%* and *y%* values of gAT.

gMOVE dx%,dY% Like gAT, this sets the location for the next graphics operation, but rather than setting an *absolute* position, it *moves* the current position *dx%* pixels to the right, and *dy%* pixels down. To move to the a left negative value for *dx%* is used, and to move up, a negative value for *dy%* is used.

The value of this command will be appreciated more when we come to the drawing capabilities of Series 3. If the move makes the current pixel fall outside the range of the current window, then any graphics produced from that pixel will not be seen.

Displaying graphics text

When you use the *graphics* print command, the pixels are 'set' to display the characters. They do not automatically 'clear' any pixel that has been previously set. This is quite different from the text PRINT command, which automatically clears any character at the print position. For gPRINT and related commands you can govern the way that the pixels are set - whether they are turned 'on' (made 'black'), off (made 'clear'), or their current state reversed. Let us first examine the gPRINT command.

gPRINT *itemlist* This is similar in some respects to PRINT, in that the item list can be variables or literals, separated by commas or semi-colons. The effect of a comma is to leave a space between two items, whilst a semi-colon simply separates the items: no space is left between them in the display. However, unlike PRINT, the next print or graphics position is always at the end of the printed data: using gPRINT on its own, for example, doesn't start a new line.

The first character to be printed in a gPRINT statement is located so that its *left side* and *baseline* are at the current pixel location. The baseline is rather like a line on writing paper: most characters 'sit' on the line, but some, like the letter 'g' or 'y' will descend below the line.

The following short procedure will show you the difference in characters between text printing and standard font graphics printing:

```
PROC gprint1:
    PRINT "This is text print"
    gAT 1,20
    gPRINT "This is graphic printing"
    GET
ENDP
```

After you have run this procedure, edit the **gAT** line to read **gAT 1,9**: you will see that the graphics print line is overwriting part of the text print line: you should also see that the graphics print line starts one pixel along to the right of the text print line.

gPRINTB *text$,w%,align%,top%,bot%,marg%*   In the last procedure, you saw how **gPRINT** can overwrite anything on the screen without clearing it first. That can be a pain if you always have to clear things - and in any event, you may not want to clear away the whole screen display, so a simple **CLS** command may not be good enough.

One solution is the **gPRINTB** statement. This 'clears' a box for the printed message. However, you have to specify information about the box and how the text will appear within it. Also, **gPRINTB** displays only one text message, as defined by *text$*, although this could of course be a concatenation of strings (my, how musical that sounds!), and you can of course use the string conversion functions to turn numbers into strings (Step 10). The permissible formats are:

```
gPRINTB text$,w%,align%,top%,bot%,marg%
gPRINTB text$,w%,align%,top%,bot%
gPRINTB text$,w%,align%,top%
gPRINTB text$,w%,align%
gPRINTB text$,w%
```

w% determines the width of the box, in pixels, that you want cleared for the text. Does that mean you have to know how many pixels there are in your text message? Yes, it does. If your box isn't wide enough, part of the message will be lost. But ascertaining the width that the box must be as a minimum is no problem, because there's an OPL function to handle it for you: gTWIDTH. We'll deal with this function in a moment.

align% controls the alignment of the text within the cleared box: the permissible values are

1	Aligned to the right of the defined box
2	Aligned to the left of the defined box
3	Centred within the defined.

The default value if you don't include the argument is 2 - left aligned. If you don't provide a value for the *align%* argument, then you cannot provide any information for the arguments that follow it either - look at the permissible formats for gPRINTB.

top% and ***bot%*** determine the clearances above and below the text in the box: again, the measure is in pixels. These values, together with the height of the current font (which you can also choose through another OPL command) determine the overall height of the cleared box. If you create above and below clearance areas that, with the font size, will be greater than 255, you'll get an error. The use of *top%* and *bot%* can give your graphics text a clearer space to 'sit' in: if you don't specify values, the defaults are '0'.

marg% controls the size of the left or right margin within the box in pixels. If the alignment is set to the left (*align%*=2), then *marg%* controls the space between the left edge of the box and the start of the text. If the alignment is set to the right (*align%*=1), then *marg%* controls the space between the end of the text and the right edge of the box. If the alignment is set to be centred (*align%*=3), *marg%* gives an offset to the part of the box in which centering is to be effective: positive values place the offset to the left, and negative values place the offset to the right of the box. If you ignore this argument, the default value is '0'.

gTWIDTH(*text$*)   This is the function to use to find out the width of a *text$* string. You need to know this (unless you're pretty accurate at guessing!) for statements such as gPRINTB. The value returned is in pixels, and takes into account the current font and style. The format is

$$w\% = gTWIDTH(text\$)$$

gPRINTCLIP(*text$,width%*)   This print *function* prints the text
    string *text$*, but only as many whole characters as the
    number of pixels determined by *width%* allows. It returns the
    number of characters actually printed. This function is
    designed more for use with windows, where a 'narrow'
    window could inhibit the printing of a complete text line.
    Knowing the width of the window, you can limit the number
    of text message characters printed to fit within that width,
    ascertain how many characters were actually printed, then
    start on a new line (using gAT) to print more of the text
    message. In this way, a graphical text display can be formed
    within a window area.

Setting the style for graphics printing

Text displayed using the graphics gPRINT, gPRINTB and gPRINTCLIP
can be in any of 64 different 'styles' - any combination, in fact, of
proportional, monospaced, bold, underlined, inverse, double height,
or italic. This is irrespective of the *font* that's used: three fonts are
built into the Series 3, and there is a facility to 'load' your own fonts.

gSTYLE *style%* This is the command that sets the style for all
    subsequent gPRINT, gPRINTB and gPRINTCLIP commands.
    The style is determined by the *style%* variable, which can be
    a combination of the following values:

style% Value	Displays text as
0	Proportional spacing
1	Bold
2	Underlined
4	Reversed white on black
8	Double height letters
16	Monospacing
32	Italicised lettering

You select the combination you want, then simply add the
relevant *style%* values together. For example, if you want
bold, italicised letters, you'd add 1 and 32 to have a value for
style% of 33.
    Note that gSTYLE has no effect on the *text* PRINT
command: these are always monospaced and 'normal'.
gFONT *fontId%* This command sets the font that will be used by the
    graphics print commands, in the current window. Three
    fonts are built into the Series 3, so they are always

197

selectable. Apart from these, there is a facility to load your own fonts, using the command gLOADFONT: when used, this function returns an 'ID' value which can be used with gFONT to select your loaded font. Such fonts can be removed by the command gUNLOADFONT. The creation of fonts is fairly complex, and well beyond the scope of this book, and so these two commands will not be discussed any further. For built in fonts, *fontId%* can have values as follows:

FontId% Value	Font
1	The standard font.
2	An emboldened font
3	Numbers only font.

Note that the third font will display only numbers, and a space. Here is a program to let you study the large number of styles available, and how they look when used with the different fonts:

```
PROC gprint2:
   LOCAL f&,s&,d%
   DO
      dINIT "Graphic Text"
      dLONG f&,"Which Font (1-3):",1,3
      dLONG s&,"Style Combination:",0,63
      dTEXT "(1 to 63)"," "   REM Note the space
      dBUTTONS "Do it",13,"Quit",27
      d%=DIALOG
      IF d%
         AT 1,1
         PRINT "This is 'text screen' text"
         gFONT f&
         gSTYLE s$
         gAT 0,50
         gPRINT "This is Font:",f&,"Style:",s&
         GET
         CLS
      ENDIF
   UNTIL d%=0
ENDP
```

You'll notice that in this program *long* integers were used for the gFONT and gSTYLE variables: this is in order, provided that their values do not exceed the integer range allowed by these commands.

Setting the way characters print

So far, we have seen that the gPRINT command prints on the screen by setting the appropriate pixels: any pixels that are previously set will remain set. However, you can change the way that gPRINT, gPRINTB and gPRINTCLIP perform their printing operations. You can arrange, for example, for the pixels to be 'unset' if they were already set.

gTMODE *mode%* This command determines how the pixels will be changed when the graphics print commands are executed, and hence how the characters will be displayed on the screen. Four possibilities are available, governed by the value of *mode%* as follows:

mode% Value	Pixels are
0	Set (black)
1	Cleared
2	Inverted
3	Replaced

The default mode is '0': this is the way that the graphics print commands normally work.

With mode 1, any clear pixels remain clear, whilst any 'blackened' pixels are made clear. Thus, this mode can be used to provide 'white' print on a previously blackened display.

With mode 2, the pixels are 'reversed': those that were clear are blackened, whilst those that were black are cleared. This is therefore a useful mode when running print from a clear area into a solid black area, and vice versa.

With mode 3, the space for a character is cleared first, then the character pixels are set black. The 'replacing' effect is fairly similar to that when using the text PRINT command - the difference being that you can set the style for the graphics print display.

Note that gTMODE determines the way the graphics print commands operate in the current window: at the moment, we are considering just one 'window' - the default window.

The Graphics

Here is a procedure that will let you examine these four modes. It includes a command we haven't discussed yet - gFILL - to blacken an area of the screen so that you can see the effects of text printed across it and into clear space.

```
PROC Gprint3:
    LOCAL x&,d%
    DO
        dINIT "Graphic Text Modes"
        dLONG x&,"Select Mode:",0,3
        dTEXT " ","(0 to 3)"
        dBUTTONS "Do it",13,"Quit",27
        d%=DIALOG
        IF d%
            gAT 0,0
            gFILL 60,20,0
            gAT 5,12
            gTMODE x&
            gPRINT "This goes over a black box"
            GET
            CLS
        ENDIF
    UNTIL d%=0
ENDP
```

Special inverse and underline printing

In addition to all the options provided by the gSTYLE command, there is another way to display a text string either underlined or inverted, and that's with the gXPRINT command.

gXPRINT text$,display% This displays the string text$ according to the variable display%, as follows:

display% Value	Displays text as
0	Normally, as with gPRINT
1	Inversed, with 'square corners'
2	Inverse, with 'rounded' corners
3	'Thin' inversed, square corners
4	'Thin' inversed, rounded corners
5	Underlined
6	Thin underlined

The 'thin' options are for those occasions when lines of text are separated by a single pixel: the bottom line of the printed line is 'shaved off'.

Note that the current font and style - as set by gFONT and gSTYLE - are still effective, even if the style itself happens to be inverse or underlined. The text mode used is as if gTMODE had been set to '3' - that is, the relevant screen area is cleared before the characters are printed.

gXPRINT can be used only with a single text string: you can of course build up a string by concatenation for display.

You should also note that the print display starts from the current graphics location.

Here's a procedure to demonstrate the seven different styles available in turn:

```
PROC gprint4:
   LOCAL c%,m$(40)
   DO
      m$="This is Style "+num$(c%,1)
      gAT 15,50
      gXPRINT m$,c%
      GET
      CLS
      c%=c%+1
   UNTIL c%=7
ENDP
```

Sizing the Cursor

The cursor display on the text screen is a fixed size. On the graphics screens, however, you can determine the size of the cursor, and its position relative to the *baseline* of any text displays. One window can have a cursor: you must specify which it is to be, and specifically switch the cursor on. The cursor is switched off by the CURSOR OFF command.

CURSOR *id%,ascent%,wid%,ht%*   This form of the CURSOR command enables you to set the shape and positioning of the cursor display on a graphics screen.

id% is the identification number of the window you wish to set the cursor in.

ascent% is the number of pixels that the *top* of the cursor should be above the baseline of any text, and has a range of

-128 to 127 (although remember that the total screen is only 90 pixels high).

wid% and **ht%** are the width and height respectively you want the cursor to be - both of which must be in the range 0 to 255, although you probably would not want to use high values!

You can, if you wish, turn a graphics cursor on by simply specifying *id%*, in which case the default values of *ascent%* (the ascent of the current font), *wid%* (2) and *ht%* (the height of the current font) are used. Here's a procedure to let you examine the way this command works.

```
PROC Cursor:
   LOCAL a&,w&,h&,d%
   DO
      dINIT "Cursor size"
      dLONG a&,"Ascent(-20 to 20):",-20,20
      dLONG w&,"Width(1 to 20):",1,20
      dLONG h&,"Height(1 to 20):",1,20
      dBUTTONS "Do it",13,"Quit",27
      d%=DIALOG
      IF d%
         gAT 0,9
         gPRINT "Cursor ascent:",a&
         gAT 0,19
         gPRINT "Cursor width  :",w&
         gAT 0,29
         gPRINT "Cursor height:",h&
         gAT 0,39
         gPRINT "Baseline of text"
         gAT 100,39
         gLINEBY 100,0          REM New command draws line
         gAT 150,39
         CURSOR 1,a&,w&,h&
         GET
         CLS
      ENDIF
   UNTIL d%=0
ENDP
```

202

STEP NINETEEN

Drawing Things

We now take a look at the graphics commands available for drawing.
The OPL words covered are gGMODE, gLINETO, gLINEBY, gPOLY, gBOX,
gFILL, gINVERT, gBORDER.

Setting the mode

We saw, in the last Step, that the way the graphics print commands
work - whether they set or clear pixels - can be determined by the
command gTMODE. There is a similar command to control the way
that the Series 3 *drawing* commands operate.

gGMODE *mode%* With this command, you determine the way that
most of the subsequent drawing commands work in the
current window: if you change the window, then for the new
window you will have to use the command again to set the
way the drawing commands work in *that* window. The action
depends on the value of *mode%*, as follows

mode% Value	Pixels are
0	Set (black)
1	Cleared
2	Inverted

The default condition, if you don't use the command, is '0' -
that is, the pixels are set to turn black. Normally speaking,
you would use a value of 1 for *mode%* if you want to clear
existing lines, or create white lines in an already blackened
area. A *mode%* value of 2 would be used if you want a line to
appear across blackened and clear areas.

Drawing the line

We have already seen that there are two ways to set the position or
pixel where the next graphics command will operate from. There is
the *absolute* way, using gAT, which takes the co-ordinates you give
as being absolute positions in the current window, with '0,0' being in
the top left corner. Then there is the *relative* way, using gMOVE,

The Graphics

which takes the co-ordinates you give and adds them to the current position in the window.

For most drawing situations, the gMOVE option is to be preferred, since it makes the construction of drawings easier. You don't have to worry so much about where in the window a line, for example, is to end, only how long the line is to be. Also, it is easier to define particular shapes by the relative positions of each line within the shape - and to position (or re-position) that shape as an entity by simply resetting the start position.

Note that any part of a drawing or text that is positioned outside the area of the current window simply isn't seen.

Three commands are available to enable you to draw straight lines in any direction.

gLINETO x%,y% This is the way to draw lines from one *absolute* position within a window, to another *absolute* position. The start position is the current pixel location, as may have been determined by gAT or gMOVE, for example. The end position is determined by x% and y%, which give the horizontal and vertical co-ordinates respectively. The pixel at the current location can be switched on (or off, depending on gGMODE) by giving x% and y% the values for the current location. For example,

```
gAT 40,50
gLINETO 40,50
```

would set the pixel at the point 40 across and 50 down in the current window.

When the line is drawn, the current location is the point at the end of the line: in other words, as determined by x% and y%.

gLINEBY dx%,dy% This command draws a line from the current pixel location to a *relative* location determined by dx% and dy%. The value of dx% determines how many pixels away the line will end in the horizontal direction: with negative values the end point is to the left of the start point, while with positive values position the end point is to the right. Similarly, dy% determines how many pixels away the vertical end point will be from the start position. Negative values position the end point towards the top, while positive values move it down.

The pixel at the current location can be set (or reset, depending on gGMODE) by using zero values for *dx%* and *dy%* - thus 'gLINEBY 0,0'. This is obviously a far simpler method than using gLINETO, since you don't have to worry about the current location.

When the line is drawn, the end position of the line becomes the new current pixel location for further graphics commands.

gPOLY a%()   There will undoubtedly be occasions when you will want to draw a series of connecting lines. You could do this using a series of gLINEBY line drawing commands. There is, however, an alternative, and that is to use an array to hold all of your line drawing information, and to use the gPOLY command.

The command works in much the same way as gLINEBY and gMOVE, that is to say, each point position is determined as a *relative* location to the previous point.

This command also allows you to move to a new position, without drawing a line. First, however, let us examine the way that you set up the array *a%()* to draw your shape. The number of 'elements' in the array will be 3 plus *twice* the number of points in your drawing, and the array is set up as follows:

a%(1)	Holds the starting *horizontal* position.
a%(2)	Holds the starting *vertical* position.
a%(3)	Holds the number of *points* that will be defined.
a%(4)	Holds the *dx%* value for the first point.
a%(5)	Holds the *dy%* value for the first point.
a%(6)	Holds the *dx%* value for the second point.
a%(7)	Holds the *dy%* value for the second point.
...	

and so on.

You'll notice that the *start* location has to be specified for this command: in this respect, the first two elements of the array behave rather like the gAT command. When the line has been completed, the *current* location is returned to the *start* location. In other words, when the command has been executed, the values in *a%(1)* and *a%(2)* determine the new current pixel location.

Now, it was stated earlier that this command could be used to *move* to the new location as well as *draw* the line. How does it know the difference?

The answer is in the way that you define the values for all of the dx% positions.

To draw a line the dx% values must be multiplied by two. (Not the *dy* values).

To simply move to the new position the dx% value must be multiplied by two, and then have '1' added to it.

Thus a dy% value of 50, and a dx% value of 20*2 will target the point 50 pixels down and *20* pixels to the right, and will draw a line to that point, which then becomes the current pixel location. If the dx% value were made 20*2+1, then the targeted point will become the new current point, but a line will not be drawn. Remember though that once the command has been executed, it is the *start* location that becomes the current location for further graphics commands. Let us first see how this command works to draw two diamond shapes.

```
PROC diamonds:
   GLOBAL a%(11)
   draw:(50,10)
   draw:(75,10)
   GET
ENDP

PROC draw:(dx%,dy%)
   a%(1)=dx%
   a%(2)=dy%
   a%(3)=4            REM The number of points we're plotting
   a%(4)=-30*2
   a%(5)=30
   a%(6)=30*2
   a%(7)=30
   a%(9)=-30
   a%(10)=-30*2
   a%(11)=-30
   gPOLY a%()
ENDP
```

Notice how, as with the other line drawing commands, a negative value for *dx%* moves the horizontal point to the left, and a negative value for *dy%* moves the vertical point upwards. Notice too that all of the *horizontal* values (the even elements of the array, from element '4' onwards) are multiplied by two.

When you have run this program, edit a%(4) by adding one to the statement line (a%(4)=-30*2+1), then translate and run it again. This time, you'll see that the shape is the same, but the line referenced by *a%(4)* hasn't been drawn.

The operation of a gPOLY command is faster than a series of gLINEBY and gMOVE commands, although you do need to take a little care in setting it up. In particular, remember to define the array with sufficient elements, and to ensure you set the element 'a%(3)' to the correct number of points or pairs of offset co-ordinates.

Boxing clever

By drawing lines or by using gPOLY, you could construct box shapes - oblongs or squares. OPL however provides three different types of box drawing command, to make life easier.

gBOX *width%,height%*   This simply draws a box *width%* pixels wide and *height%* pixels deep, in the current window, and starting from the current pixel location. The lines are drawn according to the setting of gGMODE, if present for the current window.

Once the box has been drawn, the starting point is again made the current point for further graphics commands.

gFILL *width%,height%,mode%*   This operates just like gBOX, only in this instance, the box is 'filled'. How it is filled is determined by *mode%*, which operates in the same way as gGMODE. Thus, a value of '0' blackens the boxed area, a value of '1' clears the boxed area, and a value of '2' 'inverts' the boxed area - clears all the blackened pixels, and blackens all the clear pixels. Because of the presence of the *mode%* argument, the gGMODE command has no effect on gFILL. The current position is unchanged: its the same after the command is executed as when it started.

gINVERT *width%,height%*   This operates rather like gFILL with the *mode* set to '2' - the pixels are inverted within the boxed area. The difference is that the four corner pixels are left clear to give a slightly 'rounded' effect.

gBORDER *type%,width%,height%* This is a special 'box' command, used mainly for framing windows. The formats are:

> gBORDER *type%*
> gBORDER *type%,width%,height%*

If the *width%* and *height%* are not specified, then a border is drawn one pixel wide round the inside edge of the current or active window. If *width%* and *height%* values are specified, then the 'border' is drawn not round the window, but, starting from the *current pixel location, width%* pixels wide and *height%* pixels deep. What differentiates this from the gBOX command is the fact that it can also provide various shadow effects, rounds off the corners, and can be made to clear a one pixel gap all round the edge. (Series 3 certainly provides you with plenty of options!).

type% controls three features of the box: a 'drop' shadow to the left and below, a clear gap all round, and the type of corners:

type% Value	Border effect
0	No shadow, no gap, sharper corners.
1	A single pixel shadow is drawn.
2	A *gap* for a single pixel shadow is drawn.
3	A double pixel shadow is drawn.
4	A *gap* for a double pixel shadow is drawn.

You can have any *one* of the above values, with (or without) any combination of the following two values:

type% Value	Border effect
$100	Leaves a single pixel gap round the border.
$200	Makes the corners more 'rounded'.

Thus, for a single pixel gap all round, more rounded corners and a double pixel drop shadow, type% will have a value of $303. As its name implies, this command is best suited to 'framing' windows: you can indicate an active window by using the drop shadow, clearing the shadow when the window is de-activated. However, when you do this, be sure to use related commands. For example, if you have 'more rounded corners' when the window is active ($200) but not when it is de-activated, then you will get unwanted lines on the display.

Generally speaking, this command works best when used as a window 'frame'. Here is a procedure to show the different ways you can frame a window: we first fill the screen with background shading, then create a window for the border demonstration. You can then choose the type border you'd like to examine, through our friendly Dialog.

```
PROC Borders:
  LOCAL id%,r%,f&,g%,c%
  DO
    r%=r%+8
    gAT 0,r%
    gPRINT REPT$(CHR$(176),48)
  UNTIL r%>=90
  id%=CREATE(20,20,80,40,1)
  DO
    f&=f& AND $F
    dINIT "Borders"
    dPOSITION 1,0
    dLONG f&,"Type (0-4):",0,4
    dCHOICE g%,"Gap?","Yes,No"
    dCHOICE c%,"Big Corners?","Yes,No"
    dBUTTONS "Do it",13,"Quit",27
    r%=DIALOG
    IF r%
      f&=f&-$100*(g%=1)-$200*(c%=1)
      gBORDER f&
      gAT 5,13
      gPRINT "Type",HEX$(f&)
      GET
      gCLS
    ENDIF
  UNTIL r%=0
ENDP
```

There are two commands we haven't dealt with yet in this procedure: gCREATE and gCLS. These will be discussed in the next Step.

The line 'f&=f& AND $F' ensures that the last value you set for the type is re-displayed: without this line, the value could for example be '$103', and Series 3 will adjust this to the maximum value permitted by the line dLONG f&, Type ...' - that is, '4'.

The line 'f&=f&-$100*(g%=1)-$200*(c%=1)' adds in $100 or $200 to *f*& if *g%*=1 or *c%*=1 respectively, and saves having to use a couple of IF statements.

When you run the program, examine the effects of the two different width shadows, and the way that a gap can be left for the shadow, without displaying it. The shaded background will help you to examine the 'gap all round' feature, setting the window and its border 'away' from the background.

STEP TWENTY

Windows and Bitmaps

In this Step you'll discover how to create, manipulate, use, save and restore Windows and Bitmaps.
OPL words covered are: gCLOSE, gCLS, gCOPY, gCREATE, gCREATEBIT, gIDENTITY, gINFO, gLOADBIT, gORDER, gORIGINX/Y, gPATT, gPEEKLINE, gRANK, gSAVEBIT, gSETWIN, gUSE, gVISIBLE, gWIDTH, gHEIGHT, gX, gY.

What are Windows?

So far, apart from the 'Border' demonstration program at the end of Step 19, we have used the whole screen for our displays. We can, however, select specific areas of the screen to use for our displays. Each area is known as a 'Window'.

Graphic window areas can be defined such that they overlap, cover each other up, or occupy their own discrete part of the screen. When a graphic window is defined or created, it is given an identity number - a number by which that window can be referenced when you wish to display something in it or move it. As you will see in a moment, you can also create *Bitmaps* - which are like *hidden* windows in memory. The whole screen is always available as one graphics window, and up to seven more windows and bitmaps can be created for *graphics* displays: remember that you can have the whole screen for *text* displays, or define a specific area for text using the SCREEN command.

It may be easier to consider the *graphics* windows as rectangles of 'paper' placed over the screen, each of which can be used to display graphics: anything on areas of paper hidden behind other 'paper rectangles' will not be seen. You can, however, specify which 'pieces of paper' will appear 'on top'. The *text* window must appear as one of the 'top' areas and within the current graphics window if its textual displays are to be seen.

Only one window (or *bitmap*) can be *active* at a time: that means you can only *write* information to one window at a time - and that is whichever window happens to be *current*. You can, of course, select the window or bitmap you want to be *active* or *current*.

211

The Graphics

The current window is not necessarily a *visible* window. That means you can write to window that is not visible, then make it visible for a faster, crisper display. A window may be *invisible* because it is hidden behind other windows, or because you *choose* to make it invisible.

When writing information to a window or bitmap, it has its own pixel referencing system: pixel '0,0' is always the top left corner of the *window*, whatever the position of the window on the screen. The whole window is 239 by 79 pixels in size, but the windows you define may be smaller - and anything written 'outside' of the defined window area will not be seen.

Using windows enables you to create and manage sophisticated displays more easily, and can also make animation appear smoother and faster: successive movements can be written to different windows of the same size and occupying the same screen area, then the windows selected for viewing in turn. This is quicker than writing the animation data each time.

What are Bitmaps?

A *bitmap* is the same as a window - except that it is always hidden from view: it is a window in the *memory* area of Series 3.

Bitmaps are a useful way to build up images 'off screen' for subsequent transfer to a screen window - or for saving in a file for use in other programs. Generally speaking, images can be created faster in a bitmap than in a window, and of course, the 'build-up' process is hidden from view. Bitmaps are created in much the same way as windows, and are referenced much the same way too: the 'top left corner' of a bitmap is referenced as '0,0', just like the top left corner of a window.

Like windows, bitmaps are identified by a reference number when they are created: remember, you can define up to a total of seven windows *and* bitmaps.

The Psion manual refers to bitmaps and windows as 'drawables', meaning areas on which graphics can be drawn. We shall refer to them the same way, to avoid confusion.

Creating and closing windows and bitmaps

When you create a new window, you must specify where it is to appear on the screen, and how large it is to be. Creating the window returns a 'reference' number, so that you can identify that window again for subsequent usage. For bitmaps, you don't have to specify the screen location (because there isn't one!). However, you still need to know its reference number for subsequent use. The functions for creating windows and bitmaps are gCREATE and gCREATEBIT.

gCREATE(*xloc%,yloc%,width%,height%,vis%*)   This creates a window within the screen area, with its top left corner at the pixel location defined by *xloc%* (distance in pixels from the left of the screen) and *yloc%* (distance in pixels from the top of the screen). Remember that the topmost row and leftmost columns are '0', so the top left position is '0,0'.

The size of the window is governed by the values of *width%* and *height%*, which relate to dimensions in pixels. You can define the window area such that it is not completely 'on the screen' - which you may wish to do for large displays: these can be 'scrolled' or moved into the screen area for viewing. As typical example, you might create such a window for use in a spreadsheet type of program, where the area you wish to work on is larger than the screen display area.

vis% determines whether or not the window will be visible or invisible immediately after it has been created: if *vis% has a* value of '1', it will be visible, if it has a value of '0', it will be invisible (you can always change this status later with other OPL commands). Even though the window may be invisible, you can still write to it. The format for the function is

id%=gCREATE(xloc%,yloc%,width%,height%,vis%)

The reference number for the window is returned in *id%*, which will have a value between 2 and 8. The whole screen or default window is always identified as number 1.

When you create a window, it is immediately made *current* or active, ready for you to write information to, and the pixel location for graphics commands is set to the '0,0' location within the window. (We will discuss how to make other windows current later). Note that, if you have several windows, each will have its own 'cursor' or pixel location for the next graphic command.

gCREATEBIT(*width%,height%*)   This function is very similar to that for creating a window: however, with gCREATEBIT, you don't need to specify a screen location, or whether it will be visible or not. The format is

id%=gCREATE(width%,height%)

The Graphics

The reference number of the bitmap is returned in *id%*.

There is another way to 'create' a bitmap in memory, and that is to load a bitmap *file* that has been previously saved. We will deal with this method later.

As with a window, when you create a bitmap it is immediately made *current*, and the 'cursor' or pixel location within the bitmap is set to pixel '0,0' - the top 'left hand corner'. Note that, since bitmaps are created in the RAM area of Series 3, there may be some unwanted 'left-over' information in the area used: it is advisable therefore to clear the bitmap immediately after its creation (gCLS).

With these functions you can create up to seven windows and bitmaps ('*drawables*') altogether, but it is up to you to keep track of which is which: if you're going to have a number of windows and bitmaps in your program, then probably the easiest way to keep track of them is to use an array, where you know which *element* numbers are associated with windows and which are associated with bitmaps.

There may be times when you want more than the permitted eight windows and bitmaps: if this is the case, then you will have to *close* one or more of them, in order to create new ones. The command is:

gCLOSE *id%*   This closes the window or bitmap identified by *id%*. If you close the *current* window or bitmap, then the default window (*id%*=1) is made the current window. Obviously you cannot close the default window (you'd be trying to shut down the screen!) - and if you do try, a program-stopping error will occur.

Getting information about Windows and Bitmaps

When working with windows and bitmaps, it will often be necessary to know exactly where the 'cursor' is for the next graphics command, where the window is on the screen, which window is current, which window is 'on top', and so on. There is a range of functions in OPL that enable you to determine such information, so that you don't have to keep track of it: indeed, if the user is given the facility to change things around (such as shifting a window from one place on the screen to another), it will be difficult and fairly complicated for your program to keep track without the *information* facilities.

Where's the graphics cursor? The pixel location where the next graphics command will take effect from within the *current* window or bitmap can be determined by the functions gX and gY.

gX   The format is

$$x\text{\%}=gX$$

    x% will hold the current horizontal pixel location, from the left edge of the current window or bitmap. Remember that the leftmost edge is '0'.

gY   The format is

$$y\text{\%}=gY$$

    y% will hold the current vertical pixel location from the top edge of the current window or bitmap. Remember that the topmost edge is '0'.

Where's the window? The location of a *window* on the screen can be determined by the two commands gORIGINX and gORIGINY.

gORIGINX   The format is

$$x\text{\%}=gORIGINX$$

    x% will hold the pixel location on the overall screen of the leftmost edge of the *current* window. Remember that the leftmost edge of the screen is '0'.

gORIGINY   The format is

$$y\text{\%}=gORIGINY$$

    y% will hold the pixel location on the overall screen of the topmost edge of the *current* window. Remember that the topmost edge of the screen is '0'.

These two functions can only be used with windows: if a *bitmap* is current when you use either of them, you will get a program-stopping error.

Which Window or Bitmap is current? Your program can identify which window or bitmap is current by the function

$$id\text{\%}=gIDENTITY$$

After executing this function, *id*% will hold the identification number.

The Graphics

How big is the current window or bitmap? Two functions enable you to ascertain the size of the current window or bitmap.

gWIDTH   The format is

$$width\% = gWIDTH$$

width% will hold the width, in pixels, of the current window or bitmap.

gHEIGHT   The format is

$$height\% = gHEIGHT$$

height% will hold the height, in pixels, of the current window or bitmap.

How many 'layers' down is the window? You will recall that *windows* can be placed 'on top of each other' on the screen - and that those windows concealed by others will not be seen. You can determine how far 'down' or 'back' a window is by the function gRANK:

gRANK   The format is

$$rank\% = gRANK$$

rank% will hold the position of the *current* window, with '1' being the topmost or the one that's in the foreground, and '8' being the window that's 'right down at the back'. A program-stopping error will occur if you try to use this function when a bitmap is current.

Full information about the current Window or Bitmap. As well as the *positional* information provided by the previously discussed functions, you can obtain more sophisticated data about the current window or bitmap: full details about the font, the current *text* or *graphics* mode, whether it is a *window* or a *bitmap*, and so on. Much of this information is for fairly advanced use - particularly the font data, and you will be unlikely to need it for most of your programs.

gINFO *vid%()*   This function requires *vid%()* to have been declared as a LOCAL or GLOBAL array, with at least 32 elements - although at the moment, the last three elements will not contain any relevant data: they are reserved for future use. After it has been executed, the *vid%()* array holds data as follows

vid%() element	Data held
1	The lowest character code in the current font.
2	The highest character code in the current font.
3	The height of the current font.

4	The *descent* of the current font.
5	The *ascent* of the current font.
6	The width of the zero character '0'.
7	The width of the widest character.
8	Font details (additive values):
	$1=Standard ASCII character set
	$2=A 'multilingual' character set
	(used by Series 3)
	$4=Font has been emboldened
	$8=Font has been italicised
	$10=Font has serifs
	$20=Font is monospaced
9-17	Font name[*]
18	The graphics mode, as set by gGMODE.
19	The text mode, as set by gTMODE.
20	The text style, as set by gSTYLE.
21	Cursor state (0=OFF, 1=ON)[**].
22	ID of window containing the cursor display[***].
23	The cursor width.
24	The cursor height.
25	The cursor ascent.
26	The cursor's *x* position.
27	The cursor's *y* position.
28	Window (0) or Bitmap (1).
29-32	Reserved for future use. t.

[*] The value in *vid%(9)* is an *address*. You can get the name of the font by lines such as

```
PRINT PEEK$(ADDR(vid%(9)))
font$=PEEK$(ADDR(vid%(9)))
```

PEEK and ADDR are two of the OPL words that 'access' the ROM or RAM areas of Series 3. It is not intended to discuss such words in any great detail for, whilst these two are fairly harmless in what they can do, others can cause the Series 3 to 'crash' or to wipe out valuable data if misused, and are therefore potentially dangerous for the newcomer to programming.

[**] If the cursor is switched off, then *vid%(22)* to *vid%(27)* should be ignored.

[***] The *text* screen cursor is identified by the value '-1'.

The Graphics

Reading a line of pixels. There is a function for the more advanced programmer that enables a horizontal line of pixels to be read from a window or bitmap. The information is stored 16 pixels at a time in an integer array, which must have been declared as a LOCAL or GLOBAL variable.

gPEEKLINE *id%, x%, y%,* varray%*(),* ln%   With this function:

>*id%* is the identification number for the required window or bitmap.

>*x%* and *y%* define the pixel location from which the information is to be read.

>*ln%* is the number of pixels to be read.

>*varray%()* is the array that will hold the data. The line is read from the left, information regarding the first 16 pixels being stored in the first element (*varray%(1)*), the next 16 pixels being stored in the second array element (*varray%(2)*) and so on. The *first* or *leftmost* pixel in each instance is stored in the least significant (lowest valued) bit of the array element: a set bit ('1') indicating that the pixel is switched on, and a zero value ('0') indicating that the pixel is switched off. The *dimension* or number of elements that the array must have when it is declared can be calculated from the formula:

$$((ln\%+15)/16)$$

using integer arithmetic.

Positioning and selecting windows

We have seen how to get information about the current window or bitmap: now let us look at the various ways there are to position and select windows and bitmaps.

Making a Window or bitmap current. To select a window or bitmap and make it *current,* the command is

gUSE *id%*   This command makes the window or bitmap with the reference number *id%* current, ready to receive your graphics drawings or text. Note that for windows, gUSE *doesn't* make the selected window visible: it may be hidden behind other windows, or be designated as 'invisible'. The command simply directs all subsequent drawing, graphics text and movement instructions to the selected window.

Re-positioning and re-sizing a window.   The gCREATE command allows you to define a window's size, and to position it within the overall screen. It doesn't end there, however: you can, through your program, shift it somewhere else if you wish - perhaps under 'user control' - and also change its size.

gSETWIN x%,y%,width%,height%   With this command you can move the *current* window to a new location, as defined by the values of *x%* and *y%*. The *width%* and *height%* arguments are optional, and are for use only if you wish to change the size of the window as well as move it. Thus the formats are

```
        gSETWIN x%,y%,width%,height%
        gSETWIN x%,y%
```

Positioning the 'depth' of a window. When you have a number of windows, invariably some of them will be 'hidden' behind others. You can change the 'depth' or 'level' of a window, bringing it to the top or placing it further down, with the gORDER command.

gORDER id%,level%   This command sets the 'level' of the *window* specified by *id%*, to the depth specified by *level%*. If *id%* refers to a bitmap, then an error will occur. The 'topmost' level, guaranteed to be unhidden by other windows, is level '1'. If the value of *level%* is greater than the number of windows, then the window with the highest reference number is used. Thus, if *id%* has a value of 6, and the window *id%*'s end at '4', then window '4' will be placed at the specified level. The current position of a window can be obtained by the gRANK command, remember.

To see or not to see?   When you create a window, you can determine whether or not it will be immediately visible. You can change the situation with the following command

gVISIBLE ON/OFF   To make the *current* window visible, use gVISIBLE ON, and to make it invisible, use gVISIBLE OFF. If a bitmap is current, then you will get an error.

Here's a program that will let you see the action of the gSETWIN, gORDER, gORIGINX, gORIGINY and gBORDER commands. The program creates a series of seven windows, then invites you to select a window number for movement. Notice how the gBORDER command is used to show which window is selected (and brought to the 'top'), and how the gORIGINX/Y function is used as the reference point for the desired movement. Both procedures must be entered.

```
PROC windmove:
  LOCAL c%,f%
  c%=2
  DO                          REM Create 7 windows
    gCREATE(c%*2,c%4,80,30,1)
    gBORDER 2                 REM No shadow yet
    gAT 20,17
    gPRINT "Window",c%        REM Name that window
    c%=c%+1
  UNTIL c%=9
  dINIT "Instructions"
  dTEXT "","Press a number key (2-8) to",2
  dTEXT "","select a Window and bring it",2
  dTEXT "","to the top. Use the",2
  dTEXT "","arrow keys to move it",2
  dTEXT "","(arrow+shift=faster)",2
  dTEXT "","Press ESC to QUIT",2
  DIALOG
  DO
    c%=GET
    f%=1+5*(KMOD AND 2)       REM See Note
    IF c%>49 AND c%<57        REM Number key?
      gBORDER 2               REM Yes - clear the border
      gUSE c%-48              REM Select the Window
      gORDER c%-48,1          REM ... put it on top
      gBORDER 1               REM ... and give it a shadow
    ELSEIF c%=256             REM Up
      posit:(0,-1,f%)
    ELSEIF c%=257             REM Down
      posit:(0,1,f%)
    ELSEIF c%=258             REM Right
      posit:(1,0,f%)
    ELSEIF c%=259             REM Left
      posit:(-1,0,f%)
    ENDIF
  UNTIL c%=27                 REM The ESC key
ENDP
```

```
PROC posit:(x%,y%,f%)
   gSETWIN gORIGINX+x%*f%,gORIGINY+y%*f%
ENDP
```

Note 1: This line makes f% equal to '1' if the SHIFT key is not pressed (KMOD AND 2 will equal '0', and 5*0 is 0), and '11' if the SHIFT key *is* pressed (KMOD AND 2 will be equal to '2').

As you can see from this program, you don't have to keep track of where each window is located on the screen: the gORIGINX/Y function gets the information for you.

'Filling' and clearing windows and bitmaps

There are a couple of ways that you can 'fill' a window or bitmap with information that is contained in another 'drawable': loading such information in from a previously saved file will be discussed later. First, however, let us look at the way to 'clear' a window.

gCLS   This is very much the same as the CLS command, which clears the *text* screen or window. gCLS clears the *current* window or bitmap of all data.

The whole purpose of bitmaps is to hold information or graphics displays which can subsequently be transferred to a window. Often, too, it is easier to construct an image in a window, where you can see what is happening, and then to save the image in a bitmap for subsequent use. Two commands enable you to transfer an entire area or a part of it, and to have a particular area copied as a pattern - that is, repeated as often as possible within the new area.

gCOPY *id%,x%,y%,width%,height%,mode%*   With this command, you can copy a rectangle from the window or bitmap specified by *id%*, to the *current* pixel location in the *current* window or bitmap, and set the way that the copying process is to be executed.

id% is the reference number of the window or bitmap *from* which the data is to be copied.

x% and **y%** define the top left corner of the area to be copied, within the window or bitmap.

width% and **height%** define the size of the rectangle to be copied, in pixels.

mode% determines *how* the copying process is to be executed. Both set (blackened) and clear pixels are copied, but you can change the way they are copied, in much the same way you can change the way graphics print commands (for example) work.

mode% value	Copying method
0	Copies set pixels as set pixels (black)
1	Copies set pixels as 'cleared' pixels: these will be 'seen' only over 'blackened' areas in the new location.
2	Copies set pixels as set (black) over clear areas, and as 'clear' over 'blackened' areas
3	The whole of the specified area is copied 'as is' - both clear and set pixels are copied.

As you can see, for *mode%* values of 0 to 2, only the *set* pixels are copied, either as they are, 'reversed' completely, or inverting anything that's already at the copying location. With a value of 3 for *mode%*, both the clear and the set pixels are copied, thus replacing anything previously there. After the command has been executed, the 'cursor' at both locations is restored to the original positions.

gPATT *id%,width%,height%,mode%*   This command is used to create repetitive patterns. The entire bitmap or window identified by *id%* is copied into the current window or bitmap, into a box area specified by *width%* and *height%*. The top left corner of the box is determined by the current cursor location. The copied pattern is repeated as many times as will fit within the box area.

The way that the pattern is copied into the box is determined by *mode%*, which has the same effects as detailed for gCOPY on the previous page.

If you give *id%* a value of '-1', then a built-in 'grey' pattern is used.

Here is a procedure to give you a 'feel' for the potential of the gPATT command, and to demonstrate one or two of the other commands dealt with so far. When you have run this, experiment by editing, for example, the '*mode%*' value of gPATT and the size of the area in which the pattern is to be reproduced. You can use also the program to practice creating your own patterns in the bitmap, altering the size of the bitmap at the gCREATEBIT command as necessary.

```
PROC pattern
  LOCAL id%(2),c%
  id%(1)=gCREATEBIT (20,20)   REM Create a Bitmap
  gCLS                        REM Ensure it's clear
  DO                          REM Create a pattern
    gAT c%,c%
    gBOX 2+c%,2+c%
    c%=c%+2
  UNTIL c%>=10
  id%(2)=gCREATE(2,2,200,70,1)
  gBORDER $203                REM Window and border
  gAT 100,10
  gFILL 50,50,0              REM Black box in the window
  BUSY "Press a key"        REM Wait for the magic moment!
  GET
  BUSY OFF
  gAT 2,2
  gPATT id%(1),195,65,2     REM Pattern the window
  GET
ENDP
```

Scrolling every which way

You will probably have seen how, in the text window, Series 3 scrolls
text upwards when new lines are added at the bottom of the screen.
This doesn't happen automatically on graphics screens: anything you
'send' to the screen overprints what was already there, according to
the *mode* selected. Scrolling is made possible, however, in any
direction you choose, by the gSCROLL command.

gSCROLL *dx%,dy%,x%,y%,width%,height%*   The formats for this
         command are

```
        gSCROLL dx%,dy%
        gSCROLL dx%,dy%,x%,y%,width%,height%
```

If you just specify *dx%* and *dy%*, then the display in the
entire current window (or bitmap) is scrolled by *dx%* pixels
horizontally, and by *dy%* pixels vertically. As with other
commands, negative values for *dx%* move to the left, positive

values move to the right. Similarly negative values for *dy%* move up, and positive values move down.

Note that if your window has a border (gBORDER command), then as this is within the window area, it too will scroll.

You can limit the scrolling area to a rectangle within the window or bitmap, by specifying *x%* and *y%* (to determine the top left corner of the rectangle), and *width%* and *height%* (to determine the size of the rectangle).

The area 'left behind' by a scrolling action is always left clear, and anything scrolled 'beyond the edge' of the *defined* window area is lost: scrolling back again doesn't bring it back into view. You can have a *defined* window that is larger than the actual screen: the screen then becomes a 'viewport' on your defined window. In this case, anything previously 'hidden' - because it is beyond the limits of the *screen* - can be scrolled into view. Nevertheless, areas 'left behind' are still cleared. It is up to your program to prevent wanted information from being scrolled beyond the limits of the window, or to replace cleared areas with new information, if that's what you want.

The gPEEKLINE function can be used to 'read' a horizontal line from, say, a bitmap, for inserting into a cleared horizontal line in a window: this calls for a slightly more advanced programming technique, as you must be able to 'convert' an integer value into pixel display information. We shall examine the process involved a little later.

Note that the position of the window is unaffected by the scrolling action. Also, the current cursor location within the window is not affected by the scrolling action, even if a rectangular scroll area is specified.

Here is a program that will demonstrate the scrolling process. A larger-than-screen window is created and filled to the brim with letters. You use the arrow keys to scroll in any direction - and reveal the stuff 'hidden' beyond the screen. At first, everything is scrolled: pressing 'R' will limit scrolling to a Rectangle, pressing 'A' will scroll the entire window. By scrolling to the limits of the *window* and back, you should be able to see how 'off screen' displays can be brought into view, and also how scrolled data is lost when it is taken beyond the limits of the window. When you've had enough, press the ESC key to Quit.

```
PROC scroller:
  LOCAL c%,a%
  gCREATE(-20,-20,400,200,1) REM Starts and ends 'off screen'
  c%=-20
  DO                         REM Fill window
    c%=c%+8
    gAT 1,c%
    gPRINT REPT$("AbCdEfGhIjKlMn",8)
  UNTIL c%>=200
  DO                         REM Now for the scrolls
    c%=GET
    IF c%=256                REM Up
      doscroll:(0,-1,a%)
    ELSEIF c%=257            REM Down
      doscroll:(0,1,a%)
    ELSEIF c%=258            REM Right
      doscroll:(1,0,a%)
    ELSEIF c%=259            REM Left
      doscroll:(-1,0,a%)
    ELSEIF c%=%A OR c%=%a    REM 'A' pressed?
      a%=0                   REM '0' for 'all screen'
    ELSEIF c%=%R OR c%=%r    REM 'R' pressed?
      a%=1                   REM '1' for rectangular area
    ENDIF
  UNTIL c%=27               REM 'ESC' pressed
ENDP

PROC doscroll:(horz%,vert%,area%)
  IF area%
    gSCROLL horiz%,vert%,100,50,60,30
  ELSE
    gSCROLL horiz%,vert%
  ENDIF
ENDP
```

Replacing 'lost' scrolled displays   We shall now examine how the data that's 'lost' as a result of a vertical scrolling action can be replaced, using the **gPEEKLINE** function. Here's a scrolling procedure, this time using a smaller window filled with letters. Scrolling will be limited to 'up' and 'down' directions only: as a row of pixels moves through the top of the window, it will be replaced at the bottom, and vice versa.

```
PROC scroll2:
  LOCAL k%,row%,id%
  id%=gCREATE(40,20,160,40,1) REM Create window
  k%=8
  DO                            REM Fill window
    gAT 1,k%
    gPRINT "AbCdEfGhIjKlMnOpQrStUvWxYz12"
    k%=k%+8
  UNTIL k%>=48
  DO                            REM The 'action' loop
    k%=GET
    IF k%=256                   REM Up
      row%=0                    REM so TOP line goes
      scrollit:(id%,row%)       REM Go do it
    ELSEIF k%=257               REM Down
      row%=39                   REM so BOTTOM line goes
      scrollit:(id%,row%)       REM Go do it
    ENDIF
  UNTIL k%=27                   REM esc key pressed
ENDP

PROC scrollit:(id%,row%)        REM Here's comes the tricky bit
  LOCAL ne%,bp&,a%(10)          REM Note 1
  gPEEKLINE id%,0,row%,a%(),160     REM Read line
  IF row%                       REM Means row%=39 for 'down'
    gSCROLL 0,1                 REM so scroll down
  ELSE                          REM Otherwise...
    gSCROLL 0,-1                REM Scroll up
  ENDIF
  ne%=1                         REM Set element counter to '1'
  DO                            REM For each array element
    bp&=0                       REM set bit position to '0'
    DO                          REM For each bit position
      IF a%(ne%) AND 2**bp&     REM See Note 2
      gAT ((ne%-1)*16)+bp&,39-row%  REM See Note 3
      gLINEBY 0,0               REM Plot it
```

```
        ENDIF
        bp&=bp&+1              REM Next Bit
    UNTIL bp&=16              REM Bits are 0-15
        ne%=ne%+1            REM Next array element
    UNTIL ne%=11             REM End of the array
ENDP
```

Note 1: We need to keep track of the array elements (*ne%*), and the *bits* - binary digits - that are stored in each array element (*bp&*). We are going to do some hefty multiplication, so we need a long integer for the Bit Position variable. The array (*a%()*) must be dimensioned to hold lines of 160 pixels: using the formula, '(ln%+15)/16', you'll see we need ten elements (taking the integer value).

Note 2: We have to test each *bit* in the stored value, to see if it represents a *set* bit (value of '1') or a *clear* bit (value of '0'). Each *bit* position from the lowest to the highest represents an increasing *power* of two. The first bit (bit zero) represents 'two to the power *zero*' - and *any* number to the power of zero is equal to 1. It's a fact of life. The next bit - (bit *one*) - *represents* 'two to the power *one*' and the next bit represents 'two to the power *two*' and so on. Thus, each bit represents 'two to the power of its position in the *binary number* stored in the array element'. If we AND the total value stored in the element with the different powers of two, we can test each bit in turn to see if it is set. If it *is* set, then the result of 'IF a%(ne%) AND 2**bp&' will be *true*, and so we can proceed to plot the corresponding pixel in the window. Easy, huh?

Note 3: Having ascertained that a particular *bit* in the array element is *set*, we need to plot that pixel on the display. So we need to calculate where, along the row, that bit is. Knowing the row itself is easy - we passed that information down from the main procedure. To find out which pixel along the row needs to be 'switched on' or turned black, we need to make a calculation. You will recall that gPEEKLINE stores the leftmost 16 pixels in the first array element, the next 16 in the second array element, and so on. You will also recall that the *first* pixel information in a group of 16 goes into the lowest or least significant *bit* of the number in its binary form. Thus, we know that the very first pixel will be in the *'bit zero'* position of the first element of the array. Similarly, the very first pixel in the second element of the array will be *sixteen pixels along.* So, if we deduct '1' from an array element number and multiply it by 16, we know which *band* of 16 pixels is being represented by the value stored in that array element. All we have to do then is add in the actual bit position, and lo! we have the position along the row of the pixel that must be turned on. Finally, for the **gAT** command, we need to set the row number. If *row%* is zero, it means we 'read' the pixel row from the top line - but now need to replace it at the bottom line, which will be '39'. Similarly, if *row%* was 39, we need to replace the pixel row on the top line - '0'. By deducting *row%* from 39, we get the result we want. And that's it!

Armed with the remarks given in the program and the notes above, you should be able to follow the process involved in creating a 'rolling scroll'. This program reads the information from the same window, but you could read it from a *bitmap* which would be the same width as your window, but which is 'longer' or deeper, to hold all the information. In this case, you would need to keep track of which 'row' in the bitmap needs to be 'read' - slightly more tricky, but not too difficult if you remember that the top and bottom rows that may need to be read will be the same 'distance' apart as your window's depth.

It must be said at this point that the example above is just *one* solution, and the result, although it works, is a fairly slow scrolling action: Series 3 has to make a large number (160 in this case) of calculations and plots to replace a line of pixels.

Finally you should note that, if you place a border round your window, that too will scroll unless you limit the scroll area to a rectangle *within* the border area: you would also need to adjust the row numbers being read and replaced, of course.

Saving and loading Windows and Bitmaps

Your programs can be quite lengthy if they use graphic displays of some kind, and these displays have to be created each time the program is run. Far better is to create the displays once, either in a bitmap or window, and then save them as a 'picture' file. When your program needs the saved display, it can be loaded quickly, easily and directly into a bitmap for copying entirely or in part to a window. Once a display has been saved, the 'display generating' part of your program can deleted, of course, saving space as well as speeding things up.

gSAVEBIT *name$,width%,height%*   This saves to a file the current window or bitmap, in a special way. The formats are

```
gSAVEBIT name$
gSAVEBIT name$,width%,height%
```

If you use *width%* and *height%*, then the area saved is a rectangle of the specified size, with its top left corner at the current pixel location. If you don't specify *width%* and *height%*, then the whole of the window or bitmap is saved. **name$** is the name that the file will have when it is saved, and this name must follow certain rules (the same rules, in fact, as for file names used on Desk Top computers). In essence the file name can consist of three parts:

a) A *path* to the directory in which the file is to be saved.
b) The *file name*, which must be no more than eight letters or numbers, always starting with a letter.
c) The *extension*, which is a dot followed by three letters, usually to denote the type of file.

Of these, *name$* need only specify (b) - the name you wish to give to the file. If you don't specify the *path*, then the default 'bitmap' directory '\OPD\' will be used. If you don't specify an *extension*, the default extension '.PIC' will be used.
    Note that if any file with the same name already exists at the saved location, it will be replaced by the new file.

gLOADBIT(name$,write%,i%)   Once you have bitmap files saved, you can load them again with this function. The formats are

```
id%=gLOADBIT(name$)
id%=gLOADBIT(name$,write%)
id%=gLOADBIT(name$,write%,bmnum%)
```

This loads a bitmap file into a *bitmap* (not a window) in the memory, and returns the reference number in *id%*. As with **gSAVEBIT**, if *name$* doesn't specify the path or the extension, then the default directory (\OPD\) and extension (.PIC) will be used.

If you want to prevent the bitmap restored into memory from being changed in any way, then make *write%* equal to '0': this makes the bitmap *'read-only'*, so any attempts to write new information to it will be ignored. The default value for *write%* is '1' - which means it can be changed and re-saved.

You can ignore *bmnum%*: it is used to select a particular bitmap from special files which hold more than one bitmap. The **gSAVEBIT** command will save only one bitmap in a file, and so *bmnum%* will not be needed for your OPL programs.

Now let us examine a way these two commands can be used. A typical technique could be:

1) Write your program, with all the drawing instructions.
2) Test that it works - and the drawings appear as required.
3) Add commands to *save* the windows and bitmaps, placed soon after the required drawings have been created.
4) Translate and run the program again.
5) Check that the required files have been saved successfully.
6) Make the 'drawing' and 'saving' lines 'REMarks'. Before the drawing sections, add commands to load the relevant bitmaps and, if required, create windows and copy the bitmaps to them.
7) Test the program again. If it works, you can delete all of the drawing and save commands completely.

Let us put this to the test. First, enter the following procedure

```
PROC mapsave:
  LOCAL c%,id%
  id%=gCREATE(10,10,150,60,1)
  gBORDER 0
  DO
    gAT c%*3,c%
    gBOX 20,20
    c%=c%+5
  UNTIL c%>=50
  BUSY "Press a key"
  GET
ENDP
```

That's the first step: we have created a window, with a simple border, and filled it with a few boxes. Translate and run it, to prove it works - and you'll have completed the second step.

Now edit the program by adding a line after the GET function, as follows

```
gSAVEBIT "Myboxes"
```

then translate and run the program again. This time, you should have a bitmap file called 'Myboxes' saved in memory. Check it out:

a) Press the PSION and letter 'O' keys together, to 'open a file'.
b) When the Dialog appears, press the TAB key.
c) Use the up arrow key to move the highlight to the '\' symbol at the top left of the listing, then press the ENTER key.
d) Use the up arrow key to move the highlight up, until '\OPD\' is highlit, then press the ENTER key.
e) You should now see the name of your newly saved file 'Myboxes.pic'
f) Press the ESC key twice, to cancel the two Dialogs and return to the Program Editor.

That's the fourth and fifth steps completed. Now edit the program again, so that it looks like this (notice the changes to *id%()*):

```
PROC mapsave:
   LOCAL c%,id%(2)
   id%(1)=gLOADBIT("Myboxes")
   id%(2)=gCREATE(10,10,150,60,1)
   gCOPY id%(1),0,0,150,60,0
REM  gBORDER 0
REM  DO
REM     gAT c%*3,c%
REM     gBOX 20,20
REM     c%=c%+5
REM  UNTIL c%>=50
   BUSY "Press a key"
   GET
REM  gSAVEBIT "Myboxes"
ENDP
```

Translate and run this - and you should get the same box display as before (including the border). Once that has been proved, you can delete all the statement lines with a REM in front: they're no longer needed. Two new lines will have replaced seven in the original - and that was only a simple, short program to start with, so as you can see, great savings can be achieved in memory usage by using saved files of specific displays.

Furthermore, since the files are saved in memory (or on an SSD), you can use them in *any* program you write.

STEP TWENTY-ONE

Clocks

In this Step we examine how you can have a clock displayed in your programs. The OPL words covered are gCLOCK and STATUSWIN

Time on your hands

You will be well aware that your Series 3 can display a clock - in various different sizes according to the selected function. You can have a display of a clock or clocks in your own programs - and can even reproduce the Status window on the right hand side which shows the current time, date and an icon indicating the current function or program in use.

With this facility you can, for example, show the time in two or more places in the world simultaneously, rather than having to select them individually in the 'World' function. Or you can give your programs the same 'feel' as the Series 3's facilities, where the system time panel can be made to appear (or disappear) 'permanently' by pressing the CONTROL and MENU keys. (It will always appear temporarily when the PSION and MENU keys are pressed).

Choice of clock style and size

OPL offers you the choice of two sizes of *digital* clock - small and medium, and two sizes of *analog* clock - medium and large. Depending on the type of clock you select, you can have the date, seconds and am/pm information also displayed. Digital clocks are displayed in the mode (12 or 24 hour) selected for the Series 3 system clock.

Whatever the clock type selected, it is displayed in the top left corner of the *current* window.

gCLOCK ON,*mode%,offset%*   The formats for this command are

```
gCLOCK ON
gCLOCK ON,mode%
gCLOCK ON,mode%,offset%
gCLOCK OFF
```

233

The Graphics

If you simply use the gCLOCK ON command, you will get a small analog clock, positioned in the top left corner of the current window. You can have only one clock displayed in any window.

The *mode%* argument allows you to select a type of clock, as follows

mode%() Value	Clock type
1	Small digital. This is the default.
2	Medium sized, the same as set for the Series 3 system.
3	Medium sized analog.
4	Medium sized digital.
5	Large analog.

As you can see, when selecting a medium sized clock, you can either specify digital or analog, or use the selection made by the user when setting the Series 3. You can choose any one of these values for *mode%*, and modify it by adding combinations of the hexadecimal values $10, $20 or $30 as follows

Hex	Small	Medium	Large	Function
$10	Yes	Yes	No	Display the date
$20	Yes	No	Yes	Display seconds
$40	No	Digital 12hr and Analog	No	Display am/pm

Thus, if *mode%* has a value of $53, you will have a medium sized analog clock displayed, together with the date and indication of am or pm.

Normally, the clock will display the time from the current system setting, but you can change this by using the *offset%* argument. The value of *offset%* determines how many *minutes* before (negative values) or ahead (positive values) the time on your clock display will be in relation to system clock.

To switch off a clock display, use the gCLOCK OFF command.

Here's a program that sets up a display of four clocks, to show the time in four different places round the world. The way this program is written, you can easily modify it to have your own four places, if you wish: simply enter the place name for the appropriate element of variable place$(x),

with the time difference in the associated element of variable
td%(x).

```
PROC clocks
LOCAL id%(4),c%,place$(4,12),td%(4)
place$(1)="London"
td%(1)=0
place$(2)="New York"
td%(2)=-5
place$(3)="Athens"
td%(3)=2
place$(4)="Perth"
td%(4)=8
c%=1                               REM The array counter
DO
   id%(c)=gCREATE(80*(c%-1),0,55,70,1)
   gCLOCK ON,$53,td%(c%)*60
   gBORDER 3
   gAT 7,60
   gPRINT place$(c%)
   c%=c%+1
UNTIL c%=5
GET
ENDP
```

Notice how arrays can help to shorten and simplify the
program (they save having to set each clock, and name the
places individually). The use of arrays also makes it easier
for places and time differences to be entered from a Dialog, if
you wished.

You'll see, too, that the array counter (*c%*) is also used to
position the windows for each particular clock when it is
created, thus saving the need to create each window
separately. The ability to use loops to undertake a repetitive
series of instructions is another advantage of having *arrays*
for related groups of variables.

We don't need to use the gUSE command in this program,
since a window is automatically made *current* when it is
created. As mentioned earlier, the clocks are displayed in the
very top left corner of the current window: on initiation, the
gBORDER command will 'overwrite' the edges of the clock and

235

so will be complete. But when the clock is updated, which for the clocks used in this program is every minute, the clock will 'overwrite' the border and clear a part of it in the process. So don't be surprised or think your Series 3 is cracking up!

Displaying the Status window

The status window is always available for temporary display in your programs, without you having to do anything: the PSION and MENU keys will bring up the display. However, you may choose to have the window available for permanent display, on demand by the user. Ideally, you would arrange for the same key combination to do this as other Series 3 applications: CONTROL and MENU.

The status window has no 'reference' number as other windows in your programs, and *always* appears at the very 'back' of the screen. This means *any* of your windows that occupy the same area will cover it up: 'any' includes the text screen and the default graphics window (number 1). The status window is 52 pixels wide.

It is therefore up to your program to ensure that, when and if the status window is called for, all windows (including the text and default graphics windows) are moved out of the way.

Your program can tackle this using the gSETWIN command which, you may recall, allows the size of a window to be changed as well as its position. When (and if) the status window is removed, you will probably want the windows to resume their original size. You could do this by using *actual* values in your program: all you need to do is keep check of the various locations of that the windows can have.

However, in a program which allows the windows to be moved around by the user, and for making program changes, it is better to store the window location information in array variables, to be used when required.

Any program can be made to have the status window appear. Here, we shall demonstrate how a 'three-window' program could be 'adapted' to include a status window. First, the command to use is

STATUSWIN ON

to switch the status window on, and, believe it or not,

STATUSWIN OFF

to turn it off again.

Now, let us write a program that creates two windows - making *three* altogether, with the default window. Our program will simply allow the user to change the message that's displayed in each window. As well, of course, as allowing the status window to be displayed. And for good measure, we'll use a menu for window selection, and a Dialog for the editing.

This program is fairly long - and is split up into a number of procedures *all of which must be in the same Module, and entered before the entire program can be translated and run.* Take care when entering it: bugs will be hard to find!

The program demonstrates a number of points, which are discussed after the listing. Note that you needn't enter any of the REMarks (shown in a different type in the listing): they're there to help you understand how it works.

```
PROC statdisp:
    LOCAL k%,m%,sw%
    GLOBAL wx%(6),wy%(6),wid%(6),ht%(6)
    GLOBAL msg$(3,16),id%(3)
    init:                           REM Initialise everything
    winf:                           REM Set up Window arrays
    DO                              REM The main control loop
        k%=KEY                      REM Get the input
        IF KMOD=4 AND k%=290        REM PSION and MENU keys
            IF sw%=0                REM Status window is off
                STATUSWIN ON        REM Turn it on
                sw%=3               REM =3 means On
                poswins:(sw%)       REM Re-position windows
                CONTINUE            REM Don't do 'menu' yet!
            ELSE                    REM Status Window is on
                STATUSWIN OFF       REM Turn it off
                sw%=0               REM =0 means Off
                poswins:(sw%)
                CONTINUE
            ENDIF
        ENDIF
        IF k%=$122                  REM Now deal with Menus
            mINIT
            mCARD "Quit","Quit",%q
            mCARD "Edit","A",%A,"B",%B,"C",%C
```

```
        m%=MENU
        IF m%=%q OR m%=0            REM Quit program
            STOP                    REM STOP quits
        ELSEIF m%>96 AND m%<100
            doedit:(m%-96,sw%)      REM See notes
        ENDIF
    ENDIF
  UNTIL k%=27                       REM ESC key
ENDP


PROC init:                         REM Sets up the display
  LOCAL c%
  msg$(1)="Window A"               REM For display and
  msg$(2)="Window B"               REM  editing
  msg$(3)="Window C"
  id%(1)=1                         REM The default window id
  gSETWIN 10,8,200,50              REM Resize default window
  gAT 2,30
  gPRINTB msg$(1),200-4,3          REM Print Window A message
  gBORDER 2                        REM  and Border it
  c%=2                             REM Now create
  DO                               REM  two more windows
     id%(c%)=gCREATE(c%*10,c%*8,200,50,1)
     gBORDER 2
     gAT 2,30
     gPRINTB msg$(c%),200-4,3
     c%=c%+1
  UNTIL c%=4
ENDP


PROC winf:                         REM This collates all
  LOCAL c%                         REM  the window information
  c%=1
  DO
     gUSE c%                       REM Make window current
     wx%(c%)=gORIGINX              REM Get the facts
     wx%(c%+3)=gORIGINX-5          REM  about all windows
     wy%(c%)=gORIGINY
     wy%(c%+3)=gORIGINY
```

```
      wid%(c%)=gWIDTH
      wid%(c%+3)=gWIDTH-50
      ht%(c%)=gHEIGHT
      ht%(c%+3)=gHEIGHT
      c%=c%+1
   UNTIL c%=4
ENDP

PROC doedit:(ew%,f%)              REM This is the editor
   gUSE ew%                       REM See the notes
   gORDER ew%,1
   dINIT "Edit Window"+CHR$(ew%+64)
   dEDIT msg$(ew%),"Edit it:"
   DIALOG
   gAT 2,30
   gPRINTB msg$(ew%),wid%(ew%+f%)-4,3
ENDP

PROC poswins:(f%)                 REM This positions windows
   LOCAL c%,w%
   c%=1+f%                        REM Get right array elements
   w%=1                           REM Window counter
   DO
      gUSE w%                     REM Make each one current
      gCLS                        REM Clear it
      gSETWIN wx%(c%),wy%(c%),wid%(c%),ht%(c%)
      gBORDER 2                   REM Move and re-fill it
      gAT 2,30
      gPRINTB msg$(w%),wid%(w%+f%)-4,3
      w%=w%+1                     REM Update window counter
      c%=c%+1                     REM Update array counter
   UNTIL w%=4                     REM Until done
   IF f%                          REM Status is on
      SCREEN 30,8                 REM Must position text screen
   ELSE
      SCREEN 39,8
   ENDIF
ENDP
```

The Graphics

Now for the explanation.

PROC statdisp: This is the main controlling procedure, which 'drives' the other procedures.

> LOCAL Variables
> k%   is for the input key information
> m%   is for the MENU information
> sw% is a 'flag' to hold data about the Status window. We will make this zero if the Status window is off, and '3' if it is 'on' - you'll see why it is convenient to use '3' for the 'on' condition later.
>
> GLOBAL Variables
> wx%(6), wy%(6),wid%(6) and ht%(6) are for holding all the data we need about the *six* window positions (two positions for each of three windows).
> msg$(3,16) is a string array for holding the messages to be displayed and edited.
> id%(3)   is an array for holding the identity of the three windows

The program starts by initialising the display (winit:), and then collating the window data that we shall need (winf:). This is followed by the main controlling loop for the program. The test for a keypress is made - and if so, we then see whether or not it's the PSION and CONTROL key combination. If it is, then the 'status' flag is checked to see the current status, and depending on that result, the Status window is displayed or removed by a call to poswins:, along with the *new* status as set in sw%. Now since the MENU key has been pressed, any test to see whether that key has been pressed as a request for the Menu will also be true - which we don't necessarily want at this point. And so the CONTINUE command is executed, to by-pass any further tests on the contents of k%.

If k% shows that only the MENU key has been pressed, then the menu operation is executed. Note that in this program, provision has *not* been made to act on the PSION 'short-cut keys (see Step 16).

The value returned by MENU will be the character code for a lower case q or zero, if 'Quit' was selected or the ESC key was pressed, or it will be the character code for the pressed key. If 'Quit' (or ESC) is selected, the program is terminated immediately with the STOP command. Otherwise, we're interested only in the codes for 'a', 'b', and 'c' - which have values of 97 to 99 inclusive. We therefore test for these keys, and if one of them has been pressed, we turn the value into a *window identity* number by subtracting 96, and call the editing procedure (doedit:), passing the window and the value of the status flag - either zero or '3'.

The loop - and the program stops if the ESC key is pressed.

PROC init: This is the procedure that sets up the display. The only LOCAL variable used is c%, which acts as a counter.

First the message arrays are 'filled', then the id for window '1' - the default window - is set. Since window 1 already exists and is current, we move its position, display the message for that window and order a border. The gPRINTB command is used since it enables us to centralise the message and clear anything that was there before (which will happen later when editing takes place). Then the two new windows are created and filled with the same kind of information.

PROC winf: This procedure gleans information about the three windows we now have on the screen - and adds the information that will be needed when the windows are moved.

PROC doedit:(ew%,f%) This is the editing procedure. We pass to it the current window to be edited (in ew%), and the value of the Status flag (in f%). The first thing to do is make the selected window *current*, and 'bring' it to the top of the display. A Dialog provides the editing function.

Then we use gPRINTB again to display the newly edited message: to get the correct window *width* in order to centralise the display, irrespective of whether the Status display is on, we use ew% (the window number) added to f% (which will be either zero or '3') to get the correct array element holding the window's width.

PROC poswins:(f%) This is the procedure that positions all three windows. Two LOCAL variables are used - c% is the array counter, to select the correct elements of the arrays holding the window data, and w% is the window counter. To get the right position, we need to know whether the Status window is on or not, and this is passed into the procedure through the f% variable. To set up the array counter, '1' is added to f% and the result assigned to c%. Each window display is cleared completely to prevent unsavoury lines appearing, the window re-positioned, and then 're-filled'.

It is important that the *text* screen is also moved out of the way - otherwise it would also 'cover up' the Status display. We could have just pre-set the text window 'once and for all' in this program, but you should be aware that it needs attention and so this part is included. *If your program uses the* text *screen, it* must *be positioned over the current graphics window, otherwise the graphics window could obscure it.*

You'll no doubt have noticed that the window id array (id%) wasn't used in this program, apart from assigning to it the identity of each window. It was included primarily to show it is done: your programs may need to keep track of window id's, and this array can help in that task.

The techniques used in this program are by no means the only ones available to you, but they should give you a lead on how to prepare programs of a similar nature.

PART 3

Files & Data Handling

This Part of the Book deals with the extensive file handling capabilities of OPL, which enable you to create Databases to suit your own needs.

STEP TWENTY-TWO

All About Files

*This Step takes a preliminary look at files, directories, paths and
file names, to help you understand file handling processes.*

What is a computer 'file'?

So far, we have avoided any lengthy discussion on *files*: in Step 17
on Dialogs, if you followed the `Dialog4` program explanation (page
180), you will have seen how your program modules are saved in
Series 3, both as the *source* code that you wrote, and as the
translated code. All of these, in computer terms, are files. The
information you have stored for your addresses, perhaps under the
default name of 'Data', and for any Word Processor documents you
may have written, are also *files*.

In essence, anything saved in memory is a computer file.
However, as you may by now have realised, the files all perform
different functions. Some, as just mentioned, are your instructions
in OPL, some are actual programs that can be run. Others are just
documents, or lists of records.

Each of these is different, and generally speaking, can be used
only for the purpose they were created for. Obviously you wouldn't
expect to run your Address database as a 'program': it is a listing of
records.

Nevertheless, *all* files have one or two things in common: the way
they are 'identified' or their *format*, and the way their *names* are
constructed. In both of these cases, the format used is the same as
that for your office computer or PC. This feature makes your files
compatible with the files on desk-top machines using the MS-DOS™
operating system, and vice versa. However, your programs will not
run on a desk top machine, because the *operating* system is different
- and so too is the screen size and so on. But your Series 3
document files and databases can be transferred to and copied from
PCs: document files that have been *formatted* are compatible with
the Microsoft Word™ word processor.

245

Files and Databases

The way files are named and the way they can be stored is fairly important when creating programs involving files and file-handling (such as Databases). In this Step, therefore, we shall look at the basic principles of file names, and where they can stored.

Paths and Directories

Just as you would keep related documents in one drawer of a filing cabinet, so it makes sense to keep files of a related nature in one 'area' of a computer.

The RAM memory inside your Series 3 has an area specifically allocated for saving data. You can also have SSDs fitted, specifically for saving data. Like a filing cabinet, this area is divided up into 'drawers' - only instead of being called drawers, they are called *directories*. A *directory* is really like a 'heading', under which files of a related nature are saved. All of your Database files, for example, are saved under a heading called 'DAT', your Agenda files are saved under a heading called 'AGN', and your word processor files are saved under a heading called 'WRD'.

These names are the *directories*, and each *directory* can have a 'sub-directory' - which in turn can have sub-sub directories. This is exactly the same as in office bound computers, lap-tops and so on: it is the standard practice, to keep your files organised and easy to locate.

Your SSDs can have directories, just as floppy disks can have directories. In fact, your SSDs can have the same directory names as inside the Series 3. You may ask "How does the Series 3 know the difference between a directory on an SSD and a directory of the same name stored in the Series 3's RAM area?" The answer is that each *location* is also identified individually.

Each *location* is identified by a letter: locations are usually referred to as *drives*, this term being derived from the floppy drives that are associated with desk top machines. You will be aware that your Series 3 has two slots for SSDs, referred to as 'A' and 'B'. This is the identification letter for that particular slot or drive, and serves to differentiate similar directories stored on them. The internal memory area of Series 3 that is reserved for saving files is referred to as 'drive' 'M' - which stands for 'Memory'.

PCs too can have drives labelled 'A' and 'B'. So the next question is, if you're transferring files to a drive on a PC, how do you differentiate between directories on the 'A' drive of Series 3 and directories of the same name on the 'A' drive of a PC? The answer is there is another 'location' identifier - 'LOC' for drives that are associated with the Series 3, and 'REM for the files that are associated with any externally connected computer.

Now, let us look at the way we put all of these elements together, to construct the *path* to the file that we want. First of all, the *computer* location is written as the identifier followed by two colons. Thus

      LOC::   for files on any drive inside the Series 3
      REM::   for files on any drive on an external computer

Don't confuse these two identifiers with the two OPL words REM and LOC! If you are dealing only with the series 3, then his identifier is not needed: it is assumed to be, or the 'default' location is taken as, 'LOC::'.

Next, the drive location letter must be specified, and this is done by following the identifying letter with a single colon. This is exactly the same practice as is used on PCs. Thus, an SSD in slot A of the series 3 is identified as

      A:

If you are accessing drive 'A' on an external computer, then it would be identified as

      REM::A:

If a drive is not specified when using your Series 3, it is taken to be drive 'M' - the internal memory drive. So for files saved in the internal RAM area of Series 3, you do not need to specify the "LOC::M:' part at all.

This now takes us to the directory to be used. All directories are identified by a *backslash* - '\'. And all drives have a main or *root* directory, so the 'root' or basic directory at any location is identified by '\'.

If you want to store files in this particular place - rather than under a *directory name*, then the backslash can be ignored. However, it is unlikely that you will want to save files in such a haphazard way on your Series 3, although it is a practice that is occasionally done on PCs, since some of their files *need* to be in the root directory.

Following the 'root directory' backslash comes the name of the directory, which must also be followed by a backslash. The directory where your source code files for your program modules are kept is

Files and Databases

'OPL', so to identify any file in this directory on the Series 3's internal memory, you would use

    \OPL*filename*

The same directory on an SSD (any SSD) in slot or drive A would be referred to as

    A:\OPL*filename*

and on drive A of an externally connected computer as

    REM::A:\OPL*filename*

You could have a sub-directory of the OPL directory - perhaps for your program 'Library' modules - which could be called '\LIB\'. To access such a directory (if it existed) on Series 3's internal memory, you would refer to it as

    \OPL\LIB*filename*

and on an SSD in the A drive as

    A:\OPL\LIB*filename*

This *route* to the required filename is called the **path**, and enables you to identify the files at specific locations.

It is very important to note that directories have to be created: *you cannot specify a directory in a path if the directory doesn't exist.*

Your Series 3 has a number of directories that it uses for storing your files. It stores them automatically in the correct directory for the application you're using, without you having to specify the *path*: it is only when you are writing your own programs, or wish to store information in a directory of your own choice, that you need to specify the path. As we shall see later on, you can create your own directories and sub-directories, and you can delete them, all under program control.

Here is a list of the directories that Series 3 uses as a *default* for storing files created using it's *own* applications:

Directory Name	Type of File stored
\AGN\	Agenda files.
\DAT\	Database files.
\DEF\	Word template files. and any other *default* files.
\OPD\	Bitmap files, picture files and so on.
\OPL\	OPL *source* code files.
\OPO\	OPL programs that can be run.
\WDR\	Printer driver files.

In the main, you don't have to specify these path names at all, unless you wish to store or access files in a different directory path for some reason. You *could*, for example, load a database file such as 'Data' into the Series 3 word processor, but it would look a mess of symbols and so on as well as all the records being displayed in one long list - and would be dangerous to modify if you wanted your database to work properly afterwards.

Three final points about path names. First, they can be in upper or lower case letters - all are the same as far as Series 3 (or other computers) are concerned.

Thus, 'A:\OPL\' is the same path as 'a:opL'.

Secondly, when you create a new directory you must not use the name of an existing directory.

Thirdly, when you save or copy a file or program Module to an SSD, Series 3 automatically creates the appropriate 'default' directory for it.

Naming files

We now come to the business of naming files. The Series 3 system is identical to that used on PCs. Normally, when you decide to save a file or when you create a 'new' file (such as a new OPL Module), you just give it a name of up to eight characters (we dealt with this way back in Step 2).

However, file names comprise of *two* parts: the actual *name* - such as the one that you give it when creating a new document or OPL Module - and an *extension.*

The *name* part must comprise no more than a total of eight characters and numbers.

The *extension* is separated from the name by a full stop, and comprises (up to) three letters or numbers.

Series 3 automatically adds extensions to your file names, as well as placing the files in the correct directory for storage. So normally you don't have to worry about such things. But when dealing with files on other computers, or creating your own directory or filing system, then you must start adding extension names yourself.

Extensions are used to identify the *type* of file being stored: this is not quite the same as the directory in which it is stored. For example, in your the Word processor directory, which will hold all 'word' documents, Series 3 will automatically save files with the extension '.WRD'. When you specify the file name - either when you create it or when you 'SAVE AS', you can add an extension to distinguish it - perhaps '.LET' for letters, or '.REP' for reports. However, since such files will not have the *default* extension for the directory in which they are saved, they will not appear on the main

Files and Databases

system display: you will have to use the 'OPEN FILE' and TAB key facilities to find them.

The complete file name for an OPL source code Module called 'Myprog' would be 'Myprog.OPL'. This would be saved in the '\OPL\ directory. The corresponding 'program' file, when 'Myprog' is translated, will be 'Myprog.OPO' - and this will be saved in the \OPO\ directory.

Some of the default file extensions automatically added by Series 3 when you create a new file are:

.DBF	For Database files.
.AGN	For Agenda files.
.OPL	For OPL source code files.
.OPO	For translated OPL code files.
.OPD	For bitmap and picture files.

Many of these are the same as the *directory* in which they are kept.

Wildcards

When specifying a filename for a *search* operation - when looking for a particular file to 'open' for example, you can use *wildcards* in either the *name* part or the *extension.*

A *wildcard* is a way of saying 'any letter or letters'. The wildcards are

*	Meaning 'match any number of letters'.
?	Meaning match just *one* letter in this position.

Thus, in a file search, '*.OPL' would mean 'find all the files with the extension 'OPL'. Similarly, '*.OP?' would mean 'find all the files that have an extension starting with the two letters 'OP': note that the search is made only in the current directory, if a path is not specified.

You'll find wildcards useful when writing file handling programs, for selecting specific groups of file names, or for searching records. You cannot use wild cards in directory names: these are in a path specification, which must be 'unique'.

STEP TWENTY-THREE

Database Principles

This Step introduces the concept of a database, and why you might need to create one for your own use.

What is a Database?

In simple terms, a database is a computer file that contains records. The 'address' list that is built into your Series 3 under the System option of 'Data' is a database. Each record contains information about one particular person - their name, telephone numbers, address, and any notes you may have included. The Series 3 database allows you to add or change the 'labels' that precede each item of a record, to add, change and delete records, and so on.

Each record can be likened to a card in a card-index system, where all the information related to one 'subject' is kept on one card. In an address card index system, the 'subject' is the person concerned. Each card holds all the information about that person, just like your Series 3 database records.

There is, however, a fundamental difference between a computer database and a card-index system - a difference that gives computer databases a clear advantage. (This is particularly true where your Series 3 is concerned). With a card-index system, the order of the cards is determined by the prime search requirement. For example, cards holding names and addresses are most likely to be maintained in alphabetical order, based on the person's name: it's not much fun having to search through every card to find Joe Blogg's telephone number, if the cards aren't arranged alphabetically.

With a computer, the order is completely irrelevant (unless you want to print out all of the records). The time it takes a computer to find a particular record is insignificant - faster than the bat of an eyelid.

This difference is particularly invaluable when *other* criteria form the search requirement. For example, if you have a card-index system arranged alphabetically by people's names, you'd spend some time finding all those who lived in a particular town. To a computer

251

like Series 3, this makes no difference: it's just as fast and as easy as finding the person by name.

Computer files have fields

Let us take the card-index analogy a little further. If you were to use cards to keep names, addresses and other relevant information about individuals or companies, you would undoubtedly organise each record card so that you knew exactly where to look on it for a particular item of information. In a system for keeping details of family and friends, for example, each individual record card may look like this:

```
Name: . . . . . . . . . . . . .
Phone No: . . . . . . . . . . .
Address: . . . . . . . . . . . .
Wedding Anniversary: . . . . . .
Birthday: . . . . . . . . . . .
```

Each of these lines, in computer terms, is called a *field*. On record cards, you could add other fields to some of the records, if you wanted, to meet particular needs. Generally speaking, for the databases that *you* create, it is easier to specify the required number of fields that you want at the outset: all records should have the same number of fields, if your program is to handle them properly. (It would appear that your Series 3 allows you to add *fields* by adding 'labels', but in fact this is not the case: each record has the same number of fields).

On a card-index record you can determine what fields you want, and have more or less fields on each record. On the databases you create with a program, you must determine at the outset what fields you want, and stick with them: they may be left blank, but they have to be there.

Just as you can have a whole range of card-index systems using the same format, so you can have a range of computer databases using the same format - and controlled or managed by the same program.

Why do you need to create databases?

You may well wonder, since there is a perfectly good database in Series 3, why you need to create your own database management system.

Basically, it is because the database built into Series 3 is capable of holding *alphanumeric* information, which makes calculations difficult to achieve. If you needed, for example, a stock control database - where each record held the name of an item, its part number, how many are in stock, the minimum permissible stock level, the buying and selling price of each item, and perhaps even the VAT element, then the Series 3's built in database would be pretty inadequate. With your own database management program, you could have Series 3 *automatically* give you a warning if an item was reduced below its 'minimum stock level'. You can also arrange for your program to give you the value of each item in stock, the total value of all the stock, how much it will cost to bring all the stock up to the minimum level, and so on. All under 'Menu' control, and using Dialogs for ease of entry.

The types of database that you can create to do specific types of work are limitless: you could have a program to look after your bank account for you, automatically 'transferring' funds or deducting standing orders on the appropriate date each month, to save you from having to do it (to your records). You could have a club membership database, telling you 'at the touch of a button' who owes what. And so on.

In other words, if you need to extract information and make calculations based on the records you keep, then it is well worth writing your own database manager.

However, there is a down side: database management programs tend to be fairly lengthy, if they are going to be useful (as you will see!). So they must be very carefully planned.

What a database program should include

Whatever other functions you want a database management program to perform, there are certain facilities that should be included every time. These are

1)   The ability to create a new Database file, and possibly to delete unwanted files (although deletion can be achieved using the Series 3 file handling system).
2)   The ability to add, change (update) and delete a record.
3)   The ability to search for specific records on a given clue (like 'Find' in your Series 3 databases).

Files and Databases

In addition to these, you will also want routines to extract and or manipulate data according to your requirements, and perhaps to provide a print-out onto a connected printer.

This makes for a lot of 'procedures' to build up your program. If you intend to have two or more database management programs - say one for stock control, and one for bank account management - then it can make sense to have some standard routines that are common to both placed in a Library module, which can be loaded and used as and when required by such programs.

It is not within the scope of this book to provide complete database management programs to perform a specific functions: they would be fairly long, and of no interest to those who didn't want the particular database manager discussed for their own use.

The Database Step in this Part of the book will concentrate, therefore, on the OPL commands available to you, with a 'shell' database manager program, to demonstrate as far as is practical how such commands can be used. Even as a 'simple' database manager, you'll find it requires plenty of accurate finger-tapping!

As a general guide, the approach to adopt is to write the program as simply as possible to start with, using just the basic elements required, then add and change those elements to 'improve' and enhance the way it looks when running, and the way it can be used.

In this respect, 'breaking' the program up into small discrete procedures will help considerably when the time comes to enhance it: all you need to do is replace individual procedures, and test it thoroughly again before proceeding with the next step.

Now, if your fingers are ready...

STEP TWENTY-FOUR

Database Management

In this Step, you will discover how to create and manage a database to meet your own specific requirements. The OPL words covered are APPEND, CLOSE, COUNT, CREATE, EOF, ERASE, FIND, FIRST, LAST, NEXT, BACK, OPEN, OPENR, POS, POSITION, RECSIZE, UPDATE, USE.

Planning your database

When you decide that it is time to create your own database, the very first step to take is to set down, very clearly, everything that you want it to do. This way, you can cater for all of your needs at the outset - you'll find it easier than trying to add extra facilities later on.

As a typical example, if you wanted to have a stock control database, your requirement list might look something like this:

1)   Item names and stock numbers
2)   Current stock level
3)   Minimum permissible stock level
4)   Buying and selling prices
5)   Value of each stock item
6)   Total value of the stock

In addition to these requirements to satisfy the *purpose* of your database, there are the basic needs that every database should have - as detailed in the previous Step (the ability to add, change and delete records, for example).

Having ascertained your needs,, you can then examine them to see exactly what each record should actually contain. In the stock control list, for example, items (5) and (6) needn't be a part of the actual record: they can be calculated by Series 3 for display whenever you want, thus saving record (and storage) space.

You might decide that you want to keep one type of stock separate from another - perishable goods in one database *file* and

255

non-perishables in another, for example. This is the same concept as keeping your business and personal addresses separate in the Series 3's built in database: you simply open a new record file for each type of record you wish to keep, all of them being under the control of the one database management program.

Remember, your database management program *controls* the database *files*.

The file handling process

The sequence of events for your database management program would, generally speaking, be as follows.

1) Open (or create) the database file. A file must be 'opened' before you can work on it, for reasons which you will soon understand.

2) Perform the necessary file handling operations. These include finding files, adding records, extracting information and so on - in fact, performing the tasks you wanted to achieve with your database. With Series 3, this can be achieved very easily by using the menu system available, so that you can go straight to the operation that you want to perform once a file has been opened.

3) Close the file (or files). When you leave a program that has been handling files, those files are normally closed automatically. However, it is good programming practice to ensure that such files are closed automatically.

It is possible to have more than one file open at a time - in fact, you can have up to four files open at once. You may wish to transfer information from one file to another, for example: all of this is possible, provided that you write the program accordingly.

Before we examine the many OPL words available for database management, let us create a 'shell' or 'start-up' program to handle some of the operations you are likely to need. For this, we shall use the Series 3 menu system. So that you can test this 'shell' out without having to write the entire database first, we'll provide 'dummy' procedures to 'mark' where we will ultimately have procedures: these will be expanded as we go along. We'll also have an error handling procedure, to cater for all the things that can go wrong when the program is running.

Please note that this program is just a guide: it will give you an idea of how to prepare your own database management program. It

is by no means complete, and will undoubtedly need modifying and
expanding to suit your own requirements.

```
PROC Datman:
   LOCAL m%
   DO
AGAIN::                                    REM For error trapping
      ONERR Noproc::
      scrnmsg:("Use MENU or Short-Cut keys")
      m%=GET
      IF m%=$122
         mINIT
         mCARD "Files","Create",%c,"Open",%o,
             line continues    "Read",%r,"Close",%k
         mCARD "Manage","Add",%a,"Update",%u,
             line continues    "Delete",%d
         mCARD "Analyse","Browse",%b,
             line continues    "IValue",%i,"SValue",%s
         mCARD "Quit","Quit",%q
         m%=MENU
         IF m%
            @(CHR$(m%)):
         ENDIF
      ELSEIF m% AND $200     REM Short-cut keys pressed
         m%=m%-$200          REM Strip out PSION key part
         @(CHR$(m%)):
      ENDIF
      UNTIL m%=q
      STOP                   REM The program stops here
Noproc::                     REM 'No procedure' error handler
   ONERR OFF
   showerr:(err$(err))
   GOTO AGAIN::
ENDP

PROC c:
   notimp:
ENDP                              Continues overleaf
```

257

Files and Databases

IMPORTANT: Datman must *always* be the first procedure in the Module. *Repeat the* PROC c: *procedure above for* PROC o:, PROC r:, PROC k:, PROC a:, PROC b:, PROC u:, PROC d:, PROC i:, PROC s: and PROC q:. Make sure they are all entered as they are needed in order to test Datman:. Then enter, *in the same Module:*

```
PROC notimp:
   BUSY "Not implemented yet"
   GIPRINT "Press a key"
   BUSY OFF
ENDP

PROC showerr:(msg$)
   dINIT "ERROR"
   dTEXT "",msg$,2
   DIALOG
ENDP

PROC scrnmsg:(m$)
   gAT 2,78
   gPRINTB m$,235,3
ENDP
```

The routine 'notimp:' displays a message for all of the procedures that haven't been fully written yet. Once they have been implemented, this procedure can be deleted. The 'showerr:' procedure will be used to display all (or most) of the errors that can occur when the program is running: at the moment, only incorrect 'short-cut key' combinations are 'trapped' by the error handling routine. The scrnmsg: routine allows us to display simple instructional messages on the screen from time to time.

The process we have just adopted enables us to test out our database as we write it, piece by piece, without known potential errors stopping the program from running. Test the program out thoroughly, to make sure it works properly: if it doesn't work now, it won't work when we start 'filling in' the procedures!

Creating a database file

Before your program can handle a database file, it must be opened. And before you can open a database file, it must have been created.

258

Thus, the very first time you use the program (for real), you must *create* the file you want to use. The command to use is

CREATE *file$,1fn,field1,field2...field32* This is not to be
confused with gCREATE, which is used to create a window.
As you can see, this command requires a number of
arguments. Here's what they mean:
file$ This is the name of the file that you want to create,
and where you want it to be stored. It can be just the *name*
(obeying the rules for file names, as given in Step 22), with
or without the *extension*, or it can include the full *path*, with
the directories to where you want the file to be saved (Step
22). If you omit the *extension*, the default extension (.ODB) is
used. If you omit the *path*, a path to the \OPD\ directory is
used. In most instances, this will be perfectly adequate for
your needs. If, however, you choose to save the database file
in a directory of your own choosing, and with your own
extension, then you must be sure to use the same path to
the directory and the same file extension when you
subsequently open the file again - otherwise it won't be
found.
    Note that the maximum permissible length for *file$*,
including the path and so on, is 128 characters.
lfi It has been mentioned that you can have up to four
database files opened at a time. Series 3 needs to know,
when you use a file, which of the four you intend to use (in
much the same way it needs to know which window or
bitmap file you want to use). In order to do that, each of the
four files has to be identified, and that's done by giving each
file that you create or open a *logical file identifier*. The
identifier is just a single letter - 'A', 'B', 'C' or 'D' - without
quotes, and as you will see later on, is used when *accessing*
a file and any information it contains. If, when you create the
file, you give it the *identifier* 'A', then that is how the file will
be referenced whilst the program is running. Note that, when
a file is created, it is automatically 'opened for business'.
field1..field32 In Step 23, you saw that each record in
your database has *fields* where the relevant information is
stored. You have to identify the fields that you want when
you create the file, and that is done with the *field?*
arguments. You can have up to 32 different fields in every
record of your file, but of course you will only specify as
many as you need. Irrespective of the number of *fields* you

have, the maximum length any file record can have in your database is 1022 characters, which should be more than adequate for your needs. The *fields* are, in effect, GLOBAL variables of a special kind: you specify them in the CREATE command (or in one of the OPEN commands, as we shall see later), and they are then available to *all* of the procedures in your program module.

As variables, *field* names must obey the rules of all variables: the *type* of information they are to store must be identified by an identifier symbol at the end, and they must not be more than eight characters long, including the identifier. Thus, if a field is to store integer numbers, the field might be called 'number%'. There is an important difference, however, as far as fields holding *string* information are concerned: the number of characters that they will hold does *not* have to be specified. The record will hold as many characters in a string field as are assigned to it.

When, in your program, you wish to use or assign a value to one of the field variables, you do so by prefixing it with the *logical file identifier* letter and a full point. Thus, a field named 'number%' in a file created (or 'OPENed') as file 'A' is subsequently identified as

A.number%

This differentiates that particular variable from a similar variable in, say, a file created or opened as 'B'.

Series 3 will not allow you to create a file with the same name at the same storage location. If you try to do this, then a program stopping error will usually occur. In our 'Datman' program, we are trapping *all* errors - to catch any incorrect use of short-cut keys, and so trying to create a file that already exists would be reported as a 'short-cut key' error. If we didn't have this error-trapping routine, we could use the DIALOG function's dFILE own facility for trapping 'existing file name' errors. However, as we are at the moment trapping our own errors, we must also cater for this one. The function 'EXIST' will help us out.

EXIST(*file$*) This checks to see whether the file, specified by *file$* (which *can* include the path and extension, as before) exists at the specified (or default) location. If it *does* exist, then *true*

(-1) is returned. Otherwise, *not true* ('0') is returned. The general format is

$$e\%=\text{EXIST}(file\$)$$

As a function, EXIST can of course be used as part of another statement.

For our demonstration program, we shall create a 'mini stock-control' datafile that has three fields: *item$*, *number%* and *cost*. The *item$* field will hold the name of the stock item, *number%* will hold the number in stock, and *cost* will hold the price of each item. Notice how the variables are *identified* by the type of information they are to store. To enable you to get used to the use of Dialogs, we'll use the dFILE function to get the file name: but notice that we must also provide our own error trapping routine.

Now, go into the 'Datman' Module, and edit 'PROC c:' to read as follows:

```
PROC c:                          REM The 'Create' procedure
    LOCAL fn$(128)
    dINIT "Create New File"
    dFILE fn$,"File ",9
    IF DIALOG                    REM ie, not ESC key
       IF NOT EXIST(fn$)
          CREATE fn$,A,item$,number%,cost
       ELSE
          dINIT fn$+" already exists"
          dBUTTONS "Continue",13
          DIALOG
       ENDIF
    ENDIF
ENDP
```

When you have edited PROC c: in the 'Datman' module, translate and run it again: this time, you will be able to use the 'Create' option to create a database file. If you try to create the same file name twice, you will get *our* error message Dialog box appear. Note that, if you don't enter the path for the file name, it is automatically provided by Series 3 (as you'll see if you try to enter the same name twice).

Files and Databases

Note: If you want to delete a database file that you have created - perhaps because in your experimentation you have created a number of files which you don't need - follow the following steps *carefully*:

1) Press the 'System' button to enter the main system display of your Series 3.
2) Press the PSION and 'D' keys together (or select 'Delete file' from the 'File' menu option).
3) A Dialog will appear: *do not press* ENTER: press instead the TAB KEY.
4) Use the up/down arrow keys to highlight the backslash ('\') at the top left of the screen, then press ENTER. If you have saved to an SSD, use the left/right arrow keys to select it first.
5) Use the up/down arrow keys to select '\OPD\' (or the directory in which you saved your datafiles), then press ENTER.
6) Use the up/down arrow keys to select the file you wish to delete: unless you specified otherwise, it will have the extension '.ODB'. Then press ENTER.
7) The 'Delete file' Dialog will now be displayed: check that the file you wish to delete is displayed on the 'File name' line, then press ENTER.
8) A new Dialog will ask you to confirm the deletion: press 'Y' to delete, 'N' to abort the deletion.

You can use this process to delete any file you no longer need. A similar process can be used should you want to *copy* a database file from one location to another: in this case, the main System Menu option to choose is 'File - Copy' (PSION and 'C' keys).

Opening and closing files

When you create a new file, it is automatically 'opened' for use. However, next time you come to use the program, it won't be opened: you have to open it.

Opening a database file simply means telling Series 3 you wish to perform some operations on it, perhaps adding records, or changing them. Two commands are available for opening files: one allows you to modify the file in some way, the other provides 'read-only' access. That means you can examine the contents of the file, but you can't change them.

OPEN *file$,lfn,field1,field2...field32*   You'll notice that, apart from the OPL word OPEN, this command is identical to CREATE. All the *arguments* that the command takes are the same - and as far as the fields are concerned, these must be of the same number and *type* as those used when the file was created, and though they need not necessarily have the same names, it makes sense to retain the same names. If you think about it, it is logical to have the same number of fields and field types when you open a file as when it was created: the records, after all, are for the same purpose, and have the same number and types of field.

OPENR *file$,lfn,field1,field2...field32* This is identical to the OPEN command, except for the fact that the opened file can only be *read*, it cannot be altered. A database file opened in this way could be accessed by other programs running at the same time as your database manager program.

When your database manager program is terminated, all the files are closed automatically. However, it is good practice for your program to close the files. If you want to access *more* than four files during the running of your program, then you will have to close some files down so that there are never more than four opened at a time - the maximum allowed.

Should this be one of your requirements, then you will also need to keep track of the *logical file identifiers*. Note that these are not *variables* and not *strings*, but simply a letter, without quotes. Most often, you will have different *types* of database file open at the same time. For example, in a bank-account managing program, you may have one file holding records about your current bank account, and another holding records concerning standing order payments (how much, how many, who to, and so on). You can arrange that one type is always opened as, say, the 'A' *logical file*, and the other as the 'B' *logical file*.

You will also need to CLOSE a database file that has been opened for 'Read-only' and re-open it with the OPEN command, if you subsequently decide you wish to make changes to it.

CLOSE   This command closes the *current* file (not to be confused with gCLOSE, which closes a window). That's the last one to be created or opened, or the one that has been selected to be current by the USE command.

When you close a file, memory is recovered from records that have been *deleted* - provided the file has been saved in the internal RAM of Series 3, or on a RAM SSD. Flash SSD memory is not restored until you *re-format* the SSD - which wipes all the memory clean. For this reason, it is probably better to save database files which are subject to a lot of record *changes* in a RAM memory area.

We will now edit our 'shell' database manager program, to cater for opening our database file for alteration, for read-only, and to close it. Since the action needed to open a file for alteration or read-only is almost identical, we will have one procedure to handle both cases, and call that procedure from 'PROC o:' and 'PROC r:' with an appropriate 'flag'. First of all, edit these two procedures as follows:

```
PROC o:
    openfile:(0)                    REM That's a zero
ENDP

PROC r:
    openfile:(1)
ENDP
```

Now, in the same module, add the following 'openfile:' procedure: notice how we use the 'flags' from PROC o: and PROC r: to determine the required Dialog display and action.

```
PROC openfile:(m%)
    LOCAL fn$(128),msg$(12)
    IF m%                          REM Means 'Read-only'
        msg$="Reading Only"
    ELSE
        msg$="Updating"
    ENDIF
    dINIT "Open for "+msg$
    dFILE fn$,"File ",1            REM Note the file type
    IF DIALOG
        IF NOT EXIST(fn$)
            dINIT fn$+" doesn't exist!"
            dBUTTONS "Continue",13
```

264

```
      DIALOG
   ELSEIF m%
      OPENR fn$,A,item$,number%,cost
   ELSE
      OPEN fn$,A,item$,number%,cost
   ENDIF
ENDIF
ENDP
```

By keeping both of the 'open' file actions in one procedure, we make it easy to amend and check should the need ever arise.

Remember that, when you run the program, if you cannot remember the name of your database file when the Dialog appears, simply press the TAB key, and you will be shown a list of all the files in the default directory: use the process discussed earlier to select the database file you require (extension 'ODB', unless you included your own when you created the file).

Now, to allow you to close a file that has been opened for, say 'Read-only' (for re-opening in order to make changes to it), and to give our program a clean ending, edit the 'PROC q:' and 'PROC k:' procedures as follows (note the use of TRAP to detect that a file hasn't been opened):

```
PROC q:
   k:
ENDP

PROC k:
   TRAP CLOSE
   IF ERR
      GIPRINT ERR$(ERR)
   ELSE
      GIPRINT "File Closed"
   ENDIF
ENDP
```

Adding records to the file

Without exception, you will want to be able to add records to your file. You do this by first making the required file the *current* file (if more than one is opened) with the USE command. If only one file has been opened, then it will automatically be the current file.

Files and Databases

USE *lfi*   This selects the data file previously created or opened
with the logical identifier *lfi* - A, B, C or D - as the current
file, making it ready for further actions.

To add a record to a file, you must assign values to the field
variables. You don't have to assign them all: those you don't assign
will be 'blanks' in the database file.

    You must remember that field variables have to be prefixed by
the *logical file identifying* letter (you can use either a small or capital
letter). Thus, in our database example file, the variables are
identified as

```
A.item$
A.number%
A.cost
```

This distinguishes them from similar variables in other database files
that may have been opened. The prefix, in fact, forms part of the
variable's name, so you could, for example, assign information to
'A.item$' by a statement such as

```
INPUT A.item$
```

This would take information straight from the keyboard and assign it
directly to the variable (this is the method demonstrated in the
alphabetic listing of your User Manual). More 'user friendly' would be
to use a Dialog. However, these field variables cannot be used for
data assignments in Dialogs, and so LOCAL variables will have to be
used, and the values given to the LOCAL variables re-assigned to the
field variables.

APPEND   This command adds the information *currently* in all of the
field variables to the database file as a *new* record. The new
record is 'appended' to the end of the file, and is then made
the current record. Unassigned fields are given zero values or,
for strings, 'null' values in the new record.

A file must be opened before you can assign values to its field
variables or APPEND any new records to it, otherwise a program-
stopping error will occur. We must allow for this in our 'Add'
procedure (PROC a:). Enter your Datman module, and edit 'PROC a:'
to read as follows:

```
PROC a:
  LOCAL d%,item$(16),number&,cost
  ONERR notopen::
  DO
      dINIT "Adding a Record"
      dEDIT item$,"Item:",16
      dLONG number&,"How many:",0,10000
      dFLOAT cost,"Each costs:",0,10000
      dBUTTONS "Add & End",13,
      line continues        "Add & More",9,"Cancel",27
      d%=DIALOG
      IF d%
        A.item$=item$
        A.number%=number&
        A.cost=cost
        APPEND
      ENDIF
    UNTIL d%=13 or d%=0
    RETURN
  notopen::
    ONERR OFF
    showerr:(ERR$(ERR))
ENDP
```

Notice how, in this procedure, the Series 3 error messaging system is used: it will report *any* type of error that occurs in the procedure. Notice, too, how the 'buttons' are used to enable another record to be added, just the current record, or to cancel the operation altogether. Strictly speaking, the 'Cancel' option isn't necessary: the ESC key will always exit a Dialog, with DIALOG returning the value of zero. But to help when using the program, it is a good idea to show all the options available if possible.

When you have entered this procedure, test it out by adding a few dummy records to your database file: test the error routine as well, by trying to add records without first opening the file.

Browsing through the records

One of the important features that must be built into your database manager is the ability to find records: when you want to change a record, for example, you will need some way of finding the one you want to change. You will also undoubtedly want to examine the

267

records as well: one 'set' of 'search' procedures can be used for all these and related tasks.

OPL has a number of commands that enable you to flip backwards and forwards through your records, or to find records on a specific clue - just as in the built-in Series 3 database.

When a file has been opened, Series 3 keeps track of which record is the *current* record in that file, for action or viewing. This is much the same as the way it keeps track of the screen positions for the next graphic or text action. Usually it doesn't matter where a record is, but there are occasions when you do need to know the precise *position* of a record: for example, in a *sort* routine, where the records are being sorted into some order. You can find the position with the POS function.

POS   The format for this function is simply

$$p\%=POS$$

After it has been executed, *p%* will hold the number of the record in the file, the first record being number 1. A file on Series 3 can have a maximum of 65534 records: as an integer variable, *p%* can only hold values between -32768 and 32767. Consequently, record numbers *above* 32767 are shown as negative values, ranging from -32768 (for record number 32768) down to -2 for record number 65534. If you wish to actually display the record number (rather than just use it in the file management process), then if *p%* has a negative value, 65536 needs to be added to it, to get the correct number. Thus, if you anticipate having more than a paltry 32767 records and you wish to display the record number for some reason, you will need a section of code something like this: (*don't enter this into Datman!!*)

```
IF POS<0
   PRINT POS+65535
ELSE
   PRINT POS
ENDIF
```

As well as being able to determine the number of the current record, you can also *set* the current record to a specific number or position in the file. This is like setting the cursor on the screen display, with the **gAT** or **AT** commands.

POSITION *x%* This command makes the record number *x%* the *current* record. If *x%* is greater than the number of records in the file, then the record 'pointer' will be *one* past the last record in the file - a 'blank' record since it doesn't exist yet - and the 'End Of File' function **EOF** will be *true*.

There are times when it can be necessary to know exactly how many records there are in a database file. In a stock control program, for example, the number of records in the file is an indication of how many *types* of item are being recorded.

COUNT The format is

$$c\text{\%=COUNT}$$

After this function has been executed, *c%* will hold the number of records in the file, or zero if there are no records.

There are many file management operations that you'll want to tackle, which will entail searching through *every* record and acting on the data each contains. You could perform this operation by using **COUNT** to determine the number of records, then constructing a loop with a 'loop counter' that will run through the required number of times. There is, however, an easier way.

EOF This function, which stands for 'End Of File', tests the current position of the record pointer. The format is

$$e\text{\%=EOF}$$

If an attempt is made to 'push the pointer past the last record in the file', then **EOF** returns *true* (-1). Otherwise, it returns *not true* (0). The examining loop can therefore be a simple

```
DO
     act on each record in turn
UNTIL EOF
```

269

Files and Databases

As well as the commands just discussed, there's a little group of commands that enable you to move backwards and forwards from record to record. These are now discussed:

FIRST   This command makes the first record in the file the current record.

LAST   This command makes the last record in the file the current record.

NEXT   This command makes the next record in the file the current record. If the current record is already the last record in the file, then a 'null' record is returned, and the EOF function, if used, will return a *true* condition.

BACK   This command makes the previous record in the file the current record. If the current record is the first record in the file, then this command has no effect.

Finally, there is a function to search through the entire file for a match to a specified clue.

FIND   The format for this function is

$$f\%=\text{FIND}(clue\$)$$

FIND starts with the *current* record (its important to remember that) and searches through all of the *string* fields in the data file (its important to remember that, too), until it reaches a match for *clue$*. The record with the match is then made the *current* record. Note that numeric fields are *not* searched.

Unlike the clues that you use in the Series 3 Database system, the clue that you give for *clue$* must cover the *complete* field. If you want to give only a part of the field as a clue, then you *must* use wildcards.

For example, suppose the contents of a field in one of your records is 'APPLES and PEARS'. A clue of 'APPLES' will *not* find this record. The wildcards are:

*   To match any group of letters
?   To match any *single* letter

So, to find the 'APPLES and PEARS' record, your clue must be something like 'APP*', or '*PEA*'. You can mix the wildcards in the clue. Thus '?PP*' will also find the 'APPLES and PEARS' record - and any other record that has *one* character before 'PP', and any number of characters after it.

Your clue can consist of upper or lower case letters: Series 3 treats them as the same for search purposes. Thus '*pple*' will still find a record with 'APPLES and PEARS' as one of its string fields.

We are now in a position to 'fill in' another of our 'shell' program procedures to deal with browsing through the records (PROC b:). This procedure will also be needed to find a record for updating and for deleting. We actually handle the 'browsing' operation in two procedures: one for simple back and forth viewing of records, and another for *finding* a record on a given clue. Obviously, the contents of a record must be displayed when it has been selected, and we must also allow for some errors that can occur - such as trying to search for a record in a file that hasn't been opened!

First of all, edit 'PROC b:' to read as follows:

```
PROC b:                         REM Browse thru' records.
   LOCAL b%
   ONERR notopen::
   FIRST                        REM Start from the beginning
   showrec:                     REM Show first record
   dINIT "To Search Records" REM User friendly stuff
   dTEXT "","Use left/right arrow keys",2
   dTEXT "","for previous/next record",2
   dTEXT "","Up/down arrow keys for",2
   dTEXT "","first/last records",2
   dTEXT "","'F'=Find, ESC or ENTER=Quit",2
   DIALOG
   DO                           REM Here's the action...
      scrnmsg:("Use Search keys now")
      b%=GET
      IF b%=256                 REM Up=First record
         FIRST
      ELSEIF b%=257             REM Down=Last record
         LAST
```

Continues overleaf

271

```
        ELSEIF b%=259              REM Left=Previous record
           BACK
        ELSEIF b%=258              REM Right=Next record
           NEXT                    REM But don't go past
             IF EOF                REM the last record!
               LAST
             ENDIF
        ELSEIF b%=%f OR b%=%F      REM Means 'Find'
           scrnmsg:(" ")           REM Clear current message
           dofind:                 REM and call 'Find' procedure
        ENDIF
        CLS                        REM Keep things tidy
        showrec:                   REM Now show the current record!
     UNTIL b%=27 OR b%=13          REM Until done
     CLS                           REM Then tidy up
     RETURN 1                      REM '1' for other routines
  notopen::                        REM The error handler
     ONERR OFF
     showerr:(ERR$(ERR))
  ENDP
```

We RETURN 1 from this procedure, so that a successful search can be passed back to other procedures calling this one. Now you need to enter the 'dofind:' and 'showrec:' procedures into the Module:

```
  PROC dofind:
     LOCAL f%,x%,f$(36)            REM Up to 36 character clues
     FIRST                         REM Search from the start!
     dINIT "Find"                  REM Dialog for the clue
     dEDIT f$,"Enter clue:",8
     IF DIALOG
        DO                         REM A loop, to allow for
           f%=FIND(f$)             REM repeat searches
           IF f%                   REM Means record found
           showrec:                REM so show it!
           p%=POS                  REM Hold the record number
           dINIT "Find Next?"      REM and see if more are wanted
           dPOSITION 1,1           REM Put Dialog out of the way
           dBUTTONS "Yes",%y,"No",%n
           x%=DIALOG
```

```
        IF x%=%y              REM Another to find
            NEXT              REM Finds same record otherwise!
        ENDIF
        ELSE                  REM f%=0 means past last record
        GIPRINT "No more found"
        POSITION p%           REM Re-select last found ·
        x%=0                  REM Prepare to leave procedure
        ENDIF
     UNTIL x%=%n OR x%=0
   ENDIF
ENDP

PROC showrec:
   AT 1,3
   PRINT "ITEM     :",a.item$
   PRINT "QUANTITY :",a.number%
   PRINT "COST EACH:",a.cost
   PRINT
   PRINT "Record No.",POS,"of",COUNT
ENDP
```

* Note that this will be set to the *first* record if no matching records are found.

You should now be able to run your program to create and open files, add records, and examine the records, either by using the arrow keys, or by the 'Find' function. You will undoubtedly agree that, for a 'mini' database manager, this program is becoming quite long! And we haven't finished yet...

Updating records
Updating records is a fairly similar process to adding a record. However, this time we need first to find and then to display the contents of the record to be updated. Remember that the field variables hold the contents of the *current* record in the *current* database file.

UPDATE   This command *deletes* the current record from the file, then *appends* the data held in the field variables as a new record *at the end of the file*. This newly updated record - now the last one in the file - is made the *current* record.

Files and Databases

You will perhaps appreciate, from the action of this command, that 'sorting' out the records into some kind of order can be a little futile: the order will change as soon as you alter the contents of one of the records.

Each record in a datafile is limited to a total of 1022 characters. You can test the size of an individual record with the RECSIZE function.

RECSIZE   The format is

$$r\% = RECSIZE$$

This returns the number of characters used by the current record. If you think that the records in your file may exceed the 1022 limit, then before an 'APPEND' or 'UPDATE' command, you should have a section of code which checks the size of the record first.

Now let us add an update routine to the Database Manager program, edit 'PROC u:' to read as follows:

```
PROC u:
  LOCAL d%,t%,item$(16),number&,cost
  t%=b:                      REM First find the record!
  IF t%                      REM Means OK - see PROC b:
    item$=a.item$            REM Assign the variables
    number&=a.number%        REM Watch the identifiers!
    cost=a.cost
    dINIT "Changing a Record"
    dEDIT item$,"Item:",16
    dLONG number&,"How many:",0,10000
    dFLOAT cost,"Each Costs:",0,10000
    dBUTTONS "Change",13,"Cancel",27
    d%=DIALOG
    IF d%
      a.item$=item$          REM Re-assign field variables
      a.number%=number&
      a.cost=cost
      UPDATE
    ENDIF
  ENDIF
ENDP
```

274

Notice how we're using the 'browse' procedure (PROC b:) to find the required record: when it is found, you simply press ENTER or ESC and '1' will be returned into t%. in this procedure. The 'Update' Dialog is then displayed, ready for your amendment(s). If a datafile hasn't been opened, then the 'browse' routine will detect it - and '1' will not be returned into t%: this procedure will then just terminate, the error message having already been displayed via the 'browse' routine.

Deleting a record

To delete a record, first of all you need to locate the record you wish to delete (our 'browse' function will do nicely again), confirm the deletion (just in case), then do it.

ERASE   This command deletes the *current* record from the *current* file. When the record is deleted, the next one is made the *current* record. However, if you delete the last record in the file, the *next* record is a 'null' (it theoretically doesn't exist yet), and the EOF function will return *true*. Your programs should cater for this eventuality: in Datman, the FIRST record is always chosen to start any record searches, so erasing the last record will not present any problems when displaying records.

We can now 'fill in' PROC d:. Edit it to read as follows:

```
PROC d:
   LOCAL t%
   t%=b:                    REM Find record
   IF t%                    REM Is the file open?
      showrec:              REM Yes: carry on
      dINIT "Delete Record?
      dPOSITION 1,1
      dBUTTONS "Yes",%y,"Cancel",27
      IF DIALOG             REM If not cancelled
         ERASE              REM Yes, it's that easy!
         CLS                REM Tidy up
         GIPRINT "It's deleted, oh master",0
      ENDIF
   ENDIF
ENDP
```

Files and Databases

Tailor your database

That completes all of the basic database handling functions: as you can see, it takes a considerable amount of programming just to get a simple database into action!

The good news is that most of the 'donkey work' has been done when you reach this stage: for your own database, you will need to arrange for the *fields* that you want, and change the field variables throughout accordingly.

When displaying Dialogs involving the contents of or for field variables, remember that a Dialog box can have only seven lines altogether, including the title and buttons. The alternative is to use the text screen commands (such as PRINT and INPUT).

You can of course adapt the record fields (and the number of them), and Dialog messages to suit your own particular database requirements. The Datman program should give you a good starting point, but do be careful when you change it to examine *all* the routines that the changes may affect!

It is extremely unlikely that you would want to produce a database in which you can perform just the basic functions: it would be better to use the Series 3 database. We will now examine how you can use the information that's stored in each of the records, to produce other data that you may need. Read on...

Analysing the records

This is the area where you have to write the program procedures to suit your specific needs. To demonstrate the processes that can be involved, we will fill in the so-far unused procedures 'PROC i:' and 'PROC s:' with analytical routines.

As we have a mini-stock control program, the chances are we would want to know the cost of the stock of one particular item - and the cost of all the stock added together. These two possibilities are chosen since one involves selecting a record, and making a calculation, and the other involves going through *all* the records: two of the most common requirements in Database management programs.

Let us deal with the total value of a specified stock item first. For this, we need to select the particular item (good old 'browse' again), and then make the calculation. As before, the 'browse' routine will take care of unopened files: we just need to make sure before we perform any calculations that there hasn't been an error - in other words, 'PROC b:' returned a '1'. For this demonstration procedure, the information is displayed using the text screen. You could choose to use a graphics window, in order to embolden or italicise certain parts of the display: remember to close the window at the end of the procedure though (gCLOSE), otherwise it will mask out the other displays.

Here's the procedure: edit PROC i: to read as follows.

```
PROC i:
   LOCAL t%,tc
   t%=b:
   IF t%
      tc=a.number%*a.cost
      AT 1,1
      PRINT "Item              : ",a.item$
      PRINT "Number in stock: ",a.number%
      PRINT "Each costs        : £";a.cost
      PRINT "TOTAL VALUE       : £";tc
      GET
      CLS
   ENDIF
ENDP
```

To analyse every record in the file, which must of course be opened, you need a simple loop during which each record is examined in turn, and the necessary calculations made. We want to find the total value of all the items in stock, so we need to perform the same calculation as for the value of each item, and add that value to a running total. Here's a simple procedure to tackle the job: edit 'PROC s:' as follows.

```
PROC s:
   LOCAL total,ic%
   ONERR:: notopen::
   FIRST
   DO
      total=total+a.number%*a.cost
      ic%=ic%+a.number%
      NEXT
   UNTIL EOF
   AT 1,1
```

Continues overleaf

```
        PRINT "Total Items in Stock =",ic%
        PRINT "Total stock Value =    £";total
        GET
        CLS
        RETURN
    notopen::
        ONERR OFF
        showerr:(err$(err))
    ENDP
```

When you're happy that your Datman program runs, and you have 'filled in' all of the procedures, you can delete the procedure 'notimp:'. You can leave the error handling routines in the Datman procedure itself, if you wish, as these will trap out any other errors that may crop up.

Remember though that, by having *our own* error trapping routine, we prevent Series 3 from locating the error for us: using the PSION and 'E' keys after an error has been reported will just produce a '**General failure**' message. If you want to prevent this, 'switch off' the error handling routines by preceding the 'ONERR' statements with 'REM' and a space.

STEP TWENTY-FIVE

Handling Files

This Step covers the OPL commands available for looking after all types of file. The OPL words covered are SPACE, MKDIR, RMDIR, SETPATH, DIR$, COMPRESS, COPY, RENAME, DELETE, LOPEN, LPRINT, LCLOSE.

Looking after the files

Whilst the Series 3 has excellent facilities for creating and removing directories and for file handling in general, you may wish to have your own file handling program. OPL will certainly allow you to do this, with a range of commands and functions specifically designed for the purpose.

When you first start using your Series 3, looking after the files is not much of a problem. Like Topsy, however, they have a habit of growing (in number), until one day you'll find you have long lists of files stored in various directories. Being able to handle the files - moving them around, deleting and generally keeping them organised - is good 'computer housekeeping'.

With the commands discussed in this Step - and all of the others available to you, you can create a File Handling program along the same lines as the Database Manager built-up in the previous Step. To do this, construct a 'shell' procedure to start with, using a Menu system with all of the options you wish to have. Then, for each of the individual routines, set up a 'dummy' procedure (as we did for the Database manager), so that you can test your 'shell' program as you go along.

Alternatively, you may wish to incorporate all or some of the facilities into your Database Manager program, by adding additional options to the Menu with corresponding handling procedures.

How much memory is left?

Although you can quickly look at how much memory you have used though the Series 3's system menus, it may be necessary for your *programs* to know. For example, when adding records to a file, there could well come a point when the file is then too long to fit in the memory area allocated to it.

Files and Databases

SPACE   This command returns the number of free *bytes* (or 'characters') available in the memory area *currently* being used by a file. With SSDs, the amount of space available can be as much as 2 megabytes (2 million characters) - and so the value returned is a long integer. The format is

$$s\&=SPACE$$

You could use this function to simply report the number of bytes available on the current 'drive' at any time, with a statement line such as

```
PRINT SPACE
```

or you can use it in, say, a record APPENDing routine, with statement lines such as:

```
. . .
IF RECSIZE>SPACE
    PRINT "Not enough memory for this record"
    GET
ELSE
    APPEND
ENDIF
. . .
```

The message can be displayed in a variety of ways, of course, using Dialogs or the BUSY command, and so on, to suit your program.

Creating and removing directories

To save leaving your program in order to create or remove a directory, you can incorporate appropriate routines in your program. Remember that a directory is simply a 'heading' under which files are stored. It can have sub-directories which in turn can have sub-sub directories - and so on, as requirements demand. A directory does not allocate or specify any particular amount of memory: one directory can be crammed with files, another virtually empty. As long as there is space on the 'drive', files can be added to any directory.

Series 3 maintains a number of 'default' directories for its own operations, automatically creating them if they don't exist. For example, if you decide to save a program source code module to an SSD which has just been formatted, then without any effort on your part, the default directory is created for that program.

MKDIR *name$*   This creates a new directory with the path and name specified by *name$*. The details of paths and names are given in Step 22. For example, to create a sub-directory of the word processor directory 'WRD' called 'LETTERS' the command would be

```
MKDIR "\WRD\LETTERS"
```

To create the same directory on an SSD fitted into drive 'A', the command would be

```
MKDIR "A:\WDR\LETTERS"
```

If the directory 'WRD' isn't already present on the SSD, then that would also be created. The directory names must always be preceded by a 'backslash' ('\').
      You could of course use the INPUT or the dFILE Dialog function to get the name in from the keyboard: if using the dFILE function, remember that you can set the *type* of input that can be accepted to 'Directories only'.

RMDIR *name$*   This command simply removes the directory specified by *name$*, and is used in the same way as the MKDIR command. If the directory specified doesn't exist, an error will be reported.

SETPATH *name$*   This sets the path and directory to be used for data files to that specified by *name$*: it doesn't affect the directory used by the currently running program - or the directory used for a LOADM command (to load a Module of procedures into the current program).

What's in a directory?
There may be occasions when you need to obtain a listing of what is in a particular directory. This can be achieved with the DIR$ function.

DIR$(*spec$*)   This function has two formats. The very first time it is used, *spec$* must contain the path and 'specification' of the type of files you wish to see. The *first* file matching that specification is then returned. To find the subsequent matching files, the second format is used, with *spec$* a 'null' string. When no files match the specification originally set by *spec$*, then a null string is returned. Thus, the formats are

```
d$=DIR$(spec$)          REM First time used
d$=DIR$(" ")            REM Subsequent use
```

The variable *d$* must have been declared to hold at least 128 characters. The *filename* part of *spec$* can contain wildcards, so that you could, for example, examine all the files of a specific type in a particular directory, or examine all the files in a directory - with the filename specified by wildcards only - '*.*'. Here is an example procedure.

```
PROC files:
   LOCAL spec$(128),d$(128),c%
   dINIT "Examine Files"
   dFILE spec$,"Path and ",3
   IF DIALOG
      d$=DIR$(spec$)
      WHILE d$<>""              REM If no file, don't bother
         PRINT d$
         d$=DIR$("")
         c%=c%+1                REM Line counter
         IF c%>=8               REM Screen filled?
            BUSY "More..."      REM Well, you never know...
            GET
            BUSY OFF
            c%=0                REM Reset the counter
            CLS                 REM Stop scrolling
         ENDIF
      ENDWH
      BUSY "All Done"
      GET
      BUSY OFF
   ENDIF
ENDP
```

This procedure will let you examine the files meeting your path and name specification: if more than a screen full of files are to be displayed, then the program waits for you to press a key. Notice how the full path to the file is listed during the display.

Copying files

Two commands are available for you to make a copy of a file at a different location, or to make a copy with a different name in the same directory. The commands are COPY and COMPRESS. The 'rules' for each are fairly similar, but COMPRESS is best suited for data files that have been saved on an SSD, since it doesn't copy any deleted records to the new location.

COPY *source$,dest$*   This copies the file or files specified by the directory path and filename *source$* to the directory and filename specified by *dest$*.

If there is already a file of the same name at the *dest$* specification, then *that file is deleted.*

The *source$* filename and extension can, if you wish, include wildcards, so that you could copy a whole group of files. However, if you do this, then *only* the directory path must be specified for the *dest$* (remember to use the closing backslash after the last directory name): all the files matching your 'wildcard' specification will be copied to the specified destination, deleting any files with the same names that may already exist there. If you choose to copy more than one file, then the extension *must* be specified for *source$*: either the full extension, or the wildcard '*' for all extension names.

Thus, to copy all of your OPL program files (the translated versions) from internal memory to an '\OPO\' directory on an SSD fitted to drive (slot) 'A', you would use the statement line:

```
COPY "M:\OPO\*.OPO","A:\OPO\"
```

The destination directory must, of course exist, otherwise you'll get an error : if it doesn't, you can create it with the MKDIR command. You could also copy your '.OPO' files to, say, an \OPO\ directory on the 'C:' drive of connected PC, with the statement:

```
COPY "M:\OPO\*.OPO","REM::C:\OPO\"
```

Provided that you don't use wildcards in the *source$* or *dest$* specifications, you can also change the name when you copy the file to a new location. For example, if you have a database file called 'STOCK92.ODB' in the Internal '\ODB\' directory, you could copy it to an SSD in drive 'A' with the new name 'OLD92.ODB' with the line

```
COPY "M:\ODB\STOCK92.ODB","A:\ODB\OLD92.ODB"
```

COMPRESS *source$,dest$*   When you have a data file saved on an SSD, each time a record is deleted the space it occupies is not 'restored' for use again. If you use the COPY command to copy such files to another location, the 'deleted' records are also copied. The COMPRESS command avoids this: when it performs the copy operation, it ignores any records that have been deleted. (Note that the space occupied by deleted records in files saved in RAM memory is automatically 'recovered' for further use). COMPRESS can be used *only* on data files.

The *source$* and *dest$* specifications are as described for the COPY command. However, with COMPRESS, if a file of the same name as that being copied already exists at the destination, then the file being copied doesn't replace (or 'overwrite') the existing one, but is instead *appended* to it. If you don't want this to happen - you want the file being copied to replace any existing file - then before the COMPRESS statement you need to delete the existing file. To save worrying about whether or not the file exists before you try to delete it, you can use the statement

```
TRAP DELETE fname$
```

This prevents Series 3 from stopping the program to report an error if the file doesn't exist. Since you won't be worried whether it exists or not - you just want the new file to be copied - no further action need be taken.

Renaming and deleting files

You can, from within a program, rename or delete any file at any location.

RENAME *oldname$,newname$*   *oldname$* is the directory path and name of the file being renamed, and *newname$* is the directory path and new name for the file. If you specify only the *name* part, such as 'STOCK92' for the *oldname$* and 'OLDSTOCK' for the *newname$*, then the name of the file is changed, and it remains at the same location.

    If, however, you specify a different location - or directory path - for *newname$*, then the original file is 'deleted', and copied to the newly specified destination with the new name. This provides an easy way to *transfer* any type of file from one location to another, and, if you wish, change its name in the process.

    You *cannot* use wildcards in either the *oldname$* or *newname$* specifications.

DELETE *fname$*   This command deletes the file specified by *fname$*, which can include the directory path. With this command you can use wildcards, to delete a whole range of files. For example, if you wish to delete *all* of your '.OPO' files from the '\OPO\' directory in internal ram, then the command would be

```
DELETE "M:\OPO\*.OPO"
```

You should note that, once a file has been deleted, it is irretrievable. You should be particularly careful, therefore, when deleting your *source* code files: the program-running files can always be re-created from a source file, by 'translating' it again. But there is no way back to a source file, short of re-writing it.

Printing out data files

Three commands are involved in printing out a data file to a connected printer.

LOPEN *device$*   Before any data file can be printed, the *route* or *device* must be identified to the Series 3. If a printer is being used, then one of the two following options are available:

```
LOPEN  "PAR:A"        REM For a printer connected to the parallel port
LOPEN  "TTY:A"        REM For a printer connected to the Serial port
```

Files and Databases

If you want to copy file data into another file - either in the Series 3 or on an externally connected computer, then *device$* becomes the directory path and file name of the file concerned. Thus, for externally connected computers, you could have commands such as

```
LOPEN "REM::C:\WORD\DATA.DBF"    REM For PCs
LOPEN "REM::WORD:DATA.DBF"       REM For Apple Macs™
```

When writing to computer files, whether internal or external, any existing file of the same name will be overwritten.

You can have only one device open at a time: if you wish to use another and one is already opened, the opened one must be closed first (LCLOSE)

LPRINT *expression list*   This is exactly the same as the PRINT command, with the only difference that the 'print-out' is directed to the opened device, usually a printer. A device must have been opened (LOPEN), otherwise an error will occur.

Printing to a parallel port is fairly straightforward. However, you should be aware that your data is not being formatted by any of the built in drivers: your program must incorporate all the printer commands that you wish to use - including new lines and tabs. If you simply direct a data file's output to the printer, you may or may not get a formatted display of some kind. You will need to check with your printer manual for the codes it needs to produce formatted print.

As a *guide only* to the type of programming sequence you *might* have, here is a section of a program which could send a data file to a parallel connected printer (it is assumed that a file with the logical identifier 'A' has been opened):

```
LOPEN "PAR:A"
FIRST
WHILE NOT EOF
    PRINT "ITEM :";CHR$(9);a.item$
    PRINT "QUANTITY :";CHR$(9);a.number%
    PRINT "COST EACH:";CHR$(9);a.cost
ENDW
```

The 'CHR$(9)', on most printers, issues a 'TAB' command.

Printing to a Serial port can be a little trickier: it all depends whether the default characteristics match the connected device. Full details of how to set the transmission characteristics are given in your Series 3 Programming Manual, together with a straightforward routine (rsset:) which will set the required values for you. You will be able to obtain the values you need from your Printer manual.

LCLOSE   Whilst any device that has been opened is automatically closed when your program ends, there may be occasions when you wish to open another device. As only one can be opened at a time, use this command to close the device currently opened.

Sorted print-outs

It has already been mentioned that, however careful you may be to enter your data into a file in some kind of order, as soon as you start to change that data, the order changes. This makes any print-out a little random - the records are printed in order of their position within the file.

There is a variety of different techniques for sorting individual items or complete records into some kind of required order. These routines enjoy wondrous names such as Bubble Sort, Shell Sort, Insertion Sort, Heap Sort, Quick Sort, Radix Sort ... and so on. Complete books have been written about sorting techniques alone. Each technique has some merit of some kind, although it must be said that, whatever the application, some sorting techniques are considerably faster (by a factor of ten or more) than others.

To produce a sorting program for Series 3 is next door to being a waste of time and memory storage space, for the order will be changed as soon as the file is updated again. However, it is recognised that, if you have a series of records to be printed out, it would be more practical for the print-out to be in some kind of order.

Here is a very (*very*) crude way to achieve this objective. It takes a file, and, before printing out any record, it goes through the file finding the 'first' record that should appear in the list, and prints it. That record is then 'tagged' (using an array dimensioned large enough to cope with all of the records). The process is then repeated.

This program will assume that you have a file in which the field on which the listing is to be based is *item$*, and that other fields for print-out are *number%* and *cost*: you must use the appropriate field names when adapting the program to your own needs. For demonstration purposes, the program prints to the screen: it is written as separate procedures, so that you can easily adapt it to provide for your own printer.

```
PROC prntsort:
  LOCAL fn$(128),d%
  dINIT "Sort and Print"
  dFILE fn$,"File",3
  IF DIALOG
    OPENR fn$,A,item$,number%,cost    REM Note 1
    sortit:
  ENDIF
ENDP


PROC sortit:
  LOCAL r%,c%,t%(2000),rec$(36)      REM Note 2
  FIRST
  DO
    WHILE t%(POS)=1                  REM Note 3
      NEXT
    ENDWH
    rec$=a.item$                     REM Note 4
    r%=POS
    DO
      NEXT                           REM Note 5
      IF UPPER$(a.item$)<UPPER$(rec$) AND
t%(POS)=0
        rec$=a.item$
        r%=POS
      ENDIF
    UNTIL EOF
    t%(r%)=1                         REM Note 6
    doprint:(r%)
    c%=c%+1                          REM Note 7
    FIRST                            REM Do it again
  UNTIL c%=COUNT+1                   REM for all records
  GET                               REM Note 8
ENDP
```

```
PROC doprint:(recno%)
     POSITION recno%              REM Note 9
     IF NOT EOF                   REM Note 10
         PRINT a.item$;CHR$(9);   REM Note 11
         PRINT a.number%;CHR$(9);
         PRINT a.cost
     ENDIF
ENDP
```

Note 1: Open the file (for read-only, preferably) with the field names you used for *your* database file.

Note 2: Dimension t%() so that it is large enough to hold all of the records in your data file, plus one: too few will cause an error when the program is run. The string *rec$* is for storing the information that is going to be used to determine the order. Dimension it large enough to hold the longest string. If you want the print-out to be ordered on, say, the *cost*, then this must be a *float* type of variable, and you will compare the *cost* fields rather than the *item* fields.

Note 3: We can speed things up a bit by not bothering with records that have already been tagged: this little routine takes us to the first *untagged* record.

Note 4: We store the information in the field that we want our print-out based on, ready for the comparison test. We also need to know *which record* this is, so we also save the record number (POS).

Note 5: We now select the next record, and see if the previous one should come before it, or after it. If the next record should come first *and* it hasn't already been tagged, we update the 'comparison' variable *and* the corresponding record number. This is our new 'print this first' record.

Note 6: When we've reached the End Of the File, we know that *rec$* is holding the next *item* to print (or whichever field you have chosen), but more importantly, we know its *record number* or *position*. As we are now going to print this record, we tag it in our array, so that we don't use it again.

Note 7: We've reached the end of the file, and we need to do all of this again for the next record that should be printed out. Each time round, one record number is tagged (who knows which? Only Series 3!). We need to reset the 'file pointer' back to the first record, call the print routine, and count how many records we've printed out. We'll go on until they're all done (UNTIL c%=COUNT+1).

Note 8: This is for the screen print-out - you won't see the list without this!

Note 9: In the print-out routine, we must first select the right record - passed into the routine via *recno%*.

Note 10: When EOF is *true* in the previous routine, we're actually looking at the blank record beyond the end of the file (it will usually be the very first one that's found, as it contains blanks). It will in fact have a record number one higher than the number of records in the data file: that means the *minimum* value that the t%() array should be dimensioned is the number of records plus one. We don't want this one printed, so we ignore it.

Note 11: Here we've used ordinary PRINT statements, to send the display of records to the screen: for a printer, you would use LPRINT statements, *remembering that you must have first used the* LOPEN *command.* Normally this is best located ion the very first procedure (PROC prntsort:). The CHR$(9) produces a 'TAB' on most printers: you must provide all the formatting that you want in this area, using the printer codes for your printer. Individual characters can be sent using the CHR$() format. To send two or more characters, say 'ESC' followed by the letter 'A', you can use CHR$(27);"A", the semi-colon being important. Alternatively, you can set up a variable. For example, if to embolden print on your printer requires a code of 'ESC E', you can set up a variable as follows

```
bold$=CHR$(27);"E"
```

and use 'bold$' whenever you want the next bit to be printed in bold letters. You must also, of course, send the code to clear or cancel bold printing when bold is no longer required.

Finally, any other information you want printed out - such as totals and so forth, you can tackle in a separate procedure called after the 'sortit:' procedure. Simply perform the analysis (as was demonstrated in the Datman program), then print out the results with LPRINT statements like those shown here.

EPILOG

The Last Words

EPILOG

Be careful!

The OPL functions and commands provided throughout this book will enable you to write simple or sophisticated programs to suit virtually any requirement. However, you will no doubt have seen in the Programming Manual for the Series 3 that there are other functions and commands available for you to use: in the main, these are for directly accessing the ROM or RAM areas of Series 3, and demand a sound knowledge of 'machine coding' and/or of the Series 3 operating system. Both of these topics are well beyond the scope of this book: indeed, each could be the subject of a very large book on its own.

Whilst some of the OPL words concerned are fairly harmless in what they do, others can cause serious problems if used rashly or without a thorough understanding of what they do and how they work.

These words are included in OPL for the benefit of experienced and professional program developers, and in that respect, provide a 'high level' access to the machine's operating system. Programs using these words are best developed *externally* to the Series 3, using the special Developer's Kit available from Psion. This enables programs to be written on a PC for subsequent downloading to the Series 3, without causing problems on the Series 3 through programming errors.

Brief details of some of the words concerned are given in your Programming Manual. In view of the potential problems that can arise, even with an incorrectly entered 'demonstration' program, it is not proposed to expand on those descriptions in this book: until you have the necessary background knowledge and experience, it is advised that you keep well clear of them. For your information, the words concerned, their purpose and their 'safety factor' is as follows.

Epilog

ADDR(*variable*)   This function returns the memory address in Series 3 where the specified variable is stored. As it simply returns an address, it is safe to use. The variable can be of any type - integer, long integer, string or float, and it can be an array: generally speaking, ADDR returns the first address used to store the variable. This information can be useful for those who wish to access the particular variable directly: knowledge of how each type of variable is stored is required. The format is

```
a%=ADDR(variable)
```

PEEK   There are five 'PEEK' functions which enable you to examine the contents of the Series 3 memory areas. These words can do no harm to your Series 3 even if used incorrectly: they merely 'peek' into a specified memory area, and return what is found there.

p%=**PEEKB(***address%***)**   This examines the memory address at the *byte* specified by *address%*, and returns the *integer* value of whatever is found there in *p%*. Bytes are used to store single *characters*.

p%=**PEEKW(***address%***)** This examines *two bytes* (a '*word*') starting at the address specified by *address%*), and returns the *integer* value of whatever is found there in *p%*. Integer values are stored in two bytes, the least significant byte being stored first.

p&=**PEEKL(***address%***)**   This examines *four bytes* starting at the address specified by *address%*, and returns what is found there as a *long integer* in *p&*. Long integers are stored in four bytes of memory.

p=**PEEKF(***address%***)**   This examines *eight bytes*, starting at the address specified by *address%*, and returns whatever is found there as a floating point value in *p*. Floating point values are stored in eight bytes of memory, using a special kind of format. PEEKF converts whatever is found at the eight addresses to the corresponding floating point value.

*p$*=**PEEK$(***address%***)**   This examines the address specified by *address%*, and whatever value is found there, then returns the contents of that number of following addresses as a *string*. With string variables, the very first memory byte gives the *length* of the string. The rest of the memory stores the string as *character codes*: PEEK$ converts those codes to actual string characters.

With all of these functions, ADDR can be used to specify the address of a variable. Thus,

$$p\$=PEEK\$(ADDR(var\$))$$

will return in p$ the contents of the string var$, since ADDR points to the first byte where that string is stored.

The values stored in each element of an array can be found in a similar way. For example, to use a PEEK function find the value stored in the third element of an array 'array%()':

$$p\%=PEEKW(ADDR(array\%(3)))$$

It must be pointed out that, taking this last case as example, this is the same as

$$p\%=array\%(3)$$

The difference is, with PEEK and ADDR, you are accessing the variables at the 'machine level'.

POKE *address%,value* Where the PEEK commands simply examine what is in memory, the five POKE commands (similar to the five PEEK commands) actually *overwrite* what is in memory. The 'poking' action starts at the address *address%*, and the information stored is determined by *value*.
Since this command overwrites what already exists in memory, its use is potentially dangerous: an error is specifying the address, for example, can mean overwriting valuable data and possibly corrupt files or other programs.

IO??? There is a whole range of functions which provide direct 'Input/Output' access to files, drivers, the keyboard and so on. Use of these functions demands a thorough understanding of the operating system and machine code. They can be dangerous to use, and will not be discussed any further.

KEYA/KEYC KEYA performs an asynchronous read of the keyboard, and is included for use by experienced programmers. KEYC cancels a **KEYA** operation. For normal programming, OPL words such as **GET** and **KMOD** are perfectly adequate.

USR/USR$ These commands pass *register* values to the central processor unit, and run a machine code program from a a specified address: the machine code program must have been written using *Assembly language*, which cannot be achieved on the Series 3 directly without difficulty: such programs require additional programming facilities for their creation. Without expert knowledge and the necessary facilities, they are dangerous to use.

CALL This function passes data to the *registers* of the central processing unit, and 'calls' one of the functions built into the Series 3's operating system via an *interrupt*: considerable knowledge is required of interrupts, registers and the Series 3 operating system before use of this command can even be contemplated.

OS This function is a more comprehensive variation of **CALL**, allowing values to be passed to the registers of the central processor unit, and storing the values returned by the registers. It is for professional use only.

GETEVENT, TESTEVENT, GETCMD$, CMD$ These functions and commands are used when creating an *application* that will appear on the main System screen. These applications must behave in the same way as the built-in applications in every respect, to be 'safe' when used. They test and/or return keyboard presses and commands from the system screen, enabling the program to act accordingly.

APP This is rather like 'PROC': it is used to write a small group of statements for setting up an Application on the main system screen, and is followed by the Application name, without a colon. The statements are terminated by an '**ENDA**' command. The Programming Manual discusses the operations necessary to create an application, and to install it on the main system display.

ICON This is used only within the **APP...ENDA** series of statements, to inform Series 3 of the bitmap file to be used for the display of an icon for an application to be added to the main system display. The icon is taken from the top left 24 by 24 pixels of the specified bitmap file. The file name should include the full path to the file. If no file extension is provided, '.PIC' is assumed.

TYPE   This command is used within the APP...ENDA series of statements, to specify the *type* of application that is being created. The types are discussed in detail in your Programming Manual: further explanation is not necessary.

gUPDATE   This is a graphics command that has been deliberately omitted from the 'Windows' part of this Book. Normally, the screen is 'updated' whenever anything is written to it. With this command, you can switch off the graphics updating process (gUPDATE OFF), force a graphics update to occur (gUPDATE), or switch back to the normal graphics updating process (gUPDATE ON). However, whilst this can speed up graphics operations, it can also result in the incorrect reporting of errors when the program is running. This makes programming debugging more difficult, and is the reason it has not been discussed until now. If you wish to use the commands, make sure your program is running perfectly first, then add them afterwards.

The last word...

That's it. It is sincerely hoped that this book will help you to understand how to program your Series 3, and that, armed with your new knowledge, you will get many hours of pleasure - and extra utility - from this incredible machine.

Index

INDEX

Where applicable, the main entry is shown in bold type.
OPL words are shown in capital letters.
Programs and procedures are listed under 'PROGRAMS'.

Index

Index

Index